Why Do Criminals Offend?

A General Theory of Crime and Delinquency

Robert Agnew
Emory University

OXFORD
UNIVERSITY PRESS

OXFORD
UNIVERSITY PRESS

Oxford University Press, Inc., publishes works that further Oxford University's
objective of excellence in research, scholarship, and education.

Oxford New York
Auckland Cape Town Dar es Salaam Hong Kong Karachi
Kuala Lumpur Madrid Melbourne Mexico City Nairobi
New Delhi Shanghai Taipei Toronto

With offices in
Argentina Austria Brazil Chile Czech Republic France Greece
Guatemala Hungary Italy Japan Poland Portugal Singapore
South Korea Switzerland Thailand Turkey Ukraine Vietnam

First published in 2005 by Roxbury Publishing Company
Published by Oxford University Press, Inc.
198 Madison Avenue, New York, New York 10016
http://www.oup.com

Oxford is a registered trademark of Oxford University Press

Library of Congress Cataloging-in-Publication available

ISBN 978-0-19-533046-5

Printed in the United States of America

Acknowledgments

This book is dedicated to Mary, Willie, and Jenny Agnew, with much appreciation for their love and support. I would also like to thank the following people for their very helpful comments and suggestions on earlier versions of this book: Alex Alvarez, Michael Benson, Timothy Brezina, David Farrington, Alex Piquero, and John Wright. And a special thanks to Claude Teweles for his support and advice in preparing this book. ✦

Contents

Chapter 1

Introduction

A General Theory of Crime and Delinquency

Why I Wrote This Book and What I Hope to Accomplish

I have been a criminologist for 25 years and the question I am most often asked about crime is, "Why do criminals offend?" People are intensely curious about why some individuals engage in behaviors that are generally condemned by and often harmful to others. Also, I think most people realize that we must understand the causes of crime if we are to successfully control it. But despite all my years of study, I have never been able to provide a satisfactory answer to the question. That is, I have never been able to provide an answer that is clear and concise on the one hand, but reasonably complete on the other.

Sometimes I respond to this question by listing the "risk factors" for crime. Such factors include personality traits like impulsivity, family factors like poor parental supervision, school experiences like poor grades and peer factors like gang membership (see Hawkins et al. 2000; Howell 2003; Loeber et al. 1998; U.S. Department of Health and Human Services 2001). Providing a long list of risk factors, however, tends to overwhelm my audience. It also leaves them dissatisfied, because it fails to explain such things as why these risk factors cause crime and how they are related to one another.

Sometimes I describe certain of the major theories or explanations of crime, including strain, control, and social learning theories (see Agnew 2005; Cullen and Agnew 2003). This too tends to overwhelm my audience, especially if I describe more than two or three

1

theories and try to explain how these theories are related to one another. Finally, sometimes I describe certain of the integrated theories of crime, which attempt to combine two or more crime theories into a unified whole (for overviews, see Barak 1998; Bernard and Snipes 1996; Cullen and Agnew 2003; Messner et al. 1989). Certain of these integrations, however, strike listeners as far too complex while others strike them as far too simple, and all of them seem to be incomplete—omitting key causes of crime, for example.

So for 25 years I have been unable to provide a good answer to what is perhaps the most frequently asked question about crime. My frustration over this fact led me to write this book, which represents my best answer to the question of why criminals offend. That is, *why are some individuals more likely than others to engage in crime*? The answer I provide draws on the best of current crime theory and research, and reflects my struggle to organize this theory and research into a unified whole that is clear, concise, and reasonably complete.

It is my hope that students, the general public, and policy makers will find the general theory presented in this book both accessible and convincing, and that as a result, they will take greater account of the insights of criminology when deciding how we should respond to crime. Further, it is my hope that the general theory will help criminologists better conduct their research, because the theory describes those factors that should be included in any explanation of crime and points to key areas where more research is needed.

The Questions a General Theory of Crime Must Answer

I believe that a general theory of crime must answer seven questions if it is to fully satisfy our curiosity about the causes of crime and provide maximum guidance to those seeking to control crime. These questions are briefly described below and much of this book involves an effort to answer them.

1. What Are the Major Causes of Crime?

A general theory must list those factors or variables that have a large, direct effect on crime. Research indicates that these factors include individual traits like impulsivity and irritability; family factors like poor parental supervision, weak bonding between parent and child, and harsh or abusive discipline; school experiences like low grades and low attachment to school; peer factors like association with delinquent peers and victimization by peers; and work-related factors like chronic unemployment and poor working conditions. Different theories in criminology tend to focus on different causes, but a general theory must include all of the leading causes of crime.

2. Why Do These Causes Increase the Likelihood of Crime?

Different theories provide different explanations for why the above sorts of factors cause crime. Strain theorists, for example, argue that a factor like child abuse increases crime because it upsets individuals, who then engage in crime to escape from the abuse (e.g., running away), end the abuse (e.g., assault on parents), take their anger out on others (e.g., assault on peers), or make themselves feel better (e.g., drug use). Control theorists argue that child abuse increases crime because it weakens the bond between parent and child, thereby lowering the costs of crime. Individuals who do not care about their parents have less to lose by engaging in crime, and so are more likely to respond to temptations and provocations with crime. Social learning theorists argue that child abuse increases crime because it teaches the child that aggression is an appropriate response to certain problems. A general theory must incorporate all such explanations to the extent that they are appropriate.

3. How Are the Causes of Crime Related to One Another?

A general theory must describe the relationship between those individual traits, family factors, school experiences, peer factors, and work experiences that cause crime. For example, it must take account of the fact that individual traits like impulsivity and irritability contribute to negative family experiences, low academic achievement, association with delinquent peers, and poor work histories. Likewise, it must consider the effect that family, school, peer, and work factors have on individual traits. Researchers have increasingly come to argue that the causes of crime have reciprocal effects on one another (e.g., individual traits influence family experiences, and family experiences influence individual traits), although some effects may be stronger than others (see Thornberry 1987).

4. What Effect Does Crime Have on Its 'Causes' (And What Effect Does Prior Crime Have on Subsequent Crime)?

There is good reason to believe that crime sometimes affects individual traits, family factors, school experiences, peer factors, and work experiences in ways that increase the likelihood of further crime. Engaging in crime, for example, may lead to problems with parents and teachers and to association with criminal peers. These effects, in turn, contribute to further crime. There is also reason to believe that engaging in crime *sometimes* directly increases the likelihood of further crime. Crime, for example, may provide pleasure to offenders, thereby directly increasing the likelihood of further crime. Crime, however, does not always have these sorts of effects. A general theory must therefore describe the conditions under which engaging in crime is likely to lead to further crime.

5. How Do the Causes Interact With One Another in Affecting Crime?

The effect of one cause on crime may depend on the level of the other causes. For example, we know that weak bonding between parent and child increases the likelihood of delinquency. Some evidence, however, suggests that the effect of weak bonding on delinquency depends on whether juveniles associate with delinquent peers (see Agnew 1993). Weak bonding increases delinquency by a small amount when juveniles do not associate with delinquent peers, but by a large amount when juveniles do associate with delinquent peers. We therefore state that weak bonding "interacts" with delinquent peer association in its effect on delinquency. A general theory must describe whether and how the leading causes interact with one another in affecting crime.

6. What Are the Timing and Form of Causal Effects?

The timing of causal effects refers to how long it takes the causes to affect crime. Do the causes have an immediate or contemporaneous effect on crime, or do they have a delayed effect? For example, does child abuse lead immediately to crime or does it take a period of months or even years? There has not been much research on the timing of causal effects, but it is obviously an important issue.

Likewise, there has not been much research on the form of causal effects. Most researchers assume that the causes have a "linear" effect on crime. That is, they assume that a given change in a causal variable like school grades always leads to the *same amount of change* in crime. For example, when grades decrease by one unit, crime always increases by two units. This is known as a linear effect because it can be plotted with a straight line. In Figure 1-1 below, we find that a one-unit decrease in grades always leads to two additional delinquent acts on average. This assumption of linear effects may sometimes be wrong, however. For example, it may be the case that grades have a nonlinear effect on crime, which must be plotted with a curved or zig-zagged line. Delinquency may increase by a small amount as grades move from "A" to "B," by a larger amount as grades move from "B" to "C," by a still larger amount as grades move from "C" to "D," etc. This nonlinear effect is shown in Figure 1-2. A general theory must describe the timing and form of all major causal effects.

7. What Factors Affect the Level and Operation of the Direct Causes of Crime?

A general theory must describe those factors that affect the level of the direct causes. Why, for example, do individuals differ in their level of impulsivity, parental supervision, or association with delinquent peers? Data suggest that biological factors sometimes affect the level of the direct causes. To illustrate, impulsivity may be genetically inherited to some extent, and it may be the result of certain

Figure 1-1
The Effect of Grades on Delinquency: Linear Effect

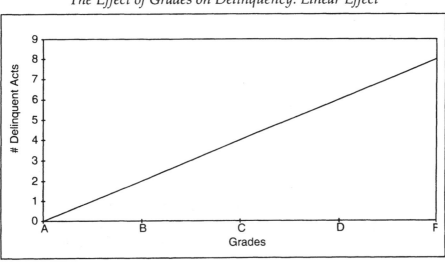

Figure 1-2
The Effect of Grades on Delinquency: Nonlinear Effect

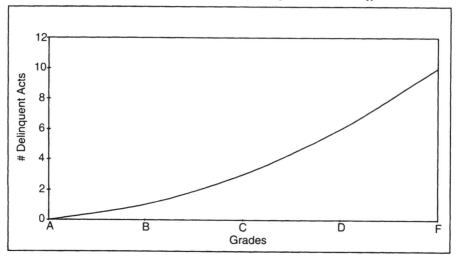

"biological harms," like certain types of birth complications and head injuries. The direct causes of crime may also be influenced by the individual's position in the larger social environment, including the community in which the individual lives and the individual's class, race/ethnic, age, and gender position in the larger society. To illustrate, females are more often subject to close parental supervision than are males (see Agnew 2005).

Biological factors and the individual's position in the larger social environment may also influence the operation of the direct causes, including the size of their effect on crime. For example, it has been argued that family factors like parental supervision and bonding have a stronger effect on crime among younger than older adolescents (Thornberry 1987). A general theory of crime, then, must describe how biological factors and the larger social environment influence the level and operation of the direct causes of crime.

Summary

Any general theory that does not answer the above seven questions is incomplete. For example, many individuals attempt to explain crime by simply listing the major risk factors for crime (#1 above). This explanation, however, does not help us fully *understand* the causes of crime. Among other things, we are left wondering why these risk factors cause crime (#2 above), how they are related to one another (#3 above), and why some people possess these risk factors while others do not (#7).

Further, this explanation is of *limited use to policy makers*. While a list of risk factors does point to the major direct causes of crime, there are other ways to reduce crime besides targeting its direct causes. One might focus on the reasons why the causes increase crime (#2). For example, if the causes increase crime by making people angry, one might develop anger management programs. Such programs may reduce crime even though they have little impact on the direct causes of crime. One might also focus on those factors that affect the direct causes (#7). For example, one might target those biological factors that contribute to traits like impulsivity and irritability. This might be done through programs that reduce birth complications and head injuries, like prenatal care programs and safety programs (see Agnew 2005).

A general theory of crime, then, must address the above seven questions if it is to fully explain crime and be of maximal use in controlling crime.

A General Theory That Answers These Questions Runs the Risk of Being Too Complex

Any general theory of crime that answers these seven questions will likely be quite complex, possibly so complex as to overwhelm the general public, policy makers, and perhaps even researchers. This is a serious shortcoming, because it may dramatically reduce the impact of the theory and may make it difficult or even impossible to test.

Certain of the general theories of crime produced in the 1980s had become rather complex. Thornberry's (1987) interactional theory is arguably the best of these. His theory of delinquency, as applied to middle adolescents (ages 15 and 16), is modeled in Figure 1-3 (Thornberry presents somewhat different models for younger and older adolescents). The model lists five major causes of delinquency (six if we recognize that prior delinquency influences subsequent delinquency). Each of these causes is broadly defined, however, and encompasses several more specific causes. For example, "attachment to parents" includes "the affective relationship between parent and child, communication patterns, parenting skills such as monitoring and discipline, parent-child conflict, and the like"

(Thornberry 1987, 866). The causes have reciprocal effects on one another (e.g., attachment to parents influences association with delinquent peers, which in turn influences attachment to parents). And the level and operation of these causes are said to be influenced by age, race, social class, sex, and community of residence, although the theory only discusses the influence of age and social class. Social class influences one's initial level on the causes of crime, such that lower-class individuals are more likely to have scores conducive to crime (e.g., score low on parental attachment). Age influences how large an effect certain of the causes have; for example, attachment to parents is said to have a stronger effect on delinquency among younger (ages 11–13) than middle adolescents.

Figure 1-3
Thornberry's General Theory of Delinquency,
Applied to Middle Adolescents (ages 15 and 16)

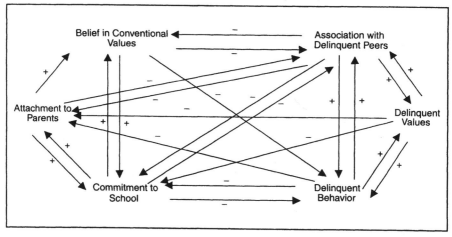

Thornberry's theory, then, addresses several of the questions listed above and is reasonably complex as a result. The theory lists many of the major causes of delinquency, draws on certain of the leading delinquency theories to describe why these causes affect delinquency (control and social learning theories), describes the relationship between these causes, describes the effect of delinquency on its causes, and describes how the larger social environment affects the causes. But as sophisticated as Thornberry's theory is, it does not address or only partly addresses certain of the above questions. It does not list some of the major causes of crime, most notably omitting personality traits (although see Thornberry and Krohn 2001); it does not fully describe all of the reasons why the causes increase the likelihood of crime, most notably omitting strain theory arguments; it does not describe how the causes interact with one another in affecting crime; it does not describe why prior delinquency only increases the likelihood of subsequent delinquency in *some* cases; it has little to say about the form and to a lesser extent the timing of causal effects; and it says little about the role of biological factors, gender, race/ethnicity, and community characteristics in affecting the level and operation of the direct causes.

So as complex as Thornberry's theory is, it is still incomplete in many ways. Building on this theory, however, would likely increase its complexity to an overwhelming level. Perhaps this is why most of the integrated or general theories developed in the 1990s and early 2000s take a different tack. They do not try to describe all of the factors that cause crime and the relationships between them. Rather, they focus on a *central causal variable* and describe in general terms how this variable affects crime. The latest of these theories is Colvin's (2000) theory of "crime and coercion." Colvin focuses on the impact of "coercion" or coercive control on crime; coercive control includes "the use or threat of force and intimidation aimed at creating compliance through fear," the "actual or threatened removal of social supports, which provide both material and emotional needs for individuals," and "the pressure arising from structural arrangements and circumstances that seem beyond individual control, such as economic and social pressure caused by unemployment, poverty, or competition among businesses or other groups" (Colvin 2000, 5). Coercion, then, is quite broadly defined.

Colvin builds his integrated theory of crime around this central causal variable. He describes the use of coercive control in various spheres, including the family, school, workplace, peer group, criminal justice system, and the immediate situations in which individuals find themselves. Specific forms of coercion in these spheres are listed, like harsh parental discipline, a range of negative school experiences, chronic unemployment and employment in "dead-end" jobs, and physical and verbal abuse from peers. He draws on the leading crime theories to explain why coercive control increases the likelihood of crime, he describes the conditions under which coercion is most likely to result in crime, and he describes the larger social forces that affect the individual's level of coercion. Colvin therefore addresses many of the questions listed above when describing the effects of coercive control. Several other recent integrated theories take a similar approach and focus on such central causal variables as disintegrative shaming (Braithwaite 1989), social support (Cullen 1994), and control imbalance (Tittle 1995).

These new integrations provide a useful means for simplifying a complex reality. Rather than trying to describe the many relationships between a large group of variables, they focus on a single, broadly defined variable that encompasses many of the more specific causes of crime. There are, however, two problems with this approach. First, the focus on a central causal variable, although broadly defined, makes it difficult for these theories to adequately address the above seven questions. These theories are especially likely to overlook certain key causes of crime (#1). Colvin's theory, for example, overlooks the fact that crime is sometimes caused by close ties to other criminals. Second, the rather abstract level of these theories limits their utility. While it is useful to speak of the effects of broadly defined variables like coercive control, the general public, policy makers, and many researchers have a need for more concrete information. They need to know what specific factors cause crime in particular spheres, like the family and school, how these factors are related to one another, and how they work together to affect crime. While the reader is provided with some guidance in these areas, most would have trouble listing all the particular causes of crime that fall under the central causal variable, describing the relationships between these causes, and noting how they work together to cause crime.

My Approach to Constructing a General Theory of Crime

Efforts to construct a general theory, then, face a major challenge: balancing the need to construct a theory that is reasonably complete with the need for a theory that is not so complex as to overwhelm readers. The general theory presented in this book takes a middle path. It does not attempt to list every cause of crime, describe all the relationships between these causes, and discuss all the ways in which these causes work together to affect crime. Nor does it limit its focus to a single, broadly defined causal variable. Rather, the general theory focuses on the major, direct causes of crime and groups these causes into a few well-defined clusters, organized by life domain (self, family, school, peer group, work). The theory then advances several general propositions that describe how these clusters are related to one another and how they work together to affect crime, with the propositions representing answers to the above seven questions. I believe this approach allows for the development of a reasonably complete theory of crime that is capable of guiding future research and crime-control efforts, but is not so complex that it overwhelms readers or impedes testing efforts.

Most of the propositions at the core of the general theory are derived from the work of others, including the integrated theories of Thornberry (1987) and Colvin (2000) discussed above. While the general theory does present some new arguments regarding the causes of crime, the theory is most distinguished by how it organizes existing theories and research into an integrated whole. The key propositions of the theory are listed below, with the chapter in which each proposition is discussed shown in parentheses.

1. Crime is most likely when the constraints against crime are low and the motivations for crime are high. (Chapter 2)

2. Several individual traits and features of the individual's immediate social environment directly influence the constraints against and the motivations for crime. Many of these traits and environmental variables are strongly associated with one another, and they can be grouped into a smaller number of "clusters" that are organized by life domain. These life domains include the self (comprised of the personality traits of irritability and low self-control), the family (poor parenting practices, no/bad marriages), the school (negative school experiences, limited education), peers (peer delinquency), and work (unemployment, bad jobs). (Chapter 3)

3. The life domains have reciprocal effects on one another, although some effects are stronger than others. (Chapter 4)

4. Crime sometimes affects the life domains in ways that increase the likelihood of subsequent crime. For example, crime sometimes contributes to irritability, poor parenting practices, negative school experiences, and association with

delinquent peers. Further, prior crime sometimes directly increases the likelihood of subsequent crime. These effects are most likely when individuals already possess traits conducive to crime and are in environments conducive to crime. (Chapter 5)

5. The life domains interact with one another in affecting crime. Each life domain has a greater effect on crime when the other life domains are conducive to crime (i.e., the individual is already at risk for crime). For example, traits like irritability and low self-control have a larger effect on crime among individuals in "negative" family, school, peer, and work environments. (Chapter 6)

6. The life domains have largely contemporaneous effects on one another and on crime, although each life domain has a large lagged (delayed) effect on itself. For example, *current* levels of crime are largely a function of *current* personality traits and family, school, peer, and work experiences, rather than *prior* traits and family, school, peer, and work experiences. (Chapter 7)

7. The life domains have nonlinear effects on crime, such that as a life domain increases in size it has an increasingly larger effect on crime. For example, the effect of negative school experiences on crime becomes progressively larger as school experiences become progressively worse. (Chapter 7)

8. Certain biological factors and features of the larger social environment affect the level and operation of the life domains. The key factors affecting the life domains are age, sex, race/ethnicity, socioeconomic status, and the characteristics of the community in which the individual lives—especially the socioeconomic status of the community. (Chapter 7)

What the Theory Is Designed to Explain

The general theory is designed to explain why some *individuals* are more likely than others to engage in *behaviors that are generally condemned* and that *carry a significant risk of sanction* by the state if detected. Such behaviors frequently cause direct harm to others, although that is not always the case. As will become apparent in the following chapters, the theory argues that some individuals engage in such behaviors because (1) they are in environments where the risk of condemnation and sanction is low; (2) they possess personality traits that reduce their concern with condemnation and sanction; and (3) they face strong pressures and incentives to engage in such behaviors. The best examples of the behaviors explained by the theory are "street crimes," like homicide, assault, robbery, rape, burglary, larceny-theft, vandalism, and illicit drug use.[1] The theory, however, also applies to some other types of crime, including white-collar crime (discussed in Chapter 10). Finally, the theory is written with the contemporary United States in mind, although it is likely applicable to other western industrialized societies. With some modification, the theory can be applied to still other societies (a topic discussed briefly in Chapter 8).

Although the theory focuses on the explanation of individual differences in the extent of crime, Chapter 9 describes how the theory can be extended to explain *group differences in crime rates*. In particular, this chapter draws on the theory to explain the fact that males have higher crime rates than females and that adolescents have higher crime rates than children and adults (sex and age being the two group characteristics most strongly related to crime). And although the theory focuses on differences in offending *between individuals*, Chapter 9 also describes how the theory can be used to explain *within-individual* levels of offending over the life course. In particular, the theory is used to explain why some individuals offend at high rates over much of their lives and others limit their offending to the adolescent years.

Testing and Applying the Theory

It should be kept in mind that the general theory is just a theory. While many key propositions of the theory have some empirical support, other propositions have not been the subject of much research. Chapter 10 briefly describes how each of the core propositions of the theory can be tested. If the theory is supported, it is my hope that it will have some impact on efforts to reduce crime. Chapter 11 draws on the theory (and the work that inspired the theory) to offer several recommendations for the control and prevention of crime. Finally, Chapter 12 provides a brief overview of the theory, noting the various ways in which the theory integrates or pulls together previous theories and research on the causes of crime.

Acknowledgments: The General Theory Is Built on the Work of Numerous Others

I would be seriously remiss if I did not acknowledge the strong debt that this theory owes to the work of numerous others, including Agnew's work on general strain theory (1992; 2001b), interaction effects (2003b), and the reasons why variables cause crime (1993; 1995b); Akers' (1998) social learning theory; Andrews and Bonta's (1998) work on rehabilitation and prevention; Bernard and Snipes' (1996) discussion of integrated theories; Braithwaite's (1989) theory of reintegrative shaming; Brezina's work on intervening processes (1998) and the consequences of delinquency (2000); Catalano and Hawkins' (1996) social development model; Colvin's (2000) theory of crime and coercion; Cullen's work on "structuring variables" (1984) and social support (1994); Elliott et al.'s (1979; 1985) integrated theory of delinquency; Farrington's (e.g., 1995) work on the causes and prevention of crime; Fishbein's (2001) and Rowe's (2002) summaries of biological theories of crime; Gottfredson and Hirschi's (1990) self-control theory; Hirschi's (1969) social control theory; Moffitt's (1993) biosocial theory of crime; Patterson et al.'s (1992) social coercion theory; Raine et al.'s (1997) work on the biosocial bases of violence; Sampson et al.'s (1989; 1995; 1997) work on crime and communities; Sampson and Laub's (1993) work on crime and the life course; Sherman's (1993; 2000) work on crime and defiance; Thornberry's (1987) interactional theory of delinquency; Tittle's (1995) masterful review of crime theories and his control balance theory of crime; and the work of many others. Since this book is relatively brief and is written for a wide audience, I do not discuss the work of these individuals in detail. My general theory, however, is built on and in large measure is an integration of essential insights from their work

Note

1. It is recognized that a given behavior, like marijuana use, may be condemned and sanctioned at one time or place, but not another. This is not a problem for the theory. The theory is designed to explain why in-

dividuals engage in behaviors that are condemned and sanctioned in particular societies at particular points in time. As a consequence, the specific behaviors explained by the theory may shift somewhat over time and from place to place (although there are a core group of violent and property crimes that are generally condemned in most societies and at most times). But in *all* cases, the behaviors explained by the theory violate strongly held social norms and carry a significant risk of state sanction.

Discussion and Study Questions

1. I claim that any general theory of crime must answer seven questions. What are these questions? Can you think of additional questions about crime that a general theory should answer?

2. I state that crime often affects individual traits and family, school, peer, and work factors in ways that increase the likelihood of further crime. Give three examples of such effects.

3. Give examples of "interaction effects," "contemporaneous" versus "lagged" or delayed effects," and "linear" versus "nonlinear" effects.

4. What is meant when we say that the causes of crime have "reciprocal" effects on one another? Give an example of a reciprocal effect.

5. What criteria do I suggest we use when evaluating a theory of crime? Can you think of any other criteria we should use (see Akers and Sellers 2004; Tittle 1995)?

6. Can you think of any potentially important causes of crime that are missing from Thornberry's model of crime (see Figure 1-3)?

7. What is "coercive control"?

8. I state that I take a "middle path" in constructing my general theory of crime. What do I mean by this?

9. What are the "scope conditions" for the general theory I present? In particular, what is the theory designed to explain (e.g., is the theory designed to explain all types of crime in all places)? ✦

Chapter 2

Crime Is Most Likely When the Constraints Against Crime Are Low and the Motivations for Crime Are High

Students in criminology courses frequently feel overwhelmed and confused. They often examine 10 or more different theories or explanations of crime, and they may examine scores of studies designed to test these theories. It is difficult to assimilate so much material over the course of a few weeks. I sometimes ask the students who are finishing my criminology classes to summarize what they have learned by providing their best answer to the question of "what causes crime?" The initial response is usually silence—they have trouble knowing where to begin. Then students usually list some of the causes we have studied, but no one comes close to offering a comprehensive explanation of crime. One of the major reasons I wrote this book was to help students and others integrate the enormous amount of material on the causes of crime.

I begin in this chapter by providing a *general* overview of the major variables that cause crime and the reasons why these variables cause crime. While there are scores of crime theories and thousands of studies testing those theories, a rather simple idea underlies most of these theories and studies: Crime is most likely when the constraints against crime are low and the motivations for crime are high (e.g., Gold 1963; Sheley 1983; Tittle 1995). Further, there are only a few *broad* constraints and motivations that we need to consider. Most refer to features of the individuals' social environment, particularly their family, school, peer, and work environments. Others refer to individuals' personality traits, which influence how they perceive, experience, and respond to their social environment. This chapter lists the major constraints and motivations affecting crime, notes that these constraints and motivations may be long-lasting or short-term (situationally based), and briefly discusses whether there are any other factors that influence the likelihood of crime.

Constraints Against Crime

"What keeps you from engaging in crime?" Your responses to this question illustrate the constraints against crime, which refer to those factors that hold individuals back or restrain them from committing crime. As depicted in Figure 2-1, these constraints might be viewed as a wall standing between the individual and crime. There are several major types of constraints: You don't engage in crime because you might be caught and punished (external control); you have a lot to lose if you are punished (stake in conformity); and you believe that crime is wrong and are a thoughtful, caring person who does not like risky activities (internal control). I describe these major

Figure 2-1
The Constraints Against Crime and the Motivations for Crime

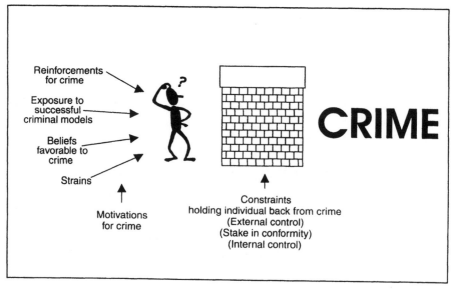

constraints below, drawing heavily on several of the leading crime theories, particularly social control theory (Hirschi 1969; Sampson and Laub 1993), self-control theory (Gottfredson and Hirschi 1990), rational choice theory (Cornish and Clarke 1986; Piquero and Tibbetts 2002), the routine activities perspective (Felson 1998), and social learning theory (Akers 1998).

External Control

External control refers to the likelihood that others will detect and sanction criminal behavior. When people think of external control they usually think of the police arresting someone and the court sending that person to prison or jail. Being arrested and incarcerated, however, is only one of many examples of external control. Other examples include your parents grounding you for your misbehavior, your friends shunning you, school officials expelling you, and employers firing you. Individuals are high in external control to the extent that others:

1. Set clear rules for them that prohibit crime and related behaviors, like staying out late at night and associating with the "wrong" crowd.

2. Monitor their behavior to detect rule violations. This monitoring may be direct, with others watching the individual (e.g., parents watching their children at home or teachers watching them at school). It may also be indirect; for example, parents may ask their children about their behavior and ask others, like teachers and neighbors, about the behavior of their children.

3. Consistently sanction their rule violations in a meaningful manner, although such sanctions should not be overly harsh or abusive, which may anger and alienate the recipient. Sanctions like time outs, withdrawal of privileges, the imposition of tasks, and clear expressions of disapproval are often recommended for children, depending on their age.

External control may be exercised by family members, friends, school officials, neighbors, employers, and criminal justice officials like the police. Most people think of the police when they think of external control, but the external control exercised by intimate others like family members is typically more influential than the control exercised by the police. Intimate others are in a much better position to monitor behavior and consistently impose meaningful sanctions.

Individuals differ dramatically in their level of external control, with some being subject to very little such control from conventional authority figures. For example, this was the case with many of the children from the "street-oriented" families in Elijah Anderson's study of violence in a poor, inner-city community. According to Anderson (1999, 69):

> At an early age, often even before they start school and without much adult supervision, children from street-oriented families gravitate to the streets, where they must be ready to "hang," to socialize competitively with peers. These children have a great deal of latitude and are allowed to rip and run up and down the street. They often come home from school, put their books down, and go right back out the door. On school nights many eight- and nine-year-olds remain out until nine or ten o'clock (teenagers may come in whenever they want to).

Stake in Conformity

External control refers to the likelihood that individuals will be caught and punished by others if they deviate. Some individuals, however, are more fearful of detection and punishment than others. One reason for this is they have a lot to lose if they are caught and punished. That is, they have a large "stake in conformity" or investment in conventional society, which may be jeopardized by crime. For example, they have good jobs that may be lost if they engage in crime.[1]

Individuals have a large stake in conformity to the extent that:

1. They have strong emotional bonds to conventional others, like parents, spouses, teachers, and employers. That is, they like, love, care about, and/or respect these others.

2. They engage in positively valued activities with conventional others or receive positive benefits from interacting with conventional others, including material benefits, emotional support, and valued information or advice.

3. They are doing well in school, like school, expect to get an advanced education, or have already obtained an advanced education.

4. They have "good" jobs that they like or they expect to get such jobs. Such jobs are prestigious, are well-paid, have good benefits, and have good working conditions

5. They have an excellent reputation among conventional others.

All of these things may be jeopardized by crime.[2] As a result, individuals with a strong stake in conformity are less likely to engage in crime.

Individuals differ greatly in their stake in conformity, with some individuals having little or no stake. Several authors, for example, point out that many inner-city youth feel that they have nothing to lose from crime. They have few close ties to conventional others; receive little of value from conventional others; are poorly educated; are unemployed or work sporadically in dead-end jobs with low pay, poor benefits, and unpleasant working conditions; are viewed negatively by others; and have no hope for a better future, with some stating that they will probably be dead or in prison in a few years' time (e.g., Anderson 1994; 1999).

Internal Control

Many individuals refrain from crime even when they are in tempting situations where there is little likelihood that their criminal behavior will be detected and punished. One reason for this is that they believe that crime is wrong or immoral. Such individuals have typically been taught this belief from an early age by parents, teachers, neighbors, religious figures, and others. Eventually, they come to accept or "internalize" this belief and it becomes a major constraint against crime. Some people, however, have not been taught or socialized to believe that crime is wrong. These individuals have an amoral orientation to crime; that is, they believe that crime is neither right nor wrong. They therefore lack a major constraint against crime.

Also, some individuals have a set of personality traits that increase their awareness of and responsiveness to the above constraints. Such individuals are thoughtful, care about the feelings and rights of others, are good tempered, have an aversion to risky activities, and have little need for the immediate gratification of their desires (see Gottfredson and Hirschi 1990; Grasmick et al. 1993). As a consequence, they are able to exercise much self-control when tempted to engage in crime. Other individuals, however, are low in self-control. They are impulsive (tend to act without thinking); care little about others; are irritable; are attracted to risky activities; and prefer the immediate rewards of crime (e.g., money, property) to the often delayed, but larger rewards of conformity. Therefore, they give little thought to and are little bothered by the negative consequences of crime. Such individuals have trouble exercising self-control when tempted by crime.[3]

Brief Summary

Individuals face strong constraints against crime when (a) their criminal behavior is likely to be detected and consistently sanctioned in a meaningful way (high external control); (b) they have a lot to lose by engaging in crime (high stake in conformity); and (c) they believe that crime is wrong and are high in self-control (internal control).

The Motivations for Crime

The motivations for crime refer to those factors that entice or pressure individuals to engage in crime. These motivations may be grouped into two broad categories (see Reckless 1961). One category focuses on those factors that *entice or pull* individuals into crime; rational choice theory, the routine activities perspective, and especially *social learning theory* focus on motivations of this type (see Akers 1998). Another category focuses on those factors that *pressure or push* individuals to engage in crime; *strain theory* focuses on motivations of this type (see Agnew 1992; 2001). These motivations are illustrated in Figure 2-1 (at the beginning of this chapter).

Factors That Entice Individuals Into Crime: Social Learning for Crime

Many individuals learn to engage in crime from others. These others include peers and gang members, who often deliberately teach individuals to engage in crime. These others may also include parents, who often inadvertently (but sometimes deliberately) teach their children to engage in crime. Individuals are taught to engage in crime in three major ways: they are *reinforced for crime, exposed to successful criminal models, and taught beliefs favorable to crime.* As a result of such learning, individuals come to view crime as a desirable or appropriate response in certain circumstances, and are thus enticed or pulled into crime.

Reinforcements for Crime

The reinforcements for crime may be positive or negative. Positive reinforcement involves the presentation of something good, like money, social approval, or the pleasurable feelings that result from drug use. Negative reinforcement involves the removal of something bad; for example, your parents stop abusing you if you run away or peers stop harassing you if use drugs. Geoffrey Canada (1995, 16–17) provides an excellent example of negative reinforcement when he notes that in the poor, inner-city community in which he grew up, the "failure to fight would mean that you would be set upon over and over again ... it was better to fight even if you couldn't win than to end up being [beaten badly] for being a coward."

We are more likely to engage in crime to the extent that our crime: "(a) is frequently reinforced and infrequently punished; (b) results in large amounts of reinforcement (e.g., a lot of money, social approval, or pleasure) and little punishment; and (c) is more likely to be reinforced than alternative behaviors" (Agnew 2005).

Crime is almost never reinforced in all settings, but is sometimes reinforced in certain settings. For example, your friends may praise you when you assault others who provoke you, so your assaultive behavior is frequently reinforced in this circumstance. Your parents, however, may punish you when you assault others, regardless of the provocation, so your assaults are usually punished in this circumstance. As you might imagine, individuals are most likely to engage in assault in those settings where it is most often reinforced.

Exposure to Successful Criminal Models

Individuals also tend to model or imitate the behavior of others, although this modeling is not simply a matter of "monkey see, monkey do." We are most likely to imitate the behavior of those we like and respect, and we are most likely to imitate their behavior when we see that it is reinforced. For example, suppose we witness a stranger being arrested for shoplifting. We are unlikely to imitate the shoplifting behavior of this person. However, suppose we witness several successful shoplifting incidents by our close friends; here, imitation is more likely.

One of the delinquents in MacLeod's (1995, 117) study of a public housing project in Boston provides a good illustration of the importance of imitation. This delinquent states that:

> We were all brought up, all we seen is our older brothers and that gettin' into trouble and goin' to jail and all that shit. . . . We seen so many fucking drugs, all the drinking. They fucking go, that group's gone. The next group came. It's our brothers that are a little older, y'know, 20-something years old. They started doing crime. And when you're young, you look up to people. You have a person, everybody has a person they look up to. And he's doing this, he's drinking, he's doing that, he's doing drugs, he's ripping off people. Y'know, he's making good fucking money, and it looks like he's doing good, y'know. So bang. Now it's our turn. We're here. What we gonna do when all we seen is fuckin' drugs, alcohol, fighting, this and that, no one going to school?

Taught Beliefs Favorable to Crime

Finally, we may be taught beliefs that are favorable to crime. Few individuals are taught that crime is *generally* good, with the occasional exception of certain minor crimes like drinking under age, gambling, and some illegal sex acts. Individuals, however, may be taught that crime is good or justified or at least excusable *under certain conditions*. Anderson (1999), for example, argues that youth in many inner-city communities are taught that violence is good or at least justified in response to a wide range of provocations and insults (also see Sykes and Matza 1957).

Agnew (1994) provides another illustration of beliefs favorable to crime. Using data from a national sample of adolescents, he found that almost all individuals felt that it was wrong to "hit or threaten to hit someone without any reason"—few people felt that violence is generally good. Agnew, however, found that many individuals felt that "it's alright to beat up people if they started the fight," "it's alright to physically beat up people who call you names," and "if people do something to make you really mad, they deserve to be beaten up." Many individuals, then, felt that violence was "alright" under certain conditions, and Agnew found that such individuals were more likely to engage in violence.

Individual Differences in the Propensity to Learn Crime

I should note that some individuals are more likely than others to find crime rewarding, to imitate the behavior of criminal models, and to adopt beliefs favorable to crime. For example, I earlier stated that some individuals have a preference for risky activities. This makes crime more rewarding to them, because criminal activities are often risky. This point is illustrated by a shoplifter who stated that "I do it for the rush. Adrenaline rush, you know. You get all excited and you feel kinda crazy inside" (Cromwell et al. 1999, 65). I also stated that some individuals prefer immediate over delayed rewards. As one delinquent put it, for example, "we don't just wanna make a buck, we wanna make a fast buck. We want it now. Right fucking now" (MacLeod 1995, 106). This desire for immediate gratification also makes crime more rewarding because the rewards of crime are often immediate (e.g., theft immediately provides money or valued goods). The rewards from conventional activities, however, are often delayed (e.g., the financial payoffs from studying hard and getting good grades are years in coming).

Brief Summary

Individuals may be pulled or enticed into crime because their criminal behavior is reinforced in certain circumstances, they are exposed to successful criminal models, and they are taught beliefs favorable to crime. Further, certain individuals possess traits such that they are more easily enticed into crime than others.

Some individuals, however, face much stronger enticements to crime than others. In particular, some individuals are in environments where they are frequently reinforced for committing crimes, regularly exposed to successful criminal models, and often presented with beliefs favorable to crime. Elijah Anderson provides a wonderful but disturbing example of this in his discussion of life in poor, inner-city communities, particularly the life of "street-oriented" children. In particular, Anderson (1994, 83, 86) observes that:

> These children of the street, growing up with little supervision, are said to "come up hard." They often learn to fight at an early age, sometimes using short-tempered adults around them as models. The street-oriented home

may be fraught with anger, verbal disputes, physical aggression, and even mayhem. The children observe these goings-on, learning that might makes right. They quickly learn to hit those who cross them. . . . Even small children test one another, pushing and shoving, and are ready to hit other children over circumstances not to their liking . . . the child who is the toughest prevails. Thus the violent resolution of disputes, the hitting and cursing, gains social reinforcement. . . . Those street-oriented adults with whom children come in contact . . . [verbalize] the messages they are getting through experience: "Watch your back." "Protect yourself." "Don't punk out." "If somebody messes with you, you got to pay them back." "If somebody disses you, you got to straighten them out." (Also see Anderson 1999.)

Factors That Pressure Individuals to Engage in Crime: Strains

Strain theory argues that a major motivation for crime is negative treatment by others. Someone treats you in a way you do not like, and you experience a range of negative emotions, like anger and frustration. These negative emotions create pressure for corrective action, and you *may* respond with crime, particularly if you lack the ability or desire to cope in a legal manner. Crime may allow you to reduce or escape from your negative treatment; for example, you may assault the people who harass you, run away from the parents who abuse you, or steal the money you cannot get through legal channels. Crime may allow you to satisfy your desire for revenge against those who have mistreated you or related targets; for example, you may "get back" at your teachers by vandalizing your school. And crime may allow you to alleviate your negative emotions; for example, you may take illicit drugs to feel better.

There are three major types of negative treatment or strain: others may (1) prevent you from achieving your goals (e.g., goals like obtaining a lot of money); (2) remove or threaten to remove positively valued things you possess (e.g., take your valued possessions); and (3) present or threaten to present you with noxious or negatively valued stimuli (e.g., verbally or physically abuse you). There are hundreds of specific types of strain that fall into these three broad categories, but Agnew (2001) argues that certain strains are more conducive to criminal coping than others. Such strains are high in magnitude, are seen as unjust, are associated with low social control, and create some pressure or incentive to engage in criminal coping. These strains include the blockage of monetary, autonomy, and masculinity goals; parental rejection; harsh or erratic discipline; child abuse and neglect; partner abuse; negative school experiences, like low grades and negative treatment by teachers; work in low-paying, dead-end jobs with unpleasant working conditions; home-lessness; peer abuse; experiences with prejudice and discrimination; and criminal victimization.

Not all people respond to such strains with crime; in fact, most live with their strain or try to deal with it through legal channels. Whether individuals respond to strain with crime is influenced by several factors, including many of the factors listed under the constraints to crime. In particular, individuals are more likely to respond to strain with crime if they are low in external control because they are less likely to be sanctioned for a criminal response. They are more likely to respond with crime if they have a low stake in conformity because they have less to lose from crime. Also, those with a low stake in conformity—like those who lack close ties to others or are unemployed—are less likely to possess the resources to cope with their strain in a noncriminal manner. Finally, individuals are more likely to respond to strain with crime if they possess personality traits like impulsivity and irritability. These traits not only reduce internal control, but they also increase the individual's sensitivity to strain. Irritable individuals, for example, are more likely to take strong offense at negative treatment and react in an aggressive manner (see Caspi and Moffitt 1995, 485–487).

Individuals are also more likely to respond to strain with crime if they have learned to engage in crime from others; that is, if they have been reinforced for crime, exposed to successful criminal models, and taught beliefs favorable to crime. Individuals in certain communities, for example, may be taught that one should respond to a range of insults and provocations with violence (Anderson 1999).

Long-Lasting and Situational Constraints and Motivations

So there are several major constraints against and motivations for crime. It is important to emphasize that these constraints and motivations may be relatively enduring or they may be more limited. In fact, the situations we encounter each have their own particular sets of constraints against and motivations for crime.

Most of the constraints I have mentioned are relatively enduring. Examples include being closely supervised by your parents, having a strong emotional bond to your spouse, having a good job, believing that crime is wrong, and being high in self-control. Likewise, most of the motivations I have mentioned are relatively enduring. Examples include being unable to achieve your monetary goals, associating with friends who reinforce your crime in certain circumstances, and holding beliefs that approve of crime in certain conditions. I do not mean to imply that these constraints and motivations never change, only that they tend to have some stability over time.

At the same time, we face certain situationally based constraints against and motivations for crime. For example, we may find ourselves in a situation where we are exposed to a lot of money and there is no one to stop us from taking it. The motivation for crime in such a situation is high (we anticipate much reinforcement if we take the money), and the level of external control is low. We may still not take the money, perhaps because of our long-term constraints and motivations. For example, we may believe that theft is bad and we may have little need for the money. Nevertheless, the situational constraints and motivations we encounter have some impact on our behavior. Rational choice theory and the routine-activities perspective describe many of the situationally based constraints against and motivations for crime (Cornish and Clarke 1986; Felson 1998; Miethe and Meier 1994; Piquero and Tibbetts 2002). We can draw on these theories and the above discussion to list the major situational constraints and motivations.

The major situational constraint against crime is the presence of others who might exercise external control over us if we engage in crime,[4] so we tend avoid victimizing people who might sanction us, like people who are bigger than us or who are traveling in groups (Felson 1996). We also tend to avoid committing crimes when conventional authority figures like parents or teachers are present. These individuals might directly sanction us or contact others, like the police, who will. That is one reason why individuals are more likely to engage in delinquency after school than during school hours, when teachers and other authority figures are present (Snyder and Sickmund 1999).

There are several major situational motivations for crime, including provocations by others (e.g., insults, threats), which is a major type of strain (Wilkinson 2002). For example, Lockwood's (1997) study of high-school and middle-school students found that almost all violent incidents began with one student provoking another, with the provocations including pushing, grabbing, hitting, teasing, and insulting. The situational motivations for crime also include the presence of "attractive targets" for crime, which signal that criminal behavior is likely to be reinforced. For example, Felson (1998) argues that potential offenders are tempted to engage in crime when they encounter property that is visible, accessible, valuable, and easy to move. Further, situational motivations include encouragement to engage in crime by peers and others, which also signals that crime is likely to be reinforced (or at least not punished). In this area, data suggest that violence is much more likely in those situations where it is encouraged by onlookers (Luckenbill 1977). Finally, situational motivations include the presence of close others who are engaging in or modeling crime. For example, we are much more likely to use drugs at a party if most of our friends are using drugs.

It is important to take account of these situational constraints and motivations. Doing so not only helps us understand why crime is more likely in some situations than others, but also helps us better explain why some people are more likely than others to engage in crime. Some people are more likely than others to encounter situations where the constraints against crime are low and the motivations for crime are high. Some people, for example, are more likely to be in situations where conventional authority figures like parents are absent or where their friends encourage crime.

Generally speaking, the *enduring* constraints and motivations we face strongly influence the *situational* constraints and motivations we encounter.[5] For example, individuals who are poorly supervised by their parents are more likely to be in situations where conventional authority figures are absent, and individuals who have delinquent friends are more likely to encounter situations where their friends encourage crime. Measures of *enduring* constraints and motivations, then, should go a long way toward indexing the *situational* constraints and motivations that individuals encounter. However, it is also desirable to directly measure the situational constraints and motivations that individuals encounter. One example of how this might be done is by asking juveniles how much time they spend in unstructured, unsupervised activities with peers (Osgood et al. 1996). In such situations, there are no conventional authority figures to sanction crime and adolescents are often provoked or encouraged to engage in crime.

In sum, we must consider both long-term and situational constraints and motivations in order to best explain why some individuals are more likely than others to engage in crime.

Is Crime Influenced by Factors Other Than Constraints and Motivations?

Can you think of any other factors that influence crime besides the constraints against and the motivations for crime? Certain criminologists have suggested that crime is also a function of the individual's opportunities for crime and skills for crime (see especially Tittle 1995). Let us consider each of these in turn.

The "opportunity for crime" refers to whether the social and physical elements necessary for crime are present; for example, is there property to steal, a person to assault, or drugs to use (see Tittle 1995, 169). I believe that most individuals encounter ample opportunities to engage in a broad range of street crimes, but opportunity as just defined is an important factor in the explanation of certain other crimes. For example, individuals who do not have white-collar jobs have little opportunity to engage in white-collar crimes like consumer fraud. This fact helps explain why blue-collar individuals and females are less likely to engage in such crimes.[6]

The "skills for crime" refer to whether individuals have such things as the physical and intellectual ability and the knowledge to commit criminal acts (Sheley 1983, 514). I believe that most individuals possess the ability and knowledge to engage in a broad range of street crimes, and that those high in motivation and low in constraint can easily obtain the knowledge they lack. For these reasons, I do not think that the skill to engage in crime is an important factor in explaining most street crimes, although it may be an important factor in the explanation of certain highly specialized crimes, like "safe-cracking."[7]

Conclusion

Crime is most likely when the constraints against crime are low and the motivations for crime are high. This chapter drew on several leading crime theories—especially control, strain, and social learning theories—to describe the major constraints against and motivations for crime. These constraints and motivations are listed in Figure 2-1 (at the beginning of this chapter). Briefly, there are three major constraints against crime: external control, stake in conformity, and internal control. There are several major motivations for crime: reinforcements for crime, exposure to successful criminal models, beliefs favorable to crime, and certain types of strain. Further, some individuals possess traits that increase their susceptibility or responsiveness to the motivations for crime. These constraints and motivations may be relatively long-lasting or limited to particular situations.

Criminologists argue that people differ in the constraints and motivations they face and these differences explain differences in crime. Consider the following two people: Joe is part of a loving family where he is closely supervised by his parents. He is doing well in school and plans to enroll in a prestigious university. He believes that crime is wrong, having been taught that by his parents and others. He is a very cautious person who always thinks before acting. And Joe's friends are like Joe: good students from loving families. Joe faces numerous constraints against crime and has little apparent motivation for crime.

Bob, on the other hand, dislikes his parents, who largely ignore and sometimes abuse him. He is flunking out of school and has no plans for the future. He is irritable, impulsive, cares little about others, and enjoys engaging in risky behaviors. He spends much time "hanging out" on the street, often getting into arguments with others. Bob's friends reinforce his crime, model crime for him, and teach him beliefs that approve of crime in certain circumstances. Bob faces few constraints against crime and has much motivation for crime.

These constraints and motivations affect individuals in several ways. Individuals usually give some consideration to the constraints and motivations they face when deciding to engage in crime. That is not to say that they carefully consider all of their constraints and motivations; their decision to engage in crime is often hurried, based on incomplete or inaccurate information (e.g., about the probability of getting caught and punished), made under the influence of alcohol or drugs, and made under great pressure (see Akers and Sellers 2004, 26–29; Cornish and Clarke 1986; Exum 2002). Nevertheless, individuals often give some rough consideration to certain of the above constraints and motivations. Burglars, for example, often give some consideration to the potential risks and gains they face when deciding whether to commit a crime. One burglar states that the "first thing ya gotta do is make sure nobody is home. It's pretty easy. I can do it driving by most times. Like, you know, cars in the driveway, front door open, kids playing, shit like that" (Cromwell et al. 1999, 52).

Further, certain of these constraints and motivations shape the nature of the decision-making process itself, influencing the factors that individuals consider when contemplating crime and how these factors are evaluated (e.g., Bouffard 2002; Exum 2002; Tibbetts and Gibson 2002). So individuals who are low in self-control are less likely to be aware of or attach much importance to the costs of crime. In this area, many criminals state that they give little thought to the potential costs of their crimes. Rather, they simply focus on the immediate benefits that might result from their crimes, like the money they might get for drugs or partying. For example, one armed robber, when asked whether he thought about getting caught, replied, "I never even think about [getting caught], I just do [the robbery]." Another stated that "If I think about [the chance of getting caught], I'm not gonna do [the stickup]. So I try not to think about it" (Wright and Decker 1997, 119)

Finally, certain of these constraints and motivations have an unconscious effect on our behavior. In particular, evidence suggests that we are often unaware of the reinforcements and punishments that shape our behavior, but such reinforcements and punishments nevertheless have a strong effect on how we behave (Claxton 1999; also see Chartrand and Bargh 2002). Short and Strodtbeck's (1965) classic study of Chicago gangs provides an example. Short and Strodtbeck found that gang leaders were most likely to engage in aggressive behavior when their status as leaders was threatened or in doubt. Their aggressive behavior served to enhance or secure their leadership status, which is to say that their aggression was reinforced. The gang leaders, however, seemed largely unaware of the fact their aggression was motivated by such forces.

So, overall, individuals are most likely to engage in crime when their constraints against crime are low and their motivations for crime are high. This is not to say that constraints and motivations *completely determine* whether individuals engage in crime. Constraints and motivations have a large impact on behavior, but there is reason to believe that individuals possess some degree of "free will" and their behavior is *not fully determined* by outside forces (Agnew 1995a). So two individuals may confront the same constraints against and motivations for crime; one may decide to engage in crime after considering these constraints and motivations while the other may not. The exercise of "free will" or "free choice" is said to have an especially strong impact on behavior when individuals face constraints and motivations *for both crime and conformity* (see Agnew 1995a). Nevertheless, the constraints and motivations described in this chapter increase the *probability* that individuals will engage in crime—with crime being quite likely when the constraints against it are very low and the motivations for it are very high.

Chapter 3 continues the discussion of constraints and motivations. Where the constraints and motivations were described in broad terms in this chapter, Chapter 3 provides a more detailed list of those factors or variables that affect these constraints and motivations. A good many variables are listed in Chapter 3, but an attempt is made to group them into a smaller number of clusters organized by life domain (self, family, school, peer group, and work).

Notes

1. Stake in conformity refers not only to what one has to lose through crime, but also to what one has gained or expects to gain through conformity. A high stake in conformity, then, not only increases the fear of punishment, but also increases the desire to conform (or motivation for conformity). In fact, many individuals with a high stake in conformity probably conform not so much because they fear punishment for crime, but because they are satisfied with their current circumstances and feel no need to engage in crime.

2. Social control theorists assume that these "stakes in conformity" are contingent on conventional behavior; that is, that they are dependent on the individual behaving in a conventional manner and would be lost or threatened if the individual engaged in crime. Social learning

theorists might argue that we should determine the extent to which these "stakes" or "reinforcers" are contingent on conventional behavior. While I think it safe to assume that most "stakes" are generally contingent on conventional behavior, it may be useful to determine the extent to which this is the case. If a significant percentage of respondents believe that their stakes are not dependent on conventional behavior, researchers should determine whether this belief conditions or influences the effect of stakes on crime.

3. Gottfredson and Hirschi (1990) argue that self-control is the *major* cause of crime and that once it is established, the other constraints against crime are unimportant. Data, however, suggest that while self-control is a very important constraint against crime, other constraints are also important. In particular, these other constraints affect crime even after we take level of self-control into account (e.g., Piquero and Tibbetts 1996; Wright et al. 1999).

4. The other constraints against crime (stake in conformity, internal control) are less likely to vary across situations, although such variation is possible (e.g., some situations may be more likely than others to activate beliefs against crime). For that reason, I believe the presence of others capable of exercising external control is the *major* situational constraint against crime.

5. Many of our enduring constraints and motivations, in fact, simply represent summaries of the situations we encounter. So when juveniles state that their parents closely supervise them, they are basically stating that they often encounter situations where their parents are present or at least have some knowledge of what they are doing.

6. Opportunity, however, may be incorporated under the constraints against and motivations for crime. Individuals without white-collar jobs are excluded from situations where white-collar crime is possible (a type of external control), and their efforts to engage in such crime are unlikely to result in reinforcement.

7. The skills to engage in crime may be also be incorporated under the constraints against and motivations for crime. Individuals lacking the skill to engage in a particular type of crime may have been deliberately prevented from obtaining that skill (a type of external control), and are unlikely to be reinforced for that crime.

Discussion and Study Questions

1. What is meant by a "constraint against crime" and a "motivation for crime"?

2. List the constraints against crime you face, as well as any motivations for crime you may face.

3. List the *major* constraints against crime and the major motivations for crime. Suppose you are developing a survey to measure these constraints and motivations. List at least two questions you would ask to measure each constraint and motivation.

4. Give examples of both long-lasting and situationally specific constraints against and motivations for crime.

5. What is meant by "opportunities for crime" and "skills" for crime? Why do I argue that these factors do not play an important role in the explanation of street crime?

6. Drawing on the above discussion about constraints and motivations, how might you explain the fact that males generally have higher rates of offending than females?

7. Given the above discussion, what specific policies would you recommend for controlling crime?

8. If you are taking a criminology, juvenile delinquency, or crime theory course, list the major theories you have studied and describe what they say about the constraints against and the motivations for crime. ✦

Chapter 3

A Range of Individual and Social Variables Affect the Constraints Against and the Motivations for Crime

Crime is most likely when the constraints against it are low and the motivations for it are high. Several major constraints against crime are listed in Chapter 2, including external control, stake in conformity, and internal control. Several major motivations for crime are also listed, including reinforcements for crime, exposure to successful criminal models, beliefs favorable to crime, and strains. Most of these constraints and motivations are quite broad and encompass many specific causes of crime. For example, numerous variables index or directly affect the individual's *stake in conformity*, like the individuals's emotional bonds to parents and teachers, grades, educational and occupational goals, and type of job. This chapter builds on Chapter 2 by listing the *specific* variables that index or directly affect the constraints against and motivations for crime. These variables constitute the leading causes of crime.

A large number of such variables can be listed. To keep the discussion manageable, I focus on those variables that likely have relatively moderate to large *direct* effects on crime.[1] This still includes a good number of variables, however. Table 3-1, for example, lists 31 variables that have sizeable direct effects on crime according to certain research with these variables, grouped into several categories. It is of course difficult to keep all of these variables in mind, which is why many students come away from criminology courses feeling overwhelmed, and why a general theory of crime is so difficult to

Table 3-1
*Variables Found to Have a Relatively Moderate
to Large Direct Effect on Crime*

A. PERSONALITY TRAITS
- impulsivity
- high activity levels
- trouble concentrating (attention deficit)
- low ability to learn from punishment
- sensation seeking
- irritability
- insensitivity to others/low empathy
- poor social- and problem-solving skills
- beliefs favorable to crime

B. FAMILY VARIABLES
- negative bonding between parent and child
- family conflict
- child abuse
- poor supervision/discipline
- criminal parents
- criminal siblings
- low social support
- (for adults) unmarried
- negative bonding with spouse/partner
- criminal spouse/partner

C. SCHOOL VARIABLES
- poor academic performance
- negative bonding to school
- little time on homework
- negative treatment by teachers
- low educational/occupational goals

D. PEER VARIABLES
- association with delinquent peers
- gang membership
- much time in unstructured, unsupervised activities with peers
- criminal victimization

E. WORK VARIABLES
- poor work performance
- chronic unemployment
- work in "secondary labor market"

develop. Any attempt to describe the relationships between all of these variables and the ways in which they work together to affect crime would be hopelessly complex.

It is possible, however, to group these variables into a smaller number of categories or clusters. Indeed, there have already been several attempts to do so. This chapter begins by briefly describing and critiquing the dominant strategy for grouping these variables, and then presents an alternative method for grouping or combining them. In particular, I argue that the direct causes of crime should be grouped into clusters organized around the life domains of self (personality traits), family, school, peers, and work. I then list the major variables in each of these life domains and describe how they index or directly affect both the constraints against and the motivations for crime.

The Dominant Strategy for Grouping the Causes of Crime Into a Smaller Number of Categories

The most obvious way to group the causes of crime is by the type of constraint or motivation they index. Those variables indexing external control can be grouped together, those indexing stake in conformity can be grouped together, those indexing strain can be grouped together, and so on. Most efforts to group these variables have employed some variation of this approach, with criminologists arguing that each variable affects a particular constraint against or motivation for crime (e.g., Elliott et al. 1985; Messner et al. 1989). In fact, a rough consensus has emerged in this area. For example, parental supervision is typically said to index external control, low grades are said to index stake in conformity, and associating with delinquent peers is said to index the social learning for crime (reinforcements, models, and beliefs favorable to crime). There is, however, a major problem with grouping variables by the type of constraint or motivation they index.

As you may have noticed in Chapter 2, many variables index or affect more than one type of constraint or motivation. For example, low grades index both stake in conformity and strain. Being abused by parents indexes stake in conformity, strain, and exposure to criminal models. Self-control indexes internal control and directly affects both strain and the social learning for crime. Many other examples can be given, and in this chapter I argue that most of the major causes of crime affect *both* the constraints against and the motivations for crime (also see Agnew 1993; 1995b). In fact, that is the reason they are the *major* causes of crime: they have far-ranging effects.

It is difficult, then, to group variables by the type of constraint or motivation they index.

An Alternative Strategy for Grouping the Causes of Crime Into a Smaller Number of Categories

I believe that there is a better way to group the causes of crime into a smaller number of categories. In particular, I propose that the causes be grouped into clusters organized around the life domains of self (personality traits), family, school, peers, and work. These domains represent the major spheres of life and they encompass all of the direct causes of crime listed in Table 3-1. Other domains—like the individual's biological state, the community in which the individual lives, and the individual's position in the larger social system (as indexed by class, sex/gender, age, and race/ethnicity)—affect crime primarily through their effect on these domains (e.g., Agnew 2005; Elliott et al. 1996; Gottfredson et al. 1991; Steffensmeier and Allan 2000; Thornberry et al. 2003b).

Grouping the causes of crime in this manner allows us to ensure that each cause is part of one and only one category. For example, low grades fall into just one category, the school domain, even though it affects both the constraints against and the motivations for crime. Abuse by parents falls into just one category, the family domain. Likewise, low self-control falls into just one category, the self domain.

A grouping scheme, however, should do more than sort each cause or variable into a single category. Ideally, the variables in each category should also have similar causes. This allows us to treat these variables as a unit when we are discussing their causes. We do not have to state that one variable in the group is caused by Y, while another is caused by Z. Also, the variables in each group will be associated with one another if they have similar causes. As the level of one variable increases, the level of the others will also tend to increase.[2] For example, an increase in family conflict will usually be accompanied by increases in negative bonding to parents and harsh discipline. This too makes it easier to treat the variables as a unit:

knowing the level of one variable tells us something about the level of the other variables.

The grouping scheme I propose increases the likelihood that the variables in each group will be caused by the same factors. Data described in Chapter 8 suggest that the variables in each life domain are caused by many of the same outside factors. For example, those family factors that increase crime, like harsh discipline and negative bonding between parent and child, are caused by many of the same outside factors, like parental stressors and parental traits like irritability. Also, the variables in each domain frequently have large causal effects on one another. For example, harsh discipline contributes to negative bonding, which in turn contributes to harsh discipline.

This is not to deny that the variables in *different* life domains share common causes or have reciprocal effects on one another, but I believe that such shared causes are fewer and such reciprocal effects are weaker. That is because of the greater social, physical, and temporal isolation between the variables in the different domains. For example, family life involves different people, occurs in different settings, and takes places at different times than school life. As a result, there is less sharing of common causes between variables in the family and school domains (e.g., the factors that cause parents to engage in poor parenting differ from those that cause teachers to engage in poor teaching). Also, the causal effects across domains are weaker (e.g., harsh parental discipline is likely to have a greater effect on parental bonding than on teacher bonding).

If these arguments are correct, those causes of crime from the same life domain should be more strongly associated with one another than those causes that index a particular constraint or motivation, like stake in conformity or strain. Not many studies have examined this issue, but the few that have been done suggest that the causes of crime do tend to cluster by life domain rather than by type of constraint or motivation (e.g., Agnew 1991b; Massey and Krohn 1986; Wiatrowski et al. 1981).

In sum, there are better reasons for grouping variables by life domain than by type of constraint or motivation.

The Key Variables in the Five Life Domains

The following sections list the key variables or causes of crime in the five life domains and describe how these variables affect both the constraints against and the motivations for crime. I begin with the self (personality traits that cause crime) and then discuss the family, school, peer, and work domains. There has been a good deal of research on *most* of the variables listed and I am reasonably confident that they have relatively moderate to large direct effects on crime.[3] Certain of the variables, however, have not been the subject of much research; nevertheless, as indicated below, there is reason to believe that they too may have relatively strong effects on crime. After discussing the five life domains, I briefly comment on their relative impact on crime during the childhood, adolescent, and adult years.

Self (Super-Personality Traits of Irritability and Low Self-Control)

Psychologists have made much progress in identifying the major traits that comprise the human personality (for overviews, see Caspi 1998; Miller and Lynam 2001; Watson et al. 1994). These traits refer to "individual differences in the tendency to behave, think, and feel in certain consistent ways" (Caspi 1998, 312). For example, if individuals tend to act without thinking, we say that they possess the trait of "impulsivity." Several specific traits have been linked to crime, including high activity levels (hyperactivity), trouble concentrating (attention deficit), impulsivity, a strong desire for thrills and excitement (sensation seeking), a low ability to learn from punishment, irritability, insensitivity to others (low empathy), poor social and problem-solving skills, and beliefs favorable to crime (see Agnew 2005; Gottfredson 2001).

It is difficult to keep all of these traits in mind, but many traits are associated with one another, that is, they tend to occur together. Researchers have argued that these traits can be grouped into a smaller number of "super-traits." There is some disagreement over whether these traits cluster into one, two, or three super-traits (e.g., Arneklev et al. 1999; Caspi et al. 1994; Miller and Lynam 2001; Piquero et al. 2000; Watson et al. 1994). Gottfredson and Hirschi (1990), for example, argue that most of these traits cluster together to form the single super-trait of low self-control. Many psychological researchers, however, argue that those traits linked to crime cluster together into two or three super-traits. The evidence is somewhat mixed in this area, although recent work in psychology suggests that these traits are best grouped into two super-traits, one of which might be termed "low self-control" and the other "irritability."

Low Self-Control. Individuals who possess the super-trait of "low self-control" are impulsive, often responding to the temptations of the moment with little thought for the long-range consequences of their behavior; they like exciting, risky, high-energy activities; they do not have much ambition, motivation, or perseverance; and they do not feel bound by conventional rules and norms. We can measure level of self-control with questions like, "I often act on the spur of the moment without thinking" (agree or disagree); "I often do whatever brings me pleasure here and now, even at the cost of some distant goal"; "Sometimes I will take a risk just for the fun of it"; "Excitement and adventure are more important for me than security"; "The things in life that are the easiest to do bring me the greatest pleasure"; and "If things I do upset people, it's their problem, not mine" (Grasmick et al. 1993). In everyday language, those low in self-control might be described as "wild" or "out of control." (Note that this definition of "self-control" is more narrow than that of Gottfredson and Hirschi [1990], whose definition of self-control encompasses the above traits *and* irritability, as defined below.)

Low self-control indexes or affects both the constraints against and the motivations for crime. Low self-control indexes internal control; in particular, those low in self-control are less aware of and responsive to the other constraints against crime, like the prospect of getting caught and jeopardizing one's stake in conformity. They are also less likely to hold beliefs that condemn crime. Further, low self-control increases both strain and the likelihood of responding to strain with crime. For example, those low in self-control are more likely to experience certain social situations as stressful; in particular, they are more likely to be bored or dissatisfied with many conventional pursuits, like attending school and working at most legal jobs. And if stressed, they have fewer inhibitions about resorting to crime. Finally, those low in self-control hold beliefs favorable to crime and are more likely to find crime rewarding because crime provides much excitement and the benefits of crime are both immediate and easily achieved.

Irritability. Individuals who posses the trait of "irritability" are more likely to experience events as aversive, attribute these events to the malicious behavior of others (believe that others are "out to get them"), experience intense emotional reactions to these events—including anger—and respond to these events in an aggressive or antisocial manner. They also show little concern for the feelings and rights of others, and tend to have an antagonistic or adversarial interactional style. We can measure an individual's level of irritability with questions like, "Some days I'm very irritable" (agree or disagree), "I can get very upset when little things don't go my way," and "My anger frequently gets the best of me" (Colder and Stice 1998). In everyday language, irritable people might be described as "mean" or "nasty" or "having a short fuse."

Irritability also indexes or affects the major constraints against and motivations for crime. Irritable individuals are lower in internal control; for example, they are less responsive to certain of the costs of crime, like jeopardizing their relationships with conventional others. Irritability dramatically increases one's level of strain and the likelihood of responding to strain with crime. Irritable individuals, in particular, are much more likely to interpret certain situations as stressful, experience intense emotional reactions to such situations, and respond in an aggressive manner. Finally, irritability also indexes and fosters the social learning of crime. Irritable individuals are more likely to hold beliefs that justify aggressive behavior and they are more likely to find crime rewarding given their hostility toward others.

Brief Summary. Low self-control and irritability both reduce the constraints against and increase the motivations for crime. It is therefore not surprising that much evidence suggests that they are among the leading causes of crime (Caspi et al. 1994; Grasmick et al. 1993; Miller and Lynam 2001; Pratt and Cullen 2000; Wright et al. 1999). Further, limited data suggest that these traits may have some association with one another and that the combination of low self-control and irritability may be especially conducive to crime. That is, these super-traits may interact in their effect on crime, such that low self-control is most likely to lead to crime among irritable people (and irritability is most likely to lead to crime among those low in self-control). More research is needed in this area, however (see Colder and Stice 1998).[4]

Other Individual Differences. Individuals differ from one another in numerous ways, only some of which are reflected in the personality traits of irritability and low self-control (see Lubinski 2000). One additional difference that has been linked to crime is that of intelligence. Much data suggest that criminals are less intelligent on average than noncriminals (Farrington 1994a; 1994b; Moffitt 1990). I do not include intelligence as one of the leading direct causes of crime, however, because I believe that its effect on crime is largely indirect. Although the data are somewhat mixed, there is reason to believe that intelligence affects crime partly through its effect on certain of the specific personality traits listed above, like impulsivity and empathy. For example, less intelligent individuals have more difficulty taking account of the future consequences of their behavior, which contributes to the trait of impulsivity. Intelligence may also affect crime through its effect on certain of the social variables that cause crime, like academic performance (see Caspi and Moffitt 1995, 477–479; Farrington 1994a; 1994b; Loeber et al. 2003; Menard and Morse 1984; Moffitt 1990).

Family (Poor Parenting and No/Poor Marriages)

Most of the family research in criminology has focused on *juvenile* delinquency, so I begin by listing those aspects of parenting that have or may have a relatively moderate to large direct effect on delinquency (see Agnew 2005; Brezina 1998; Campbell 1995; Coie and Dodge 1998; Colvin 2000; Farrington 2002; Fox and Benson 2000; Loeber and Stouthamer-Loeber 1986; Patterson et al. 1992; Sampson and Laub 1993; Wright and Cullen 2001; Wright and Wright 1995).

Negative Parent/Juvenile Bonding. Delinquency is more likely when family members hate or reject one another and spend little time together in pleasurable activities. Negative bonding reduces one's stake in conformity and functions as a major source of strain (see Agnew et al. 2000).

Poor Supervision/Discipline. Delinquency is also more likely when parents *fail* to set clear rules prohibiting delinquency and related behaviors, effectively monitor rule compliance, and consistently discipline the child in an appropriate manner for rule violations. Delinquency has been linked to such disciplinary problems as the failure to sanction rule violations (lax discipline), the erratic or inconsistent use of sanctions (sometimes punish, sometime ignore misbehavior), unfair punishment (undeserved or excessive punishment), and the use of harsh punishments (e.g., physical punishments and threats, screaming, verbal abuse). Poor supervision/discipline most obviously reduces external control. It also increases strain, with erratic, unfair, and harsh punishments being a major type of strain (see Agnew et al. 2000). Poor supervision/discipline also fosters the social learning of crime. Most notably, parents who employ harsh punishments provide aggressive models for their children and implicitly teach them that violence is an appropriate response to certain problems.

Family Conflict and Child Abuse. Family conflict between parents and the juvenile and between parents themselves is related to delinquency. This is especially true if the conflict involves screaming, insults, threats, expressions of contempt, and physical violence. Likewise, delinquency is related to child abuse, including physical, sexual, and emotional abuse as well as neglect (the failure to provide adequate food, shelter, medical care, and/or attention/affection). Family conflict and abuse reduce the juvenile's stake in conformity, are a major source of strain, and foster the social learning of crime (juveniles are exposed to aggressive models and implicitly taught beliefs favorable to crime). Also, data suggest that family conflict often results in the reinforcement of aggressive behavior. When a parent and juvenile behave aggressively toward one another, the parent sometimes "gives in" to the juvenile or retreats, thus reinforcing the aggressive behavior of the juvenile (see Patterson et al. 1992).

Absence of Positive Parenting. Delinquency may also be related to the absence of "positive parenting." Positive parenting has two related dimensions. First, parents teach their children the social, academic and problem-solving skills they need to form close ties to conventional others, do well in school, and resolve problems in a non-delinquent manner (Catalano and Hawkins 1996; Hawkins et al. 2003). Such skills are best taught through a combination of direct instruction, parental modeling, practice combined with feedback, and reinforcement for successful performance. Second, parents provide support to their children, particularly when the children face problems or challenges they are not equipped to handle. Such support includes emotional support and several types of instrumental support, including information, advice, material/monetary assistance, and advocacy (Cullen 1994; Wright and Cullen 2001). Positive parenting has not received as much attention as the other dimensions of parenting, but the absence of positive parenting may reduce the juvenile's stake in conformity, increase strain (the absence of positive parenting may be experienced as a type of strain or stress), reduce the ability to cope with strain in a legal manner, and increase the likelihood that individuals will find crime reinforcing.

Criminal Parents/Siblings. Criminal parents usually do not *deliberately* teach their children to engage in crime. That is, such parents usually do not intentionally reinforce their children's crime, model crime for them, and teach them beliefs favorable to crime. Rather, criminal parents tend to produce criminal children because they engage in the types of poor parenting described above, like poor supervision (Sampson and Laub 1993; Wright and Wright 1995). Some criminal parents, however, do provide deliberate instruction in crime (see Anderson's 1999 discussion of "street families"; also see Canada 1995; Miller 2001). The same is even more true for criminal siblings. Anderson's study of a poor, inner-city community illustrates the ways in which criminal parents, siblings, and others sometimes provide deliberate instruction in crime, including beliefs favorable to crime and negative reinforcement for crime:

> The street-oriented adults with whom children come in contact at home and on the street—including mothers, fathers, brothers, sisters, boyfriends, cousins, neighbors, and friends—[verbalize] the messages these children are getting through public experience: "Watch your back." "Protect yourself." "Don't punk out." "If somebody disses you, you got to straighten them out." Many parents actually impose sanctions if a child is not sufficiently aggressive. For example, if a child loses a fight and comes home upset, the parent might respond, "Don't you come in here crying that somebody beat you up; you better get back out there and whup his ass. I didn't raise no punks! If you don't whup his ass, I'll whup yo' ass when you come home." Thus the child gains reinforcement for being tough and showing nerve. (Anderson 1999, 70–71)

Brief Summary. The key family variables impacting delinquency are poor supervision/discipline, negative parent/juvenile bonding, family conflict and child abuse, the absence of positive parenting, and criminal parents/siblings. These variables are associated with one another, partly because they are caused by many of the same outside factors (see Chapter 8) and partly because they have causal effects on one another. For example, family conflict increases the likelihood of negative bonding between parent and child. Further, at least some of these variables may interact in their effect on delinquency. For example, poor supervision may be more likely to cause delinquency when there is negative bonding between the parent and child. Other family variables, like divorce/separation and family size, affect delinquency primarily through their effect on these key variables.

What About Adults? Much less research has focused on the relationship between family factors and adult crime (although see Farrington and West 1995; Giordano et al. 2002; Horney et al. 1995; Laub et al. 1998; Laub and Sampson 2001; Piquero et al. 2002; Sampson and Laub 1993; Simons et al. 2002; Wright and Wright 1995; Wright et al. 1999). Some data suggest that adults who are *unmarried or negatively bonded to their spouses* have higher levels of crime than adults who are positively bonded to their spouses (i.e., love and respect their spouses, engage in positively valued activities with them). Having children does not appear to be strongly related to offending. While children may provide some stake in conformity, the association between children and offending may be weakened by the fact that criminals are more likely to engage in frequent and unprotected sex, thus increasing the likelihood they will have children (Farrington and West 1995; Thornberry et al. 2003b). However, we might expect that *strong bonds to children* would reduce the likelihood of offending, especially for females. Miller (2001), for example, found that having children caused many female gang members to leave the gang or reduce their level of criminal activity (also see Chapter 9; Giordano et al. 2002; Laub and Sampson 2001).

It seems reasonable to suppose that other dimensions of adult family life are related to crime. Limited data suggest that having a *criminal spouse or partner* increases the likelihood of crime, especially for women (Simons et al. 2002). The amount of *supervision/discipline exercised by one's spouse* might also be related to crime. Spouses may not supervise and discipline one another in the same way that parents supervise/discipline their children, but spouses may still vary in the level of supervision and discipline they exercise. For example, spouses may vary in the extent to which they express disapproval of crime and related behaviors, monitor their partners' behavior, and sanction criminal behavior in an appropriate manner. The amount of *conflict/abuse between spouses* and the amount of *social support provided by spouses* may also be related to crime, with these variables affecting crime for the same reasons that parental conflict and support affect juvenile delinquency.

School (Negative School Experiences and Limited Education)

Although the evidence is somewhat mixed, there is reason to believe that several school-related variables have relatively moderate to large direct effects on delinquency (Agnew 2005; Colvin 2000; Gottfredson 2001; Thornberry et al. 2003b). You might notice that these variables roughly parallel those listed for the family. The key school variables affecting delinquency include:

Negative Bonding to Teachers and School. Delinquency is more likely among juveniles who report that they hate teachers and school, dislike the time they spend at school, and get nothing of value from school. Like negative bonding to parents, negative bonding to teachers and school reduces one's stake in conformity and is a major type of strain.

Poor Academic Performance. There is no doubt that poor academic performance is *associated* with delinquency, with delinquents having poorer grades, lower scores on standardized tests, and being more likely to be held back in school. Some researchers claim that this association is due to the fact that both poor academic performance and delinquency are caused by the same third variables, like low self-control (see Gottfredson 2001; Gottfredson and Hirschi 1990; Maguin and Loeber 1996). Others state that poor academic performance also has a direct causal effect on delinquency (Thornberry et al. 2003b). I lean toward the latter argument, as there is good reason to believe that poor academic performance reduces one's stake in conformity and often increases strain.

Little Time Spent on Homework. Delinquents spend less time on homework than do nondelinquents, which reduces their stake in conformity.

Lower Educational and Occupational Goals. Delinquents *desire* less education and less prestigious jobs and they *expect* to get less education and less prestigious jobs than nondelinquents. For example, one individual involved in much delinquency stated that "I ain't goin' to college, who wants to go to college? I'd just end up gettin' a shitty job anyway." When asked what his life will be like in 20 years, he replied "I don't fucking know. Twenty years. I may be fucking dead. I live one day at a time. I'll probably be in the fucking pen" (MacLeod 1995, 3, 7). These lower goals reduce stake in conformity and may increase strain (see Agnew 2002 on anticipated strain).

Poor Supervision/Discipline. There is reason to believe that delinquents are more likely than nondelinquents to be poorly supervised and disciplined by teachers and school officials. In particular, delinquents are less likely to be in situations where rules for behavior are clearly communicated, behavior is well monitored, conventional behavior is reinforced, and rule violations are consistently sanctioned in an appropriate manner (see Gottfredson 2001). This poor supervision/discipline reduces their external control and may function as a source of strain.

Negative Treatment by Teachers. Delinquents are more likely to report that they are treated in a negative manner by teachers; for example, that their teachers frequently "talk down" to them, verbally abuse or insult them, threaten them, and otherwise treat them unfairly. For example, one delinquent had this to say about his high school teachers: "They make you feel like shit. I couldn't take their shit" (MacLeod 1995, 108). This negative treatment reduces their stake in conformity, increases their strain, and may foster the social learning of crime by providing negative models and implicitly teaching that aggressive behavior is sometimes acceptable.

Absence of Positive Teaching. Finally, some evidence suggests that delinquency is higher when teachers fail to set high standards for students; make little effort to effort to provide students with the skills, knowledge, and opportunities they need to do well in school; and fail to provide social support when needed (see Gottfredson 2001).

Brief Summary. The key school variables impacting delinquency are negative bonding to teachers/school, poor academic performance, little time on homework, low educational and occupational goals, poor supervision/discipline, negative treatment by teachers, and the absence of positive teaching. These variables are associated with one another, with part of the association being due to the fact that these variables have causal effects on one another. For example, poor academic performance reduces bonding to teachers and school. Also, certain of these variables may interact in their effect on crime (e.g., negative treatment may be more likely to lead to delinquency among those with poor academic records).

The following quote from Jay MacLeod provides a sense of the school experiences of many delinquents. MacLeod spent much time observing a group of delinquents (the "Hallway Hangers") in a public housing project in Boston. He states that:

> The Hallway Hangers' attitudes toward the educational system can be summed up by Stoney's words: "Fuck school. I hate fucking school." Most of the Hallway Hangers have dropped out. While officially enrolled, most spent little time in class, preferring the fun, companionship, and drugs at Pop's. When in class, they were generally disruptive and undisciplined. None of the Hallway Hangers participated in any extracurricular activities. By their own accounts, they were high or drunk much of the time they spent in school. (MacLeod 1995, 97)

What About Adults? The school research has of course focused on juveniles, because most adults are not in school. Nevertheless, it is reasonable to suppose that crime will be higher among adults with limited educations. Surprisingly, there has not been much research in this area, but the few studies that have been done provide some support for this proposition (see especially Crutchfield and Pitchford 1997; Thornberry and Farnworth 1982; Wright et al. 1999). *Level of education* affects one's stake in conformity, one's level of strain (it may be stressful to have a poor education in our society), the likelihood of reacting to strain with crime (education increases conventional coping skills), and the likelihood that one will find crime reinforcing. I should note, however, that much of the effect of education on crime is probably indirect. In particular, education influences the constraints against and motivations for crime primarily through its effect on the individual's work, marital life, and peer associations (more below).

Peers (Peer Delinquency)

The juvenile's relations with peers have a strong effect on delinquency, with several dimensions of peer interaction being important (Agnew 2005; Akers 1998; Aseltine 1995; Cernkovich and Giordano 2001; Colvin 2000; Haynie 2001; 2002; Huizinga et al. 2003; Thornberry et al. 2003a; Warr 2002).

Close Friends Engage in Delinquency. Peers vary a good deal in their orientation toward delinquency, with some peers openly engaging in delinquency and encouraging their friends to do likewise, and much data suggest that the delinquent orientation of one's peers has a major effect on delinquency. Certain studies, in fact, suggest that associating with delinquent peers is the most important predictor of delinquency other than prior delinquency. Variables like peer bonding and the supervision/discipline exercised by peers are important, but their importance is conditioned by the level of peer delinquency. That is, the effect of variables like peer bonding on delinquency depends on whether or not the individual's friends are delinquent, with positive bonds to *delinquent* peers *increasing* delinquency (Agnew 1991a). So individuals are more likely to engage in delinquency if their friends are heavily involved in delinquency, especially their close friends and especially if these friends exercise much control over them. This may explain why gang membership has such a large effect on delinquency; gang members are often strongly bonded to one another and they frequently face much pressure to engage in delinquency (Thornberry et al. 2003a, 140–162).

Having close friends who engage in delinquency reduces our concern with external sanctions, because these friends empower us and we see that their crime is seldom sanctioned (Piquero and Pogarsky 2002; Stafford and Warr 1993). It reduces our stake in conformity, because engaging in crime is not likely to jeopardize our relations with delinquent friends. It increases our strain, because delinquent friends more often abuse one another and get into conflicts with others. It increases the likelihood of responding to strain with crime, because delinquent friends encourage delinquent responses. And it fosters the social learning of crime, because delinquent friends are more likely to reinforce crime, model crime, and teach beliefs favorable to crime.

Peer Conflict/Abuse. Some evidence suggests that being verbally and physically abused by peers increases the likelihood of crime. This is especially the case when this abuse involves criminal victimization (Agnew 2002; Anderson 1999; Cernkovich and Giordano 2001; Colvin 2000; Eitle and Turner 2002; Huizinga et al. 2003). Such abuse may reduce stake in conformity (ties to others), increase strain, and foster the social learning of crime. Abused individuals are exposed to aggressive or criminal models and they often develop beliefs favorable to crime, like the belief that society is a "jungle" and only the strong survive.

Time Spent With Peers in Unstructured, Unsupervised Activities. Such time is perhaps the best indicator of the extent to which individuals encounter situations conducive to crime, that is, situations in which external control is low, strain is high (provocation from other peers), and crime is likely to be encouraged (peers reinforce crime, model crime, and present beliefs favorable to crime) (see Hawdon 1999; Osgood et al. 1996). Data suggest that time spent on the "street" with peers is especially conducive to crime; youth who live on the street or spend large amounts of time on the street with peers are much more likely to engage in crime (Hagan and McCarthy 1997).

Brief Summary. There is reason to believe that the above three dimensions of peer interaction are associated with one another: individuals with delinquent friends are more likely to get into conflicts with others and to spend unstructured, unsupervised time with peers (Colvin 2000; Hoyt et al. 1999; Huizinga et al. 2003; Miller 2001). These dimensions may also interact with one another in their effect on crime. For example, delinquent friends have a greater effect on crime when we spend a lot of time with them (Agnew 1991a).

What About Adults? Peer delinquency is much less common among adults. Adults are less likely to have friends who engage in crime, given the sharp drop in offending that occurs when individuals become adults (see Warr 2002). Adults generally spend less time with peers, given their work and marital commitments. And adults are generally less influenced by peers, given the centrality of their work and marital commitments. Nevertheless, some adults are high in peer delinquency, especially adults who are unmarried, unemployed, or employed in "bad jobs," and peers may occupy a central role in the lives of such adults. So even though peer delinquency is less common among adults, it should have a major effect on crime among certain adults (see Cernkovich and Giordano 2001; Crutchfield and Pitchford 1997; Warr 2002).

Work (Unemployment and Bad Jobs)

Most of the work research focuses on adult crime (although see Wright et al. 1997), with the following work-related variables having some effect on crime (Baron and Hartnagel 1997; Colvin 2000; Crutchfield and Pitchford 1997; Fagan and Freeman 1999; Giordano et al. 2002; Laub and Sampson 2001; Piquero et al. 2002; Rutter et al. 1998; Sampson and Laub 1993; Shover 1996; Shover and Wright

2001; Sullivan 1989; Thornberry and Christenson 1984; Uggen 2000; Wright et al. 1999):

Unemployment. Some studies find that unemployment increases the likelihood of at least certain types of crime, although not all studies agree. This difference in findings likely stems from the gross way in which unemployment is sometimes measured; for example, studies often fail to consider the length of unemployment and the prospects for finding work. Also, studies frequently compare unemployed individuals to individuals in *all types of jobs*, including the "bad jobs" described below. Unemployed individuals should be more involved in crime than people with "good jobs," but not necessarily more involved than people with "bad jobs." Long-term unemployment with little prospect for future work should reduce stake in conformity, increase strain, and increase exposure to situations conducive to crime ("hanging out" on the street with peers), especially among young adults.

Poor Supervision/Discipline. Limited data also suggest that crime is more likely among individuals who work in environments that lack clear rules regarding appropriate behavior, where behavior is poorly monitored, and where rule violations are seldom sanctioned in an appropriate manner. Consider, for example, a 1991 fire at a chicken processing plant in North Carolina that killed 25 workers (see Aulettte and Michalowski 1993). The company management had deliberately locked the fire doors that would have allowed the workers to escape. According to some workers, this was done to prevent employees from stealing chicken nuggets. Aulette and Michalowski argue that this tragedy was partly due to the fact that several federal, state, and local agencies failed to adequately monitor conditions at the plant and sanction rule violations, thereby making it easy for management to engage in illegal behavior.

Negative Bonding to Work. Individuals who dislike their work (or conventional work in general) and their coworkers should be more likely to engage in crime; among other things, such workers have a lower stake in conformity and are higher in strain. As an example of negative bonding, consider the following quote from one offender:

> I worked as a busboy for one week. It was like being a pig in everyone else's slop. Why should I put up with that shit? . . .

Doing crime is a lot more fun and pays a lot better. (Fleming 1999, 73)

Poor Work Performance. Individuals with poor work performance frequently miss work and do a poor job when at work. Poor performance is indicative of a low stake in conformity and it too should increase the likelihood of crime.

Poor Working Conditions. Crime should be higher among individuals in jobs that involve unpleasant tasks (e.g., simple, repetitive, physically demanding, or subservient work), little autonomy or freedom, frequent use of coercive control (e.g., threats, ridicule), low pay, few benefits, little prestige, limited opportunities for advancement, and high turnover. These characteristics tend to be found in jobs that are in what is known as the "secondary labor market" (see Crutchfield and Pitchford 1997). Such jobs reduce the individual's stake in conformity, increase strain, increase the likelihood that individuals will find crime reinforcing, and increase exposure to situations conducive to crime.

Criminal Coworkers. Individuals with criminal coworkers should be more likely to engage in crime because their coworkers are less likely to sanction crime (reducing external control), are more likely to treat the individual in a negative manner (increasing strain), and are more likely to reinforce crime, model crime, and teach beliefs favorable to crime (see Wright and Cullen 2000).

Brief Summary. The key work variables affecting crime are unemployment, poor supervision/discipline, negative bonding to work, poor work performance, poor working conditions, and criminal coworkers. These dimensions are associated with one another and may interact in their effect on crime.

One of the criminals in Baskin and Sommer's study of female offenders (1999, 35) provides a sense of certain of the work variables that contribute to crime. She states that:

I worked for minimum wage at Duane Reed Pharmacy.... I never liked a job that would be just standing in one place, you know, like doing the same thing over and over. I got tired of it—the monotony, the routine everyday, so I stopped showing up. I lasted there about four months. Then, I worked in McDonald's for maybe four weeks. I hated McDonald's. It was boring. I was there for about four weeks. (Baskin and Sommers 1999, 35)

The Relative Importance of the Life Domains at Different Stages in the Life Course

The five life domains—self, family, school, peers, and work—generally have large effects on the individual's level of offending. Some life domains, however, have larger effects than others. It is difficult, however, to compare effect sizes without taking account of the individual's stage in life. For the sake of simplicity, I divide the individual's life into three stages: childhood, adolescence, and adulthood.[5] A domain like work has a relatively large effect on crime among adults, a relatively small effect on crime among adolescents, and is largely irrelevant to the explanation of crime among children, as few children in the United States are involved in paid work.

The relative effect of a life domain on crime at any given life stage depends on several factors. First, it depends on the role that the life domain plays in the individual's life at that time. For example, parents play a central role in the lives of their pre- and elementary school–age children. Parents have primary responsibility for socializing and meeting the needs of such children, and the "intensity of interaction" between parents and such children is quite high. It is often the case that two parents are responsible for one or a few children, they spend much time with these children, they have much control over them, and the emotional ties between parents and these children—whether positive or negative—are typically quite strong. Partly as a consequence, the things that parents do (*and do not do*) have a relatively large effect on whether these children engage in crime. Second, the relative effect of the life domains depends on the level of competition between the life domains at that time. For example, few groups seriously compete with parents in their effort to influence their pre- and elementary school–age children, which also accounts for the relatively large effect of parents on such children. Third, it depends on the individual's traits, abilities, and interests at that time. For example, pre- and elementary school–age children are very dependent on others to meet their needs, which further accounts for the relatively large effect of parents on such children.

Criminologists recognize that the relative effect of variables on crime often changes over the life course. In fact, several crime theories devote much attention to these changes (e.g., Catalano and

Hawkins 1996; Moffitt 1993; Sampson and Laub 1993; Thornberry 1987; also see Benson 2002; Piquero and Mazerolle 2001). Work in this area is discussed further in Chapter 9, when I offer an explanation for the relationship between age and crime. For now, I briefly describe the relative effects of the life domains on crime during the childhood, adolescent, and adult years, making a rough distinction between relatively large versus relatively small to moderate effects.

Childhood. The most important causes of crime during childhood are poor parenting practices and the personality traits of irritability and low self-control. The traits of irritability and low self-control emerge very early in the life course and—regardless of age—they have a major influence on how individuals perceive, experience, and respond to their environment. And through this influence, these traits have a major effect on many of the constraints against and motivations for crime. Poor parenting has a relatively large effect on crime among children given the central role of parents at this time, the limited competition they face from other groups, and children's dependency. School and peers have relatively small to moderate effects on crime at this time, as the life of the child is dominated by the family.

Adolescence. The most important causes of crime during adolescence are irritability/low self-control and peer delinquency. As noted in certain accounts (e.g., Agnew 2003a; Aseltine 1995; Sim and Vuchinich 1996; Thornberry et al. 2003b; Warr 2002), peers come to play a more central role in the lives of adolescents and adolescents become more sensitive to peer influences. The family has only a moderate effect on adolescent crime, as it faces stiff competition from peers and, to a lesser extent, from school. Also, adolescents are less dependent than children. The school has a moderate effect on crime, largely because teachers play a smaller role in the lives of most adolescents than do peers and parents.[6] Many adolescents work at part-time jobs during adolescence (and full-time jobs during the summer), but their work experiences have a relatively small effect on crime as work does not yet play a central role in their lives.

Adulthood. The most important causes of crime during adulthood are irritability/low self-control, peer delinquency, no/poor marriages, and unemployment/bad jobs. Most adults have completed their schooling, although the extent of their education has a relatively small to moderate (direct) effect on crime. As indicated, the effect of education on crime is largely indirect, through work,

Figure 3-2
The Relative Effects of the Life Domains on Crime During
the Childhood, Adolescent, and Adult Years (Relatively
Large Effects Illustrated With Thick Lines)

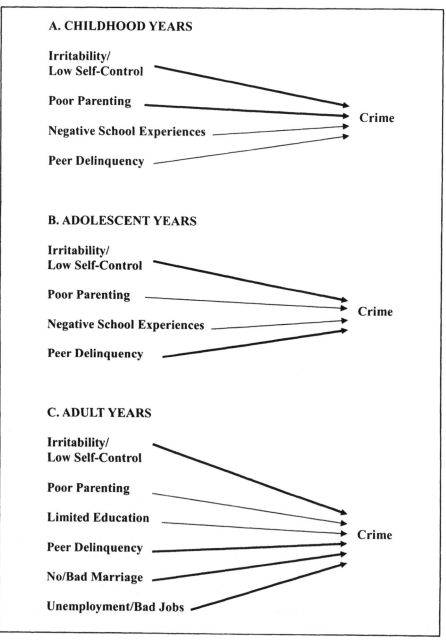

marriage, and the nature of peer associations. It is through these in-direct effects that education exerts its greatest impact on the con-straints against and the motivations for crime. Poor parenting has a relatively small effect on crime, because parents play a limited role in the lives of their adult children; parents face intense competition from others, like spouses and coworkers, and adults have achieved much autonomy from parents. Spouses/partners and work, how-ever, play a central role in the lives of most adults, and, as indicated earlier, delinquent peers play a central role in the lives of some adults—especially those who are unmarried, unemployed, or in-volved in "bad jobs."

These relative effects are shown in Figure 3-2. Relatively strong effects are illustrated with thick lines and relatively moderate to small effects with thin lines.

Conclusion

A large number of variables may affect the constraints against and the motivations for crime. In fact, the above discussion listed more than 30. In order to simplify a complex reality, these variables were grouped into five clusters organized by life domain: self (the super-personality traits of low self-control and irritability), family (poor parenting and no/poor marriages), school (negative school experiences and limited education), peers (peer delinquency), and work (unemployment and bad jobs). The variables in each category tend to be associated with one another, which makes it easier to treat them as a unit.

The variables in each of the life domains affect both the con-straints against and the motivations for crime. This argument runs counter to the prevailing view in criminology, which tends to asso-ciate particular variables with particular theories.[7] For example, bonding between the parent and child is usually seen as a "social control" variable and is said to affect delinquency because it reduces the constraints against crime. As suggested above, there is little ba-sis for this view. Most variables affect crime for reasons related to most or all of the leading crime theories; that is, they affect many of the major constraints against *and* motivations for crime (also see Agnew 1993; 1995b). Chapter 10 describes certain strategies that can be used to test this idea.

The arguments presented in this chapter are summarized in Figure 3-3, which lists the major variables that cause crime, organized into the five life domains, and shows that these variables affect crime both by reducing the constraints against crime *and* increasing the motivations for crime.

Figure 3-3
The Major Causes of Crime, Organized Into the Five Life Domains

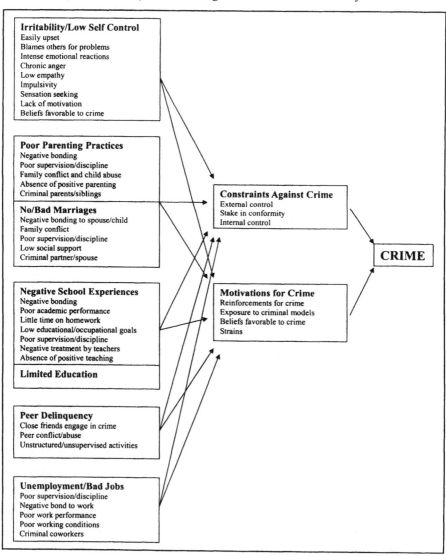

A theory of crime, however, does more than simply list the variables that cause crime and describe the reasons why they do so; it also describes the relationships between these variables. This is the task that I take up in Chapter 4. While it would be quite difficult to describe the relationships between the many individual variables listed in this chapter, I focus on the relationships between the five major life domains—a much more manageable task.

Notes

1. I somewhat arbitrarily define "moderate to large" effects as standardized effects that average .10 or greater across studies, meaning that the variable in question explains at least 1 percent of the variation in crime (see Bachman and Paternoster 1997). I do not discuss variables that have relatively small direct effects on crime, like religion and exposure to mass-media violence (see Agnew 2005; Baier and Wright 2001). I also do not discuss variables that have largely *indirect* effects on crime, that is, variables that affect crime primarily through their effect on other variables (e.g., low family income affects crime primarily through its effect on other variables, like bonding to parents and parental supervision).

2. I am assuming that all variables are scored in the same direction, such that as a variable increases in size crime goes up.

3. I say "reasonably confident" because much of the research suffers from one or more problems, including the following: Sometimes the research is based on unrepresentative samples; that is, samples of respondents that do not represent the population from which they were drawn (e.g., sample members may be wealthier than members of the population). As such, we cannot be sure whether we can generalize the findings from our sample to the population as a whole. Sometimes variables are poorly measured; for example, peer abuse might be measured by a single question that does not distinguish minor from serious instances of abuse. Sometimes cross-sectional data or data collected at one point in time are used, so that we cannot determine whether the association between variable X and crime is due to the causal effect of variable X on crime or to the causal effect of crime on variable X (e.g., does child abuse cause delinquency or does delinquency cause child abuse?). And sometimes the research fails to adequately take account of other variables that may affect the relationship between variable X and crime. For example, suppose we find a relationship between poor grades and delinquency. This relationship may

be due to the fact that poor grades cause delinquency or it may be due to the fact that poor grades are associated with some other variable, like low self-control, that causes delinquency. In order to determine if poor grades really do cause delinquency, we must take account of self-control when examining the effect of grades on delinquency (i.e., we examine the effect of poor grades on delinquency among those low in self-control and among those high in self-control). As a result of these sorts of problems, there is still some uncertainty about whether certain of the variables I list have relatively moderate to large direct effects on crime (see Agnew 2005 for a fuller discussion).

4. More research, in fact, is needed in several areas regarding personality traits and crime. Most notably, research should examine which of the specific components of low self-control and irritability best explain crime, the extent to which low-self-control and irritability are associated, and the extent to which the causes and consequences of low self-control and irritability are similar and different. So there is still much to learn about the relationship between personality traits and crime.

5. Other criminologists employ finer age divisions. Thornberry (1987), for example, distinguishes between younger, middle, and older adolescents. Piquero et al. (2002) distinguish the stage of "emerging adulthood" (between ages 18 and 25) from the rest of the adult years. Future work on the general theory in this book should move in the direction of such finer divisions.

6. Teachers have less responsibility than parents and peers for socializing and meeting the needs of adolescents; in particular, their role is generally limited to fostering adolescents' academic development. Adolescents do spend a lot of time at school, but much of this time is spent interacting with peers. A single teacher typically instructs a large number of students, has little control over these students outside the immediate context of the classroom, and has weak emotional ties to them.

7. According to the prevailing view in criminology, each of the leading theories of crime "owns" a particular set of independent variables and these variables affect crime for the reasons specified by that theory (see Bernard and Snipes 1996; Hirschi 1989). Control theory, for example, owns variables like parental supervision, parental attachment, commitment to school, and self-control, which affect crime by reducing the constraints against crime. Strain and social learning theories, however, own different sets of independent variables, which affect crime for the reasons specified by those theories. Efforts to integrate theories typically reflect this perspective. Most commonly, integrated theories attempt to describe the relationship between the variables owned by dif-

ferent theories by employing "end-to-end" integrations (see Bernard and Snipes 1996; Elliott et al. 1979; 1985; Hirschi 1979; Messner et al. 1989; Paternoster and Bachman 2001; Thornberry 1987). The independent variables owned by one theory (e.g., social control variables like parental attachment and school commitment) cause the independent variables owned by another theory (e.g., association with delinquent peers). The intervening mechanisms associated with each variable are preserved in the integration; for example, control variables are said to "free" the adolescent to associate with delinquent peers. Less commonly, integrated theories employ the strategy of "conceptual integration," wherein the variables of one theory are used to subsume the variables of other theories, but the intervening mechanisms associated with the first theory are retained. Akers (1989), for example, argues that the concept of differential reinforcement in social learning theory can subsume the concepts of attachment and commitment in social control theory (also see Akers 1985; 1998; Pearson and Weiner 1985).

Discussion and Study Questions

1. Why do I feel it is so important to group the causes of crime into a smaller number of clusters?

2. What characteristics should a good "grouping scheme" have?

3. Why do I argue that we should not group the causes of crime by the type of constraint or motivation that they index?

4. Why do I argue that it is best to group variables by life domain?

5. Why did I select the five life domains of self, family, school, peer group, and work? Can you think of other important life domains that were neglected?

6. Name any three specific causes of crime listed under the life domains. Discuss how these causes affect both the constraints against and the motivations for crime.

7. Can you think of any specific causes of crime that are not listed in this chapter?

8. Several specific causes of crime are listed under each life domain. Do you notice any common dimensions underlying

these causes—that is, dimensions that cut across the life domains (e.g., bonding to others is a dimension that is listed under the family, school, peer, and work domains).

9. Why do some life domains have a larger effect on crime than others at a given stage in life?

10. Related to the above question, why does the effect of a life domain on crime vary over the life course? For example, why do parenting practices have a larger effect on crime among children than among adults? ✦

Chapter 4

The Web of Crime

The Life Domains Affect One Another, Although Some Effects Are Stronger Than Others

The lives of many criminals are a mess. As juveniles, they tend to be irritable and low in self-control, they do not get along with their parents, they have poor grades and hate school, most of their friends are delinquent, and they spend most of their free time "hanging out" with these friends. As adults, they remain irritable and low in self-control; they are involved in bad marriages, if they are married at all; they work sporadically at "dead-end" jobs; and they often continue to hang out with their criminal friends.

Many criminals, in fact, tend to experience most of the causes of crime listed in Chapter 3. These causes were grouped into five clusters, organized by life domain: self (irritability and low self-control), family (poor parenting and no/bad marriages), school (negative school experiences and limited education), peers (delinquent peers), and work (unemployment and bad jobs).

It is no accident that many criminals have problems in all these domains. These domains not only affect crime, they affect one another as well. For example, individuals with the traits of irritability and low self-control are more likely to experience poor parenting, partly because they upset their parents, who respond by employing harsh disciplinary techniques or withdrawing from them. Poor parenting practices, in turn, contribute to irritability and low self-control. Problems in the life domains, then, tend to mutually reinforce or contribute to one another. This argument is illustrated in Figure 4-1, which to some extent resembles a spider's web.

Figure 4-1
The Mutual or Reciprocal Effects of the Life Domains on One Another

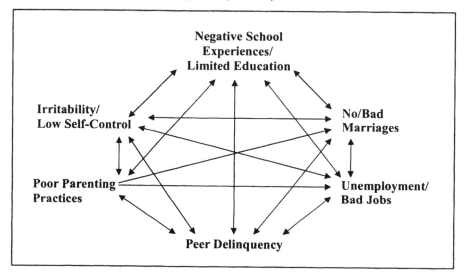

Many criminals are trapped in this web; that is, their personality traits and family, school, peer, and work experiences are all conducive to crime and all work to mutually reinforce one another. These criminals tend to offend at high rates. Some do manage to escape from the web when they make the transition to adulthood, usually because they get involved in good marriages and become bonded to decent jobs. Those who do not escape continue to offend at high rates well into their adult years.

This chapter elaborates on these points by describing the effects of the five life domains on one another. Understanding these effects is important because it sheds light on how the life domains work together to affect crime. While the variables in each life domain have a direct effect on crime, they also affect crime indirectly through their effects on the other domains. Poor parenting, for example, has a direct effect on crime and indirectly affects crime by contributing to irritability/low self-control, negative school experiences, peer delinquency, and unemployment/bad jobs. Understanding these effects also has important policy implications, because it can help us better control crime. Efforts to reduce poor parenting, for example, will be more effective if they take account of the ways in which poor parenting is fostered by the other life domains.

I begin by describing the effects of irritability and low self-control on the other life domains, then focus on the effects of the family, school, peer, and work domains. Drawing on relevant theory and research, I make a rough distinction between *relatively* large versus small to moderate effects. I also discuss how the effects of the life domains on one another often change over the life course, from childhood to adolescence to adulthood.

The Effects of the Self (Irritability and Low Self-Control) on the Other Life Domains

To refresh your memory, individuals who possess the traits of irritability and low self-control are impulsive, have a preference for exciting and risky activities, are low in motivation and perseverance, are easily upset, have an antagonistic interactional style, and are generally unconcerned with the feelings and rights of others. Studies suggest that low self-control and irritability have large effects on all of the other life domains, contributing to poor parenting, no/bad marriages, negative school experiences, limited education, association with delinquent peers, unemployment, and employment in bad jobs (e.g., Agnew et al. 2002; Barrick et al. 2001; Brief et al. 1988; Caspi 1998; Evans et al. 1997; Nagin and Paternoster 1994; Peterson and Hann 1999; Wright et al. 1999; 2001). For example, Caspi et al. (1989) followed a sample of males from childhood through adulthood, and discovered that those who had irritable dispositions obtained less education, were more often unemployed, more often worked in "bad jobs," were less likely to be married, and were more likely to be divorced than their less irritable counterparts. Irritability had similar effects for females.

Why do irritability and low self-control have large effects on the other life domains? Several reasons have been advanced (see Caspi 1998; Caspi and Moffitt 1995; Caspi et al. 1989). You can best appreciate these reasons when you imagine people with these traits. Such people are basically "out of control" and mean.

First, do you think such people would want to establish close ties with conventional others or invest a lot of time and effort in conventional pursuits, like school and work? Probably not. Such activities require more effort than they are willing to give and are not likely to be experienced as rewarding. In fact, individuals with these traits often find conventional activities like school to be boring and restrictive. Such individuals, however, may find activities like cutting school and associating with delinquent peers quite rewarding. As a consequence, those high in irritability and low in self-control *often choose to devote little effort to conventional pursuits and frequently prefer to be in social environments conducive to crime;* for example, they choose to ignore their parents and neglect school and they prefer to associate with delinquent peers.

Second, do you think people with the traits of irritability and low self-control would do well in conventional pursuits even if they wanted to? Again, probably not. Individuals with these traits often lack the abilities necessary to do well in many conventional pursuits. For example, they have trouble getting along well with others, following directions, and persisting in a line of action (e.g., doing their homework on a regular basis, showing up for work every day). As a consequence, these individuals often *fail at conventional pursuits and are forced into social environments conducive to crime.* For example, conventional peers reject them, so they are forced to associate with delinquent peers. They fail at school, so they are forced to take "bad jobs."

Third, do you think other individuals would like interacting with people who are irritable and low in self-control? Once more, probably not. People with these traits are unpleasant and create much strain for others. As a consequence, other individuals often treat people with these traits in a hostile manner or withdraw from them. The parents of children with these traits, for example, quickly find themselves in a desperate state. Their children frequently engage in risky and harmful behaviors, they are not very responsive to disciplinary efforts, and they are generally unpleasant. These parents may come to dislike their children and, in their desperation, they may employ harsh or abusive disciplinary techniques or may simply withdraw from them. Teachers, peers, and employers may likewise start treating individuals with these traits in a negative manner. So individuals with these traits often provoke negative reactions from others, both in specific situations and on a regular basis over long periods of time. People with these traits, then, *create social environments conducive to crime.*

Finally, do you think people with these traits view or perceive their social environment in the same way as others? For example, suppose we have two people: one who is irritable and low in self-control and the other who is not. These two people experience an identical event: someone bumps into them as they are walking down a school hallway. Do you think they will perceive the event similarly? Again, probably not. The irritable and low in self-control person is more likely to view this event as a deliberate offense, as opposed to an accident, because people with these traits are more likely to believe that others are deliberately mistreating them. In particular, they are more likely to perceive "ambiguous provocations" (e.g., someone spilling water on them during lunch) as malicious acts (see Coie and Dodge 1998).

People who are irritable and low in self-control are also more likely to perceive the costs of crime as low and the benefits as high in a given environment. One experiment, for example, described several criminal events to students who varied in their level of self-control. These students were then asked about the potential costs and benefits associated each event (e.g., the likelihood the offender would be caught and suffer certain consequences, how much "fun or kick" the event would provide). The students who were low in self-control were more likely to state that the potential costs of the criminal events were lower and the potential benefits were higher (Nagin and Paternoster 1993).

So individuals with the traits of irritability and low self-control are more likely to *perceive a given environment in ways conducive to crime.* For example, they are more likely to believe that their parents are deliberately mistreating them, that their teachers will not discover their misdeeds, and that engaging in a particular criminal act will be "fun." These differences in perceptions are important. Psychologists make a distinction between the "actual" and the "perceived" social environment, and both have large effects on behavior (Magnusson and Stattin 1998).

Summary. So the traits of low self-control and irritability increase the likelihood that individuals will experience poor parenting, fail to marry or become involved in bad marriages, have a range of negative school experiences, obtain little education, associate with delinquent peers, be unemployed, and work in "bad jobs" when they are employed. These effects occur for four reasons: people with these traits devote little effort to conventional pursuits and sometimes prefer to be environments conducive to crime (e.g., associating with delinquent peers), they often fail at conventional pursuits and are forced into environments conducive to crime (e.g., bad jobs), they provoke negative reactions from others and thereby create environments conducive to crime (e.g., harsh or abusive parenting), and they are more likely to perceive given environments in ways conducive to crime.

The Effect of the Family (Poor Parenting and No/Bad Marriages) on the Other Life Domains

The major family variables affecting delinquency include negative bonding between parent and child, poor supervision/discipline, family conflict and abuse, the absence of positive parenting, and criminal parents/siblings. A similar set of variables dealing with marital/partner relations affects adult crime. These variables tend to have relatively moderate to large effects *on the other life domains,* with parenting practices during the childhood years being especially important. It is useful to describe the reasons why the family is so important because these reasons also shed light on the effects of the other domains.

Explaining the Size of Family Effects. The family tends to have relatively moderate to large effects on the other domains partly because family life *occurs prior to and overlaps with* these domains. That is, individuals experience family life before and during the period of time that their traits develop, they attend school, and they form peer associations. This allows family life to influence the formation of traits and patterns of interaction in the school and peer domains. Once traits and patterns of interaction are formed, they tend to be somewhat resistant to change, for reasons described in Chapter 7. The family also has a sizeable effect on the other domains because of the *large role that the family plays in the life of the individual.* As described in Chapter 3, parents have primary responsibility for socializing and meeting the needs of their children. Also, the "intensity" of interaction between parents and children is high (e.g., parents spend much time with their children, have much control over them, emotional ties between parents and children are quite strong). Finally, the family has a sizeable effect because *no other group seriously challenges or competes with the efforts of family members to influence their children*—at least during the childhood years.

Irritability and Low Self-Control. Research suggests that parenting practices *during the childhood years* have a large effect on irritability and low self-control (Campbell 1995; Caspi 1998; Colvin 2000; Hay 2001; Peterson and Hann 1999; Wright et al. 1999).[1] This is not surprising; these traits are in the process of being formed, the family dominates the life of the child during this time, and one of the major functions of the family is to shape the child's personality. The effect of parenting practices on traits declines to a small to moderate level during adolescence. Traits are largely formed and somewhat resistant to change by this time. Further, the family now competes with peers and to a lesser extent the school in its efforts to shape the child. During adulthood, the quality of ones marriage has a small to moderate effect on traits for the same reasons. Parenting practices (and marital relations) affect the traits of irritability and low self-control in two ways.

First, individuals must be taught to exercise self-control and manage their anger.[2] Very young children are generally low in self-control and quick to anger (think about the behavior of young children when they do not get something they want or someone does something they do not like). Parents teach their children to exercise *self*-control and manage their anger partly by exercising *external* control over them. That is, parents set clear rules for their children, closely monitor their behavior, and consistently sanction rule violations in an appropriate manner. This external control eventually teaches children to control their anger, pause before acting, consider the consequences of their behavior, and refrain from inappropriate behavior. Parents also teach their children to exercise self-control and manage their anger using those techniques that are part of "positive parenting," like modeling self-control for their children and reinforcing them when they exercise self-control. All of these efforts are enhanced to the extent that children have a close bond with their parents. *Poor* parenting practices, like poor supervision and the absence of positive parenting, are therefore associated with irritability and low self-control.

Second, parents (and spouses) influence the above traits, particularly irritability, by affecting the level of strain that their children experience. Exposure to high levels of strain or negative treatment may eventually lead children to develop irritable dispositions. A variety of parenting practices contribute to strain, including unfair punishment, harsh punishment, high levels of family conflict, and child abuse, and data suggest that many of these practices increase levels of irritability (Agnew et al. 2000; Belsky 1990; Elder et al. 1985; Hops et al. 1990).

Negative School Experiences. Poor parenting practices have a large effect on school experiences, like negative bonding to teachers and poor academic performance (Bankston 1999; Patterson et al. 1992; Riordan 1997). When parental supervision and discipline are poor, parents often *fail* to monitor their children's school performance and take appropriate action when problems arise. And when "positive parenting" is low, parents fail to teach their children the skills and attitudes necessary to do well in school and fail to provide their children with social support when needed, like assistance doing homework. Further, parents may create much strain for their children, making it difficult for them to concentrate on school work. So poor parenting practices contribute to negative school experiences.

Peer Delinquency. Likewise, parenting practices have a large effect on peer delinquency. Data suggest that many of the poor parenting practices described above increase the likelihood of association with delinquent peers, the time spent in unsupervised activities with peers, and possibly peer abuse (Agnew 2005; 2002; Elliott et al. 1985; Thornberry et al. 2003a; Warr 2002). Certain of these parenting practices, like negative bonding and poor supervision/discipline, reduce the desire and ability of parents to influence their children's peer associations. In fact, parents who poorly supervise their children may not even know that the children are members of delinquent groups like gangs (Decker and Van Winkle 1996, 235–240). Other poor parenting practices, like family conflict and child abuse, create strain for children. This strain creates a desire to escape from home, which increases the likelihood of associating with peers, including delinquent peers. Miller (2001) provides an excellent illustration of this in her study of female gang members, when she states that many females join gangs to escape abuse and other problems at home. For example, Miller (2001, 49–50) provides the following description of the experiences one female gang member:

> Brittany described a terribly violent family life. She lived in a household with extended family—12 people in all— including her mother, grandmother, stepfather, and an adolescent uncle who was physically abusive. Her aunt's boyfriend had sexually assaulted her at the age of 5, but

family members didn't believe her. Although she didn't know her father, who was in jail, she had early memories of him physically abusing her mother. . . . [She states] "I felt that my family didn't care for me . . . that when I was on the streets I felt that I got more love than when I was in the house so I felt that that's where my love was, on the streets, so that's where I stayed."

Marital status and the quality of one's marriage also have a large effect on peer associations. Individuals who are unmarried or involved in bad marriages often spend much time with peers, including delinquent peers. There is nothing to prevent them from doing so: they are unmarried or, if married, they do not care about their spouses. Further, the strain they experience may drive them away from their spouses and toward peers. Good marriages, however, may reduce peer associations, especially delinquent peer associations, because people desire to spend much time with their spouses and their spouses are able to exercise some control over them. Good marriages, then, dramatically reduce association with delinquent peers; in fact, some data suggest that most of the effect of good marriages on adult crime is explained by the impact of these marriages on peer delinquency (Warr 2002; although see Simons et al. 2002).

Marriage. Parenting practices have a small to moderate *direct* effect on marital status and the quality of one's marriage. I predict a small to moderate effect because parents play a small role in the lives of their *adult* children and adults are subject to the strong influence of other life domains, like peers and work. Nevertheless, parenting practices may have some direct effect on marital status and quality (Faust and McKibben 1999; Treas and Lawton 1999). Parents often provide their adult children with much social support, which may include introducing their children to potential spouses and providing them with financial and other assistance after marriage, which can improve marriage quality. (Note: Parents do have a large *indirect* effect on marital status and quality through their effect on the traits, school experiences, peer associations, and delinquency of their children).

Work. Parenting practices also have a small to moderate *direct* effect on work experiences, with parental social support being most relevant here. Parents may influence the occupational aspirations of their children, encouraging them to pursue decent jobs or, in some cases, failing to do so. MacLeod (1995, 57), for example, reports that the delinquents in his study generally received little encouragement from parents to raise their aspirations. One delinquent gave the following reply when asked what kind of work his mother wanted him to do for living: "Anything, man. Somethin.' I dunno. Just a fuckin' job."

Parents may also influence the work experiences of their children by using their resources—like money and job connections—to help set their children up in business or find them jobs (Lin 1999). Sullivan (1989), for example, describes how the parents in one working-class community were often able to use their connections to secure decent, blue-collar jobs for their children, thus reducing the likelihood that their children would continue to engage in crime as they became adults. The parents in two other, poorer communities, however, lacked the job connections to help their children. As a consequence, these children were more likely to continue engaging in crime as they entered their adult years. So strong parental social support may increase the likelihood of employment and work in a good job, while poor social support may reduce it. (Note: Parents have a large *indirect* effect on adult work experiences through their effect on the traits, school experiences, peer associations, and delinquency of their children [see Sampson and Laub 1993]).

Marital experiences have a small to moderate effect on work experiences as well. Being unmarried or involved in a bad marriage increases unemployment and reduces bonding to work, work performance, and the quality of one's job (Ferber and O'Farrell 1991; Haas 1999). Among other things, unmarried individuals and those in bad marriages have less incentive to do well at work, have less social support, and are under greater strain. (It should be noted, however, that the effect of marriage on work sometimes differs by gender. For example, marriage increases the likelihood that men work but may reduce the likelihood that women work, especially if children are present [see England et al. 2001; also see Chapter 9 for further discussion of the impact of gender on family and work effects]). One reason for the small to moderate effect of marriage on work is that work experiences are insulated from the demands of family life in the United States. As Messner and Rosenfeld (2001) point out, the economy—including work—is the dominant institution in the United States. People are expected to sacrifice their family lives for the sake of work, but not the reverse. Reflecting this fact, people more often state that work interferes with family life than that family life interferes with work (Ferber and O'Farrell 1991, 55; also see Haas 1999).

Summary. Poor parenting and marital experiences affect all of the other life domains, although effect sizes vary. Poor parenting affects the traits of irritability and low self-control (large effect during childhood), negative school experiences (large effect), association with delinquent peers (large effect), marital quality (small to moderate effect), and unemployment and bad jobs (small to moderate effect). Being unmarried or in a bad marriage affects personality traits (small to moderate effect), delinquent peers (large effect), and unemployment/bad jobs (small to moderate effect). I should emphasize that these statements regarding effect size are not always based on extensive research and should be viewed as tentative.

You may have noticed that many of the effects described above were explained in terms of control, social learning, and strain theories: the three leading theories of crime (described in Chapter 2). Parents who engage in poor parenting practices *fail to teach* their children self-control, anger management, and the skills and attitudes necessary to do well in school. Such parents also *fail to sanction* their children when they display low self-control or irritable behavior, have problems at school, or associate with delinquent peers. These are social learning and control arguments. Further, poor parenting increases the strain that juveniles experience, which makes them irritable, interferes with their school work, and drives them away from home, increasing the likelihood of delinquent peer association. Social learning, control, and strain theories not only help us understand why individuals engage in crime, but they also help us understand the effect of poor parenting on the other life domains. And as you will see below, they also help us understand the effect of school, peer, and work experiences on the other life domains.

The Effect of School (Negative School Experiences and Limited Education) on the Other Life Domains

Negative school experiences include negative bonding to teachers and school, poor academic performance, little time spent on homework, low educational and occupational goals, poor supervision/discipline, negative treatment by teachers, the absence of positive teaching, and limited education (for adults). Negative school experiences affect the other four life domains, although effect sizes vary by domain.

Low Self-Control/Irritability. Negative school experiences should have a small to moderate effect on irritability/low self-control. These traits are largely formed by the time the child enters school. It is difficult for teachers to deliberately affect these traits because they are responsible for many students and must often focus on the achievement of other goals, so their role in the lives of juveniles is limited. Further, teachers compete with others, like parents and peers, in trying to influence these traits. Nevertheless, school experiences may have some effect on traits. Good school experiences, like good supervision/discipline and positive teaching, may foster self-control and reduce irritability, while poor school experiences may have the opposite effect. School strain, in particular, may increase irritability. Overall, however, negative school experiences are more a consequence than a cause of irritability and low self-control.

Poor Parenting Practices. Negative school experiences should have a small to moderate effect on poor parenting practices. Parenting practices are largely established by the time the child enters school. School officials typically make little effort to change parenting practices, and the school competes with other groups in affecting parenting practices, like peers (also see the discussion of parenting practices in Chapter 8). Nevertheless, poor school experiences may create strain for parents, and this strain may weaken the bond between parent and child and contribute to harsh discipline or neglect.

Peer Delinquency. School experiences should have a large effect on peer delinquency during the adolescent and adult years. School experiences are temporally prior to and overlap with peer delinquency, and the school is perhaps the central context for the development of peer ties. The peer interaction that occurs at school, in fact, is often more important to students than the academic work. When students are asked to list "the one best thing about school," their most common response is "my friends" (Riordan 1997, 205). School experiences influence the nature of this peer interaction, especially the types of peers that students are exposed to and their reaction to these peers. Good students who like school are more likely to be exposed to other good students, in part because of ability grouping (tracking, and ability groups within the classroom). They are more likely to be attracted to these students, given that we are attracted to similar others. And they are more likely to be fearful of associating with delinquent students, because this may jeopardize their stake in conformity. As a consequence, good students are *less* likely to associate with delinquent peers (who tend to be among the poorer students, for reasons indicated in Chapter 2). Conversely, poor students who dislike school are more likely to come in contact with, be attracted to, and associate with one another. Further, the strain they experience at school may sometimes function as a bond that unites them. These arguments find support in studies that indicate that negative school experiences have a large effect on delinquent peer association (Colvin 2000; Elliott et al. 1985; Thornberry et al. 2003a; 2003b).

Work and Marriage. School experiences have a large effect on work experiences, particularly the type of work one does. The primary function of school in the United States is to prepare individuals for work and to provide them with the credentials that grant access to certain types of jobs. No other group seriously competes with the educational system in this area.

School experiences, including length of education, should have a small to moderate effect on marital experiences. Marriage often occurs after schooling is complete, and other factors—like peer and work experiences—have a strong effect on marital experiences. Nevertheless, school experiences influence such things as the timing of marriage, the potential marital partners one is exposed to, and one's appeal or attractiveness to these potential partners. Individuals with advanced educations are likely to marry at older ages (which increases the likelihood of a successful marriage), be exposed to more potential partners with desirable personality traits (higher self-control, lower irritability), and be more attractive to such individuals. They are more attractive in part because of their advanced education and in part because that education may have improved their interpersonal skills. These effects help explain why an advanced education generally decreases the likelihood of divorce for men; the effect of education on divorce for women is more complex (see Faust and McKibben 1999).

Summary. Negative school experiences increase low self-control/irritability (small to moderate effect), poor parenting practices (small to moderate effect), peer delinquency (large effect during adolescence and adulthood), unemployment/bad jobs (large effect), and no/bad marriages (small to moderate effect).

The Effect of Peers (Peer Delinquency) on the Other Life Domains

Peer delinquency includes having close friends who are delinquent, being verbally and physically abused by peers, and spending much time with peers in unstructured, unsupervised activities. These peer variables are especially important during the adolescent period, although they remain important for some people into the adult years.

Low Self-Control/Irritability. Peer delinquency should have a small to moderate effect on low self-control and irritability (Asendorf 1998). These traits are largely formed by the time that peer associations develop. Nevertheless, peer delinquency may exert some effect on these traits. In particular, delinquent peers may model and reinforce impulsive, risky, and aggressive behavior. They may teach beliefs favorable to crime, and the strain associated with delinquent peer association, including peer conflict and abuse, may contribute to irritability. There has not been much research on the effect of peer delinquency on individual traits, although data do suggest that association with delinquent peers increases the likelihood that individuals will hold beliefs favorable to delinquency (see Agnew 2005).

Poor Parenting. Peer delinquency should have a small to moderate direct effect on parenting practices. Like traits, parenting practices are well-established prior to the development of peer delinquency. Nevertheless, the demands of the peer group, especially the delinquent peer group, may draw juveniles away from the family. Further, peer delinquency may create strain for family members. Parents, in particular, may become concerned about the friends their children are associating with and the deviant activities in which they engage. This strain may weaken the bond between parents and juveniles and contribute to harsh disciplinary techniques (or lead frustrated parents to give up on their children).

Negative School Experiences. Peer delinquency should have a large effect on negative school experiences during the adolescent years. The demands of delinquent peers may interfere with school work and such peers may challenge the juvenile's commitment to school (Thornberry et al. 2003a). Based on their study of St. Louis gangs, Decker and Van Winkle (1996, 187, 190) state that:

> In most cases, gang life has an obsessively deadly attraction for our subjects, one which constricts and diminishes their life to the friendship group of the gang. Indeed, nearly two-thirds of our subjects could not or did not identify any activities they participated in outside of the gang. . . . Attending school, being on time, paying attention to teachers and other staff, getting passing grades . . . are not high priorities for most gang members. (Also see Riordan 1997.)

Peer delinquency can also create strain for teachers, who may respond by rejecting students who are members of delinquent groups and treating them in a negative manner.

Marriage and Work. Finally, peer delinquency should have a large direct effect on marriage and work. Delinquent peers may discourage the juvenile from marrying and peer activities may make it difficult to marry or at least form a good marriage. The same may be true of delinquent peers and work (see Thornberry et al. 2003a). As Decker and Van Winkle (1996, 221–2) note of the gang members in their study, "the main reason most of our subjects do not work is because they are gang members, whose lives and time are focused on street and peer-group activities that they find more rewarding." Associating with delinquent peers like gang members, however, may increase the likelihood of early pregnancy and teenage parenthood—but these tend to limit opportunities for future success (Thornberry et al. 2003a). All of this is not to deny that many juveniles leave delinquent peer groups for good jobs and marriages, but only to claim that it is more difficult for them to do so.

Summary. Peer delinquency affects low self-control/irritability (small to moderate effect), poor parenting practices (small to moderate effect), negative school experiences (large effect), no marriage/bad marriage (large effect), and unemployment/bad jobs (large effect). These effects are most pronounced during the adolescent years, when there is much variation in peer delinquency and peers play a central role in the lives of individuals. Peer delinquency becomes much less common among adults, but may still have a large effect on certain adults.

The Effect of Work (Unemployment and Bad Jobs) on the Other Life Domains

Those work experiences contributing to crime include unemployment, poor supervision/discipline, negative bonding to work, poor work performance, poor working conditions, and criminal coworkers. Few children are involved in paid work in the United States, and work plays only a small to moderate role in the lives of most adolescents. Work, however, occupies a central role in the lives of adults.

Low Self-Control and Irritability. Work in bad jobs should have a small to moderate effect on irritability and low self-control. Such jobs do little to teach self-control and the strain associated with them may foster irritability. Work in good jobs, however, may increase self-control and lower irritability (Brief et al. 1988; Crouter 1994).

Peer Associations. Developing an attachment to a decent job should have a large effect on delinquent peer associations. Individuals with strong work ties should have less time and less desire to associate with delinquent peers (see Simons et al. 2002).

Marriage. Work experiences should have a large effect on family life among men. Men who are unemployed or in bad jobs are less likely to marry, in part because they cannot afford to support families and potential marriage partners find them less desirable. And if married, such men are more likely to experience marital problems, in part because they have a lower stake in conformity and in part due to the strains associated with their low incomes and poor working conditions. The effect of women's work on marital status and quality is generally smaller than the effect of men's work (see Chapter 9). This may partly reflect the fact that women's work sometimes has contradictory effects. For example, women's work may reduce financial strain in the household, thereby improving marital quality, but lead to conflicts over who should perform household tasks, thereby reducing marital quality. Further, the effect of women's work on family life appears to depend on a range of factors, making it difficult to draw general conclusions in this area (for overviews on work and family life, see Haas 1999; Faust and McKibben 1999; Ferber and O'Farrell 1991; Kashefi 1999; Larson et al. 1994).

Summary: The Effects of the Life Domains on One Another Over the Individual's Life

A large number of effects are described in the above discussion. Figures 4-2 through 4-4 summarize this discussion by showing the effects of the life domains on one another and on crime during the childhood, adolescent, and adult years. Large effects are illustrated with thick lines and small to moderate effects with thin lines.

As can be seen, each life domain directly affects crime and indirectly affects crime through its effects on the other domains. For example, negative school experiences have a direct effect on crime and an indirect effect through the other life domains, especially peer delinquency. Also, the life domains tend to mutually reinforce one another. For example, poor parenting contributes to irritability/low self-control, while irritability/low self-control contributes to poor parenting. These mutually reinforcing effects are what I refer to as the "web of crime." This web goes a long way toward explaining why some individuals offend at high rates over much or part of their lives.

Criminals who offend at high rates usually develop low self-control/irritability and experience poor parenting in childhood (Chapters 8 and 9 explain why). It is difficult to say which comes first, the traits or the poor parenting. But the traits and poor

Figure 4-2
The Effects of the Life Domains on One
Another and on Crime During CHILDHOOD

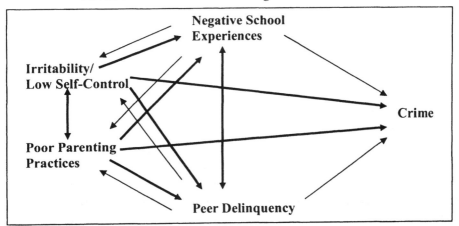

Figure 4-3
The Effects of the Life Domains on One Another
and on Crime During ADOLESCENCE

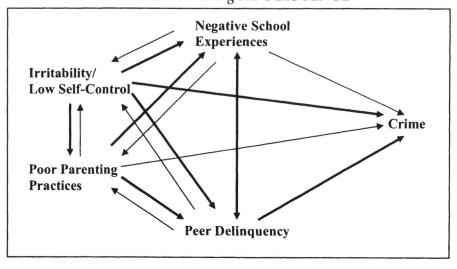

Figure 4-4
The Effects of the Life Domains on One Another
and on Crime During ADULTHOOD

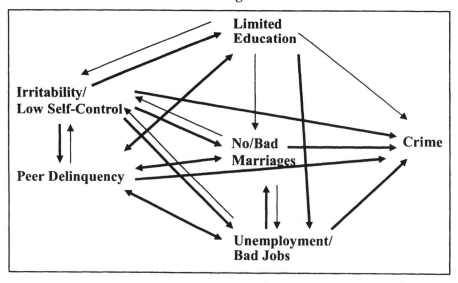

parenting mutually reinforce one another: irritability/low self-control fosters poor parenting, which in turn fosters irritability/low

self-control. As the child becomes older, irritability/low self-control and poor parenting lead to problems in school and to association with delinquent peers. These school and peer problems, in turn, reinforce poor parenting and irritability/low self-control (as well as one another). While some individuals are able to escape from this web of crime when making the transition to adulthood, many others remain trapped, although poor parenting is replaced by marital problems and negative school experiences are replaced by bad jobs. Such criminals continue to offend at high rates well into their adult lives.

Not all criminals, however, are high-rate, chronic offenders. Most criminals, in fact, tend to limit their offending largely to the adolescent years. As described in Chapter 9, the social and biological changes associated with adolescence often contribute to irritability/low self-control, poor parenting, negative school experiences, and peer delinquency during the adolescent years. So for a few years, some individuals become trapped in this web; however, they are not as deeply immersed as chronic offenders, and so they have a much easier time escaping from it when they reach adulthood.

Conclusion

This chapter focuses on the effect of the five life domains on one another. A large number of effects are described, with most of the life domains affecting one another. These effects vary in size, with such variation often being linked to stages in the life course (childhood, adolescence, adulthood). Further, the variables in the different life domains affect one another for a variety of reasons, with these reasons often being related to social learning, strain, and control theories. The models in Figures 4-2 through 4-4, which summarize the major effects described in this chapter, are filled with thick and thin arrows pointing in many directions.

Some might argue that the general theory of crime depicted in these models is not very simple or parsimonious. In fact, it may appear rather complex. Nevertheless, I believe that the general theory represents the best possible approach for understanding the causes of crime. First, the theory does reflect reality—the life domains are truly interdependent. What happens in one sphere of life typically has repercussions for the other spheres. Any theory of crime that fails to acknowledge this is seriously deficient, providing incomplete and misleading information about the causes of crime (see Thornberry 1987; Thornberry et al. 2003b).

Second, the general theory provides a more parsimonious approach than any alternative theory that focuses on the specific causes of crime. Imagine, for example, what the models in Figures 4-2 through 4-4 would look like if they listed the 30+ specific causes of crime listed in Chapter 3. It is true that the general theory is more complex than alternative theories that focus on one or a very few broadly defined causes of crime, like coercive control, social support, or reintegrative shaming. But as argued in Chapter 1, these theories fail to present readers with a clear sense of what the causes of crime are in the various life domains, how these causes are related to one another, and how they work together to affect crime.

Finally, I would argue that while the general theory of crime presented up to this point is complex on one level, it is quite simple on another. In fact, there is a certain simplicity in its complexity. The theory basically argues that the life domains mutually reinforce one another; that is the central point of this chapter. If you understand this, you have come a long way toward understanding the causes of crime. While effect sizes do vary, there are only a few such variations to keep track of at each life stage. In particular, traits and parenting practices are the key domains during the childhood years: they have large effects on one another, the other life domains, and crime. Traits, parents, and peers are the key domains during the adolescent years, and traits, marital relations, peers, and work are the key domains during the adult years. There are also a number of reasons why the life domains affect one another, but most of these reasons are related to control, social learning, and strain theories.

So while the general theory presented up to this point is not the most parsimonious of theories, is not as complex as certain alternatives, it is not as complex as it might first appear, and it strikes the best balance between the need for simplicity on the one hand and the need to accurately reflect reality on the other.

My presentation of the general theory, however, is not yet complete. We have so far treated crime as a "dependent variable," examining those variables that affect crime. But crime exerts some important effects of its own. In particular, there is reason to be believe that engaging in crime often increases the likelihood of further crime. I examine this argument in Chapter 5.

Notes

1. It is also the case that individual traits have a large effect on family factors: as indicated, children who are irritable and low in self-control increase the likelihood that their parents will engage in poor parenting practices. Further, the relationship between poor parenting and traits like irritability and low self-control is partly due to the fact that both are caused by the same third variables, like the parents' irritability and low self-control (Caspi and Moffitt 1995).

2. As argued in Chapter 8, some children are easier to teach than others because of their biological characteristics.

Discussion and Study Questions

1. What is meant by "the web of crime"?

2. Why is it important to examine the effects of the life domains on one another?

3. Give an example where a life domain has a small or moderate *direct* effect on crime, but a large *indirect* effect through the other life domains.

4. I argue that the effect of one life domain on another can often be explained in terms of control, social learning, and strain theories. Give an example of each of these explanations.

5. What factors determine whether a life domain has a small to moderate or a large effect on another life domain?

6. The size of effects often varies over the life course, from childhood to adolescence to adulthood. Give an example of such variation and discuss the possible reasons for this variation.

7. Why do the traits of irritability and low self-control increase the likelihood of poor parenting, negative school experiences, peer delinquency, no/bad marriages, and no/bad jobs?

8. The effect of "no/bad jobs" on the other life domains varies by gender. Give an example. How might we explain such variation?

9. What are the most important life domains at each stage of the life course? Describe their effects. ✦

Chapter 5

Crime Affects Its 'Causes,' and Prior Crime Directly Affects Subsequent Crime

We have now examined most of the major direct causes of crime, but there is one important cause that we have over-looked—in fact, it is perhaps the most important cause of crime. Studies suggest that engaging in crime at one point in time substantially increases the likelihood of offending at a later point in time (Akers 1998; Bushway et al. 1999; Elliott 1994; Elliott et al. 1985; Hawkins et al. 2000; Nagin and Paternoster 2000; Patterson 1992; Sampson and Laub 1993; 1997; Wright et al. 1999). This effect constitutes another strand in the "web of crime," and it too helps explain the fact that *some* individuals commit crimes over much of their lives (see Cairns and Cairns 1994; Caspi and Moffitt 1995; Sampson and Laub 1993, 9–17). Any general theory of crime, then, must model and explain the large effect of *prior crime* on *subsequent crime*.

Fortunately, this effect is easily explained using the arguments described in Chapters 2 through 4. Prior crime affects subsequent crime largely because of its effects on the five life domains. In particular, engaging in crime often (but not always) contributes to irritability/low self-control, poor parenting, bad marriages, negative school experiences, peer delinquency, unemployment, and bad jobs. Prior crime, then, *indirectly affects* subsequent crime through the five life domains. The first part of this chapter describes these indirect effects.

Prior crime also has a *direct effect* on subsequent crime. Most studies suggest that prior crime affects subsequent crime even after we take account of the effect of prior crime on the life domains. This is because prior crime may directly impact certain of the constraints against and motivations for crime. Engaging in crime may reduce the fear of external sanctions, increase certain types of strain that do not involve the life domains, and provide certain benefits to the individual, like money and status. The second part of this chapter describes these direct effects. Figure 5-1 illustrates both the direct and indirect effects of prior crime on subsequent crime.[1]

Figure 5-1
The Direct and Indirect Effects of Prior Crime on Subsequent Crime

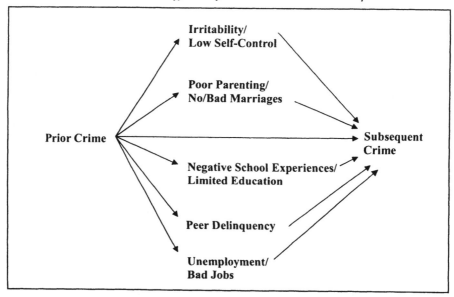

The argument that prior crime increases the likelihood of subsequent crime draws heavily on labeling theory. According to this theory, individuals who are labeled criminals by others are more likely to engage in crime (see Cullen and Agnew 2003, Part VIII for an overview). This is because others treat these individuals as "criminals" or "bad people." In particular, conventional others reject them and employers do not want to hire them. Eventually, labeled individuals end up associating with one another. The result of being labeled a criminal, then, is a reduction in the constraints against crime and an increase in the motivations for crime.[2] Labeling theorists tend to focus on individuals who have been "formally labeled" criminals by the police and courts, individuals who have been arrested and officially sanctioned. But a number of labeling theorists also examine individuals who have been "informally labeled" criminals by parents, teachers, and others (e.g., Matsueda 1992). Whatever the focus, labeling theorists argue that being labeled a criminal increases the likelihood of further crime by reducing the constraints against and increasing the motivations for crime.

I make many of the same arguments below. I do not focus on "formal" labeling in this chapter; rather, I delay my discussion of the impact of arrest and official sanction until Chapter 11. But I do deal with "informal labeling." In particular, I argue that people like parents and employers may become aware of the individual's crime and label the person a "criminal." They may then treat him or her in a negative manner, thereby contributing to poor parenting, bad marriages, negative school experiences, peer delinquency, unemployment, and bad jobs.

The arguments I make below also move beyond labeling theory. In particular, I argue that prior crime may increase the likelihood of subsequent crime *even if others never find out about the prior crime or label the individual a criminal.* For example, prior crime may increase the likelihood of subsequent crime if individuals make a lot of money from their crime. This occurs even if the prior crime does not become known to others; in fact, this effect is *more* likely to occur if the crime does not become known to others. Prior crime may also increase the likelihood of subsequent crime because engaging in crime makes individuals realize that the risk of external sanction is low (see Stafford and Warr 1993). This effect is also more likely if the individual's prior crime remains unknown to others. I argue that prior crime increases the likelihood of subsequent crime for a number of reasons, some derived from labeling theory and some not.

Having said all this, I should note that while engaging in crime generally increases the likelihood of further crime, it does not always lead to further crime. In some cases, prior crime has no effect on further crime or actually reduces the likelihood of further crime. Criminologists have devoted much effort in recent years to figuring out why this is so, and I explore the issue in the final part of this chapter. Drawing on the work of several criminologists, I argue that the effect of prior crime on subsequent crime depends on (1) how others react to the crime, and (2) the characteristics of the criminal (Braithwaite 1989; 2002; Sherman 1993; 2000; Stafford and Warr 1993).

The Effect of Crime on the Life Domains

Irritability/Low Self-Control. Crime should have a small to moderate effect on irritability and low self-control.[3] Irritability and low self-control typically develop before criminal behavior emerges. Nevertheless, engaging in crime may impact irritability and self-control in several ways. As Matza (1964) suggests, the experience of committing a criminal act often reduces the individual's level of self-control. Many individuals are initially fearful of engaging in crime. However, when they do engage in crime—for whatever reason—they often find that their crime is not sanctioned or even discovered by conventional others. This reduces their fear and emboldens them—thereby resulting in a reduction in self-control. Further, individuals who commit criminal acts often feel under some pressure to justify or excuse their acts, both to reduce any guilt they might feel and to deflect possible sanctions by others. As a consequence, engaging in crime leads them to develop beliefs that justify or excuse crime (Thornberry et al. 2003b). In addition, some crimes, like *certain types* of illicit drug use, may make individuals more irritable and less able to exercise self-control (White and Gorman 2000). Finally, crime increases the likelihood of negative treatment by others, which may increase the individual's level of irritability. Crime, then, may increase irritability and reduce self-control for several reasons.

Family, School, Peers, and Work. Engaging in crime has a large effect on the family, school, peer, and work domains. The reasons for this effect are similar to the reasons why irritability and low self-control affect these domains. Engaging in crime may *create a preference for environments conducive to crime.* For example, criminals may prefer to associate with other criminals (we prefer to associate with people who are similar to us). Or criminals who make a lot of money from crime may prefer unemployment over legal work.

Engaging in crime may also *affect our performance in the life domains.* Frequent drug use, for example, may lead to school failure and problems at work. Further, this poor performance may *force individuals into environments conducive to crime,* like bad or no jobs. Cromwell's study of burglars provides an example of this effect. Cromwell et al. (1991, 54) state that:

Once [the burglars] began to use drugs regularly . . . they usually begin to rely, at least partially, on criminal activity to maintain the habit. As their drug use intensified, the users (particularly heroin addicts) found regular employment increasingly difficult to maintain, and they often dropped out of legitimate society and into a drug-using, criminal subculture.

This effect may be stronger if the individual's crime is known to others, because others may react more harshly if they attribute the individual's poor performance to crime.

Finally, engaging in crime may *create strain (or the anticipation of strain) for others,* like parents, peers, teachers, spouses, and employers (e.g., Ambert 1999). This is especially true if the crime is directed against these others or occurs in the family, school, peer, and work environments. These *others may respond by avoiding the criminal or treating the criminal in a negative manner.* This effect obviously requires that the crime be known to others. Decker and Van Winkle provide an example of this effect. Based on their observations and interviews with gang members and others, they state that:

Schools do not want students who sell drugs, fight with rivals, show disrespect for teachers and staff, and carry weapons. Employers would rather not hire young men and women who wear gang colors, throw signs, and say 'what's up cuz.' Gang members and gangs bring danger to their environs and the people around them. Legitimate social institutions, therefore, distance gang members from their provinces. . . . (Decker and Van Winkle 1996, 228–9)

So engaging in crime may negatively affect the life domains for several reasons, some of which require or are enhanced to the extent that the crime is known to others. This is one reason why crime that results in arrest and formal sanction is more likely to affect the life domains—such crime is more likely to be known to others (Hagan 1991; Sampson and Laub 1993; 1997; Stewart et al. 2000; 2002b; Tanner et al. 1999). A number of studies have examined the effect of crime on the life domains, and they suggest that crime contributes to poor parenting, bad marriages, negative school experiences, peer delinquency, unemployment, and bad jobs (e.g., Benson 2002; De Li 1999; Fagan and Freeman 1999; Hagan 1991; 1993; 1997; Moffitt et al.

2001; Peterson and Hann 1999; Rutter et al. 1998; Sampson and Laub 1993; 1997; Simons et al. 2002; Thornberry and Christenson 1984; Thornberry et al. 2003a; 2003b). Let me provide a few examples.

Gerald Patterson and his associates have spent much time studying the impact of the child's delinquent behavior on parenting practices (see Patterson et al. 1992). They have observed and interviewed a good many children and their parents, following some families over several years. Patterson's research suggests that the delinquent behavior of the children has a large effect on parenting practices. Delinquent behavior increases the likelihood that parents will dislike their children, poorly supervise them, and treat them in a harsh manner. (And these parenting practices, in turn, contribute to delinquent behavior). Further, Patterson and his associates have found that delinquent behavior increases the likelihood of rejection by conventional peers, association with delinquent peers, and academic problems.

Elliott and Menard (1996) examined the relationship between juvenile delinquency and association with delinquent peers in a nationally representative sample of 1725 juveniles. These juveniles were 11 to 17 years old when they were first interviewed and most were then re-interviewed each year over the next several years. Elliott and Menard found a close relationship between delinquency and association with delinquent peers. Most commonly, a nondelinquent individual would get involved with slightly delinquent peers and, following this involvement, would start engaging in minor offending. This minor offending would then lead to involvement with somewhat more delinquent peers, which would lead to more serious offending, which in turn would lead to involvement with even more delinquent peers. So this study, like many others, suggests that delinquency increases the likelihood of association with delinquent peers (and that association with delinquent peers increases delinquency; also see Matsueda and Anderson 1998; Thornberry et al. 2003b). Further, additional research suggests that engaging in delinquency increases the likelihood of peer conflict and abuse. In particular, our criminal acts frequently upset others, particularly the victims of these acts, and they sometimes respond by attacking us (see Lockwood 1997). Reflecting this fact, studies indicate that engaging in crime increases the likelihood of criminal victimization (Agnew 2002).

Tanner et al. (1999) examined the effect of crime on a range of educational and occupational outcomes in a nationally representative sample of approximately 2,500 individuals. These individuals were first interviewed when they were 14–17 years old and were again interviewed about 13 years later, when their educational and occupational outcomes were measured. Tanner et al. found that those who engaged in crime *as adolescents* obtained less education, were more likely to be unemployed, and worked in lower status jobs as adults (although the effect of crime on unemployment and occupational status only held for males). This was true even after Tanner et al. took account of race, age, parents' socioeconomic status, family structure (two-parent family or not), number of siblings, "cultural resources" in the parents' home (magazines, newspapers, library card), cognitive skills, and educational expectations.

So crime often negatively affects the life domains and thereby contributes to further crime.

The Direct Effect of Prior Crime on Subsequent Crime

While prior crime affects subsequent crime primarily through its effect on the life domains, it also has a *direct* effect on subsequent crime. This effect is also easily explained, because there is good evidence that engaging in crime directly reduces certain of the constraints against crime and increases the motivations for crime.

Crime May Reduce the Fear of External Sanctions. Engaging in crime often reduces our fear of external sanctions, thereby lowering one of the major constraints against crime. Individuals who engage in crime usually discover that their crime is seldom sanctioned, and as a consequence they are more likely than others to believe that the risk of external sanction is low (see Horney and Marshall 1992; Paternoster and Piquero 1995; Piquero and Pogarsky 2002; Pogarsky and Piquero 2003; Stafford and Warr 1993).[4]

Crime May Increase Strain. Engaging in crime also increases our motivation for crime, with many crimes increasing our level of strain. In particular, crime may not only cause parents, peers, and others in the life domains to treat us in a negative manner, but may also cause people like neighborhood residents to treat us in a negative manner. The individuals we victimize may seek revenge against us (Cairns and Cairns 1994, 73–76; Lockwood 1997). Certain criminals are tempting targets for others; drug dealers, for example, are often targeted by robbers because they carry a lot of money and drugs, and are unlikely to call the police. Drug dealers are also targeted by other dealers seeking to control their turf (see White and Gorman 2000). Further, engaging in crimes like drug use and gambling may create a desperate need for cash, thereby contributing to monetary strain (see White and Gorman 2000). For example, one of the armed robbers in Wright and Decker's (1997, 39, 35) study stated that he engaged in robbery because "I might need some money to buy me some drugs when I'm really desperate. . . . I might go get 80 dollars [on a stickup]. Well, 80 dollars ain't gonna be no drugs. I know this cause I done be through this situation [before] and that's when I'm gonna [end up coming] back outside again and do the same thing. That starts a pattern." Another robber stated that "I [have] a gambling problem and I . . . lose so much I [have] to do something to [get the cash] to win my money back. So I go out and rob somebody."

Crime Often Has Short-Term Benefits. The effects of crime, however, are not all bad. Crime often benefits the individual (or as social learning theorists would state, crime is often reinforced). These benefits are frequently short-lived and, over time, they may be overwhelmed by the negative consequences of crime like bad marriages and bad jobs (see Hagan 1997). But for a period of time, criminals may find that the benefits of crime outweigh the costs. Certain of the benefits of crime are obvious, like money, and data suggest that some individuals can make more money from crime than they can from legal activities. One review of the literature in this area concludes that "even when incarceration costs are factored in, the hourly rewards from crime seem to exceed legal wages for unskilled young men subject to many of the risk factors for crime and incarceration" (Fagan and Freeman 1999, 256–7).

Other benefits of crime are less obvious. Crime may be a source of status or prestige, especially for lower-class individuals who find it difficult to achieve status through legal channels. Anderson (1999) and others state that criminals in certain communities are treated with great respect, although this respect is at least partly rooted in fear. Another, related benefit of crime is that it may increase the individual's self-esteem (Brezina 2000; Rosenberg et al. 1989). Crime, in particular, may allow powerless and subservient individuals to demonstrate their control and dominance over others. Yet another benefit is that crime may provide intrinsic satisfaction to certain individuals, especially individuals with a strong need for thrills and excitement. Wood et al. (1997) asked prison inmates and college undergraduates about the "types of feelings a person may have when committing different crimes." The inmates were much more likely than the students to state that individuals committing the crimes would feel "on a high or rush," "pumped up," "on top of the world," "happy/excited," and other positive feelings. The inmates were much less likely to state that individuals committing the crimes would feel "worried," "under stress," "guilty," "depressed," and other negative feelings. So, for some individuals, crime may be exciting or thrilling.

Researchers such as Akers (1998), Brezina (2000), Katz (1988), and Wood et al. (1997) describe many of the benefits that may result from crime, including tangible benefits like money and intangible benefits like status and thrills. As Brezina (2000) points out, these benefits receive special emphasis in strain and social learning/rational choice theories. Strain theorists argue that crime is sometimes an effective method for coping with a variety of strains or stresses (see Agnew 1992; Brezina 1996). In particular, crime may be a means for achieving goals that are not available through legitimate channels, including monetary, status, and autonomy goals. Crime may be a means for retrieving or protecting valued possessions. Crime may be a means of escaping from or ending negative treatment; for example, adolescents may run away from abusive parents or attack the peers who harass them (see Brezina 1999). Crime may also be a means of alleviating the negative emotions that result from strain (e.g., through illicit drug use). Brezina (1996) stated that if these arguments are correct, strained individuals who engage in crime should experience some relief from the negative emotions that accompany strain. This is precisely what he found in a study of adolescent males: Strained individuals who engaged in crime were less likely to be angry, resentful, anxious, and depressed than strained individuals who did not engage in crime.

Social learning theorists also state that crime is sometimes a successful method for coping with problems (or strains). Patterson's research on the family provides an excellent example (see Patterson et al. 1992, Chapter 4). Patterson discovered that children sometimes respond to parental disciplinary efforts with aggressive behaviors like arguing, yelling, and throwing things. He further discovered that such aggressive behaviors are sometimes "successful," causing parents to "back down" or give up on their disciplinary efforts. For example, a parent tells a child to stop watching TV and do her homework. The child argues with and eventually ends up screaming at the parent. The parent then backs down, saying something like "you need to do your homework later" or "I don't care what you do." The child's aggression is thus reinforced by the parent's backing down.

Social learning theorists, however, also argue that many individuals are in environments where crime is reinforced even when it is not committed in response to some problem. Most notably, crime is often reinforced among those who associate with delinquent peers. Such reinforcement frequently comes in the form of social approval and status, as when friends congratulate the individual for shoplifting a CD or winning a fight. So some individuals benefit from or are reinforced for their crime.

Summary. Prior crime may have a direct effect on subsequent crime for several reasons: Engaging in crime may reduce the fear of external sanctions, increase strain, and result in short-term benefits or reinforcements.[5]

The Effect of Prior Crime on Subsequent Crime Depends on the Reaction to Crime and the Characteristics of the Criminal

The mechanisms by which prior crime may increase the likelihood of subsequent crime are shown in Figure 5-2. In certain cases, these mechanisms require that the crime be known to others or they are enhanced if the crime is known to others. In other cases, these mechanisms do not require that the crime be known to others or they are enhanced if the crime is *not* known to others.

As indicated above, however, prior crime does not always increase the likelihood of subsequent crime. Sometimes it has no effect on subsequent crime and sometimes it reduces the likelihood of subsequent crime. I believe that we now have a good idea why this is so (see especially Braithwaite 1989; 2002; Sherman 1993; 2000; Stafford and Warr 1993). The effect of prior crime on subsequent crime depends on how others react to the crime and on the characteristics of the criminal.

How Others React to the Crime

There are four key ways in which others might react to the individual's crime: Others may (1) *fail to respond to the crime;* (2) respond in a *harsh/rejecting manner;* (3) respond in a manner that is *approving/ supportive of the crime;* or (4) respond in a manner that *firmly rejects the crime, but is accepting of the person.*[6] The first three responses increase the likelihood that prior crime will lead to subsequent crime, while the fourth response reduces the likelihood. I should note that individuals may experience more than one type of response; for example, they may experience a "harsh/rejecting" response from their parents and an "approving/supportive of the crime" response from their peers.

Figure 5-2
The Mechanisms by Which Prior Crime May Increase Subsequent Crime

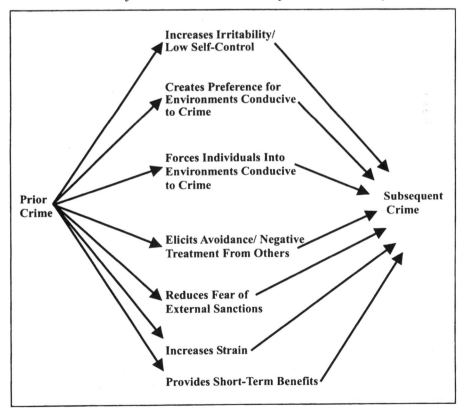

Increases Irritability/ Low Self-Control

Creates Preference for Environments Conducive to Crime

Forces Individuals Into Environments Conducive to Crime

Prior Crime

Subsequent Crime

Elicits Avoidance/ Negative Treatment From Others

Reduces Fear of External Sanctions

Increases Strain

Provides Short-Term Benefits

Failure to Respond to the Crime. The first and perhaps most common response to crime is that *others do little or nothing about the individual's crime.* This typically occurs because others do not know about the individual's crime. Most crime is never detected, at least by conventional others like parents and teachers. Others, however, may fail to respond to the individual's crime even if they do know about it: perhaps they do not care about the individual or they are afraid of responding. This failure to respond increases the likelihood of further crime for certain of the reasons indicated above and in Figure 5-2. Most notably, the failure to respond reduces the constraints against crime (e.g., perceptions of the likelihood of external sanction) and it enhances certain of the benefits of crime (e.g., it is easier to make money from crime if others fail to respond to your crime). These effects are usually not considered by labeling theorists, who sometimes argue that the best response to crime is to ignore it (and thereby avoid labeling the person a "criminal").

Harsh/Rejecting Response. The second response to crime is to reject the criminal and treat him or her in a harsh manner (similar to what Braithwaite [1989] calls "disintegrative shaming"). This response requires that others know about the individual's crime and it is especially likely when these others label the individual a "criminal" or a "bad person" or something similar. This response increases the likelihood of crime primarily because of its effect on the life domains; rejection and mistreatment lead to irritability, poor parenting, bad marriages, negative school experiences, peer delinquency, unemployment, and bad jobs. These effects are emphasized by labeling theorists. According to Braithwaite, this harsh/rejecting response to crime is common in the United States, where high levels of urbanization and mobility often prevent people from developing close ties to one another.

Approving/Supportive of the Crime Response. The third response is to approve of, justify, or excuse the individual's crime (under certain conditions), and perhaps encourage further crime. This response increases the short-term benefits of crime and may foster low self-control, and is most likely to come from deviant or criminal others, especially criminal peers.[7] (I should note that individuals who experience this response from peers often have parents who fail to respond to their crime or respond in a harsh/rejecting manner. As indicated in Chapter 4, association with delinquent peers is related to poor parental supervision and harsh parental discipline.)

Firmly Reject the Crime, but Accept the Person Response. The final response is to firmly reject the crime, but continue to accept the individual who committed the crime (similar to what Braithwaite calls "reintegrative shaming"). In particular, others sanction the individual's crime in a meaningful, but not overly harsh manner. After the crime is sanctioned, the individual is forgiven. The individual's ties to conventional others and institutions are maintained or, if need be, strengthened. For example, suppose parents discover that their child is using drugs. The parents sanction the drug use in a firm manner, but they do not abuse or reject the child. In fact, they continue to express their love for the child and make an effort to address the problems that contributed to the drug use.[8] As Braithwaite points out, this type of response is reflected in sayings like "condemn the offense, but not the offender" and "hate the sin and love the sinner." The "firm but accepting" response does not increase the likelihood of subsequent crime and may even reduce it. The individual is sanctioned for his or her crime in a meaningful way, but the sanctions are not overly harsh and the individual is not rejected. As a consequence, the life domains are less likely to be negatively affected. In fact, there may be an effort to strengthen the life domains. I should note that this type of response is at the heart of the "restorative justice" movement, which is starting to have an important impact on the juvenile and criminal justice systems (see Chapter 11 and Bazemore 2000; Braithwaite 2002).

Summary. The nature of the response to crime, then, has a big impact on whether prior crime increases the likelihood of subsequent crime. The first three responses described above increase the likelihood that prior crime will lead to subsequent crime. These responses to crime are common in the United States, and this helps explain why prior crime often increases the likelihood of subsequent crime in this country (and many other countries as well). Even so, the "firmly reject the crime, but accept the person" response to crime does occur, which helps explain why prior crime does not always lead to subsequent crime.[9] A key question, however, is what determines the type of response to crime.

What Determines the Type of Response to Crime? The type of response is largely determined by the individual's standing on the five life domains (this section draws heavily on Braithwaite 1989). The three types of responses that lead to further crime are most likely when individuals possess the traits of irritability and low self-control and are in social environments conducive to crime (poor parenting, no/bad marriages, negative school experiences, peer delinquency, unemployment/bad jobs). There are several reasons for this. First, such individuals are less likely to have their crime detected, as they are poorly supervised by others (which of course contributes to the failure to respond to crime). Second, such individuals are more likely to be labeled "criminals" by conventional others if their crime is detected. That is because they fit the stereotype of a "criminal" or "bad person"; they are irritable and "out of control," come from "bad" families, do poorly in school, associate with other criminals, etc. This labeling increases the likelihood of a "harsh/rejecting" response to their crime. Third, other individuals like parents do not care about these people, do not know how to properly sanction them, and lack the skills and resources to address their problems. This increases the likelihood of the "failure to respond" and "harsh/rejecting" responses. Finally, such individuals are, by definition, more likely to have delinquent friends. This increases the likelihood of an "approving/supportive of the crime" response by peers.[10]

The Characteristics of the Criminal

The effect of prior crime on subsequent crime not only depends on how others react to the crime, but also on the characteristics of the criminal. Two individuals may commit the same crime and experience similar reactions from others, but respond quite differently to their crime and these reactions. The first individual, for example, may derive much pleasure from the crime (e.g., thrills, excitement) and may be angered by the negative reactions of others. The second individual may derive little pleasure from the crime and may be quite anxious about the negative reactions of others. Prior crime is obviously more likely to lead to subsequent crime in the case of the first individual. What determines this difference in reaction? The same factors that influence how others respond to the individual's crime also influence how the individual responds to his or her own crime and to the reactions of others. That is, the individual's response is influenced by his or her standing on the five life domains.

Consider individuals who are high in irritability, low in self-control, experience poor parenting, have negative school experiences, and are high in peer delinquency. Such individuals are more likely to react to their crime in ways that increase the likelihood of further crime. Most notably, they are more likely to benefit from their crime. For example, they find crime exciting, and they have a range of problems for which crime is often an effective solution, especially given their limited coping skills and low social support. Now imagine that these individuals receive one of the three responses to crime that increase the likelihood of further crime (failure to respond to crime, harsh/rejecting response, approving/supportive of the crime response). They are also more likely to react to these responses with further crime. Take, for example, the harsh/rejecting response. They are less likely to be deterred by the negative reactions of others (see Sherman 1993; 2000). Being low in self-control, they are less concerned about the negative consequences of crime. They also have less to lose from crime.[11] In addition, they are more likely to become angry at the negative reactions of others and respond with crime, because they have an irritable disposition and are otherwise disposed to crime because of their standing on the life domains.

Now imagine individuals who are low in irritability, high in self-control, and in social environments opposed to crime. They are less likely to benefit from their crime. For example, they do not find crime exciting; in fact, their crime makes them feel anxious and guilty. They also have fewer problems for which crime is an effective solution. Further, imagine that these individuals receive one of the three responses that increase the likelihood of further crime, like the harsh/rejecting response. They are more likely to be deterred by the negative reactions of others, less likely to become angry in response to such reactions, and less likely to respond to whatever anger they do experience with crime.

Summary. So the effect of prior crime on subsequent crime also depends on the characteristics of the individual. Individuals who are irritable, low in self-control, and in social environments conducive to crime are more likely to respond to their own crime and to the criminogenic reactions of others in ways that increase the likelihood of further crime.[11]

Summary

Prior crime usually increases the likelihood of subsequent crime, because prior crime often has a negative effect on the life domains. That is, crime often contributes to irritability/low self-control, poor parenting, negative school experiences, peer delinquency, limited education, bad marriages, unemployment, and bad jobs. Also, prior crime often *directly* increases the likelihood of subsequent crime. In particular, prior crime may reduce the fear of external sanctions, increase strain, and benefit the individual in various ways.[1]

Prior crime, however, does not always increase the likelihood of subsequent crime: Sometimes prior crime has no effect on subsequent crime and sometimes it reduces the likelihood of subsequent crime. This is because the effect of prior crime on subsequent crime is conditioned by the reaction to crime and the characteristics of the criminal. Prior crime is more likely to lead to subsequent crime when others (1) fail to respond to the prior crime; (2) respond in a harsh/rejecting manner; or (3) approve of, justify, or excuse the crime. These responses are most likely when individuals are irritable, low in self-control, and in social environments conducive to crime (poor parenting, negative school experiences, peer delinquency, etc.). Prior crime is also more likely to lead to subsequent crime among individuals who are not easily deterred by others, who are likely to benefit from crime, and who are quick to anger. Such individuals tend to be irritable, low in self-control, and in social environments conducive to crime.

So, prior crime is most likely to lead to subsequent crime among individuals who are irritable, low in self-control, and in social environments conducive to crime. We might say that these individuals suffer a "double whammy," as others are more likely to react to their crime in ways that increase the likelihood of further crime. And they are more likely to respond to the reactions of others and to their own crime in ways that increase the likelihood of further crime.

Notes

1. Prior crime is also related to subsequent crime because both prior and subsequent crime are *caused* by the same third variables, like low self-control (e.g., Gottfredson and Hirschi 1990). This explanation for the relationship between prior and subsequent crime is sometimes referred to as the "population heterogeneity" explanation, referring to the fact that relatively stable differences in the tendency for individuals to commit crime contribute to the association between prior and subsequent offending. For example, low self-control leads to offending

at Time 1 and to offending at Time 2, thereby contributing to the association between Time 1 and Time 2 offending. But most studies find that prior crime affects subsequent crime even after we take account of these stable individual differences in the tendency to commit crime (caused by third variables like self-control). Bushway et al. (1999) and Nagin and Paternoster (2000) provide excellent summaries of the research in this area.

2. Labeling theorists also argue that labeled individuals may come to view themselves as criminals, because that is how others view and treat them. They then act in accord with this criminal self-image. I incorporate this argument into the general theory by arguing that the reactions of others may alter the individuals' personality traits in ways conducive to crime; in particular, individuals may become more irritable and lower in self-control.

3. Crime and irritability/low self-control are closely related, with some claiming that crime is one of the best indicators of irritability/low self-control (Gottfredson and Hirschi 1990; also see Pratt and Cullen 2000). But like most criminologists, I argue that low self-control/irritability are personality traits that are distinct from crime and that can be measured independently of crime, most often with questions that focus on the individual's beliefs, preferences, emotions, and intentions to behave in certain ways (see Grasmick et al. 1993).

4. As indicated, crime also has an *indirect* effect on the constraints against crime, through its effect on the life domains. For example, crime may reduce parental supervision (external control), reduce bonding with parents (stake in conformity), hurt school and work performance (stake in conformity), and reduce self-control.

5. You may notice a seeming paradox here: prior crime increases subsequent crime both because it increases strain *and* it provides relief from strain (a benefit of crime). I believe that both processes are often operative. For example, the following may occur: An individual commits an act of violence, which provokes retaliation from others. The individual responds to this retaliation or strain by counterattacking (so prior crime increases strain, which increases the likelihood of subsequent crime). The counterattack is successful, which increases the likelihood that the individual will respond to similar situations in the future with violence (so crime provides some relief from strain, which increases the likelihood of further crime). While I think this and similar scenarios are plausible, one might reasonably pose the following question: If prior crime increases the likelihood of strain, why doesn't that strain reduce the likelihood of subsequent crime? The strain is basically a cost of crime. I answer this question in the latter part of Chapter 5. In

brief, the strain that may result from crime does deter some individuals from further crime, especially those high in self-control, low in irritability, and with a strong stake in conformity. But this strain fails to deter others, especially those low in self-control, high in irritability, and with a weak stake in conformity. Such individuals are angered rather than frightened when others treat them in a negative manner and they have less to lose from crime. Further, the strain that results from their crime is not well-suited for deterrence. This strain usually does not involve the consistent application of meaningful sanctions (see the discussion of external control in Chapter 2). Rather, it usually involves the erratic application of harsh sanctions.

6. It is possible to list other responses to crime. This becomes apparent if one creates a typology of responses with several dimensions (e.g., approve of versus condemn crime, reject person versus accept person, ignore/fail to respond to crime versus react to crime). The responses listed in this book, however, are believed to be the most common and theoretically relevant.

7. As indicated in Chapter 3, parents may sometimes approve of and encourage crime under certain conditions. Anderson (1999), in particular, notes that a small minority of parents in poor, inner-city communities encourage their children to respond to minor slights and provocations with violence. These parents reward their children when they successfully do so and sometimes punish them when they fail to resort to violence.

8. The parents may even challenge the efforts of others, like school officials or police, to label their child a "criminal" or a "bad person" (although the parents do not deny the child's drug use or try to prevent these others from administering reasonable sanctions).

9. I might note that tests of labeling theory usually fail to consider the four different responses to crime. Rather, they usually compare people who receive the harsh/rejecting response (or people they *assume* receive the harsh/rejecting response) to all other people. They neglect to take account of the fact that these other people receive different responses to their crime, and that certain of these responses (failure to response, accepting/supportive of crime response) may also increase the likelihood of further crime. This fact partly explains the weak support for labeling theory.

10. Conversely, the "firm but accepting" response to crime should be more likely when individuals are low in irritability, high in self-control, and in social environments opposed to crime (e.g., good parenting practices, positive school experiences). Such individuals are *more* likely to have their crime detected, they are *less* likely to be labeled criminals,

they are surrounded by others who care about them and have the skills and resources to properly sanction and help them, and they are less likely to have delinquent friends.

11. You might be wondering how individuals with these characteristics would respond to the fourth reaction to crime: the "firmly reject the crime, but accept the person" response. You may think that such individuals would simply dismiss the efforts of others to firmly sanction their crime, and there is some truth to this. Even so, the "reject the crime, but accept the person" response should lead to a greater reduction in crime among such individuals than among those who are low in irritability, high in self-control, and in environments opposed to crime. This response does little to provoke further crime and actually tries to improve the individual's standing on the life domains. Individuals who are irritable, low in self-control, and in environments conducive to crime can benefit more from this response because they are more strongly disposed to engage in crime. Individuals who are low in irritability, high in self-control, and in environments opposed to crime have little disposition for crime. This sort of response is therefore of little benefit to them; they are likely to refrain from further crime regardless of how others react to their crime (see Wright et al. 2001; Note 2 in Chapter 11).

Discussion and Study Questions

1. Prior crime is said to *directly* and *indirectly* increase the likelihood of subsequent crime. Give an example of a direct and an indirect effect of prior crime on subsequent crime.

2. Can you think of any other reasons why individuals who engage in crime at one point in time are more likely to engage in crime at a subsequent point in time, besides the direct and indirect effects of prior crime on subsequent crime (see Note 1)?

3. Describe the central arguments of labeling theory. What is the difference between "informal" and "formal" labeling?

4. I argue that prior crime increases the likelihood of subsequent crime for several reasons, some of which require that the prior crime be known to others and some of which do not. Give an example of an effect of prior crime on subsequent crime that requires that the prior crime be known to

others. Give an example of an effect that does not require that the prior crime be known to others.

5. Describe the reasons why engaging in crime may increase irritability and reduce self-control.

6. Describe the reasons why engaging in crime may negatively affect the other life domains (i.e., lead to poor parenting, negative school experiences, peer delinquency, bad marriages, unemployment, and bad jobs).

7. Describe the ways in which engaging in crime may increase the individual's level of strain.

8. Describe the types of benefits that may result from crime.

9. The effect of prior crime on subsequent crime depends on how others react to the prior crime. What types of reactions increase the likelihood that prior crime will lead to subsequent crime? What type of reaction reduces the likelihood that prior crime will lead to subsequent crime?

10. Can you think of other ways of reacting to crime beyond those discussed in this chapter?

11. Based on this chapter, what advice would you give to parents who discover that their child has committed a crime?

12. Do you think that police, court, and correctional officials in the United States react to crime in an appropriate manner? If not, what changes would you suggest they make?

13. Describe how the individual's standing on the life domains influences how others react to their crime.

14. Labeling theorists sometimes argue that the best reaction to crime is to do as little as possible about the crime. Why do some labeling theorists make this argument? Drawing on this chapter, do you agree with argument?

15. Describe the different ways in which individuals might react to their own crime. Describe the different ways in which they might react to the reactions of others.

16. Describe how the individual's standing on the life domains influences how they react to their own crime and to the

"criminogenic" reactions of others (failure to respond to crime, harsh/rejecting response, approving/supportive of the crime response).

17. The "firmly reject the crime, but accept the person" response often leads to a reduction in subsequent crime. Why do I argue that this response will lead to a greater reduction in crime among those who are high in irritability, low in self-control, and in social environments conducive to crime? (See Note 11.)

18. I conclude this chapter by stating that those who are high in irritability, low in self-control, and in environments conducive to crime suffer a "double whammy." What do I mean by this? ✦

Chapter 6

The Causes of Crime Interact in Affecting Crime and One Another

We have come a long way since Chapter 1. Most of the key arguments of the general theory of crime have now been presented. Before we proceed any further, it might be useful to review these arguments.

The Core Propositions of the General Theory (Up to Now)

1. Crime is caused by five clusters of variables, organized into the life domains of self (irritability/low self-control), family (poor parenting practices, no/bad marriages), school (negative school experiences, limited education), peers (peer delinquency), and work (unemployment, bad jobs). The effect of the life domains on crime often varies over the life course.

2. The variables in each domain increase crime by reducing the constraints against crime and increasing the motivations for crime. The constraints against crime include external control, stake in conformity, and internal control. The motivations for crime include strain, reinforcements for crime, exposure to successful criminal models, and beliefs favorable to crime.

3. Each life domain affects the other domains, although some effects are stronger than others and effect sizes often change over the life course. These effects are such that problems in

109

one domain contribute to problems in another; for example, irritability/low self-control contributes to poor parenting, which in turn contributes to irritability/low self-control. Problems in the domains, then, tend to mutually reinforce one another (the "web of crime"), and each domain has both a direct effect on crime and an indirect effect through the other domains.

4. Prior crime has a direct effect on subsequent crime and an indirect effect through the life domains. These effects are conditioned or influenced by the individual's standing on the life domains. Prior crime is most likely to lead to further crime when the individual is high in irritability, low in self-control, and in social environments conducive to crime.

The Causes of Crime Interact in Affecting Crime and One Another

This chapter extends these arguments in an important way. The core proposition of the general theory is that the five life domains cause individuals to engage in crime. However, that is not always the case. While the factors in each life domain increase the likelihood that individuals will engage in crime, they do not cause everyone to engage in crime. For example, individuals who experience poor parenting are more likely than others to engage in crime, but not all individuals who experience poor parenting engage in crime. Poor parenting practices, then, lead to crime among some people but not others. How can we explain this fact? Answering this question is important, because it can dramatically improve our ability to explain crime. It may also improve our ability to control crime. If we can determine why the factors in a life domain lead to crime among some people but not others, we may be able to develop programs that help people resist the criminogenic effect of such factors. This chapter addresses the question of why the life domains increase crime among some people but not others.

The answer given to this question will sound familiar to you. I argue that the effect of each life domain on crime is influenced or conditioned by the individual's standing on the other life domains. For example, the effect of poor parenting on crime depends on whether individuals are irritable and low in self-control, have negative school experiences, are high in peer delinquency, etc. Poor parenting is more likely to lead to crime among irritable individuals, those low in self-control, and those in aversive social environments. The same is true for the effect of the other life domains on crime. This argument was used in Chapter 5 to explain why prior crime increases the likelihood of subsequent crime among some people but not others.

This argument has also been used to explain the phenomena of "resilient youth." You may know some people who grew up in aversive environments, perhaps troubled families or crime-ridden neighborhoods, but they somehow managed to avoid becoming delinquents. Criminologists call such people "resilient youth." Several criminologists have asked how we can explain the behavior of these youth; that is, how is it that they avoid delinquency when so many of their peers in similar circumstances become delinquent? The answer is that the effect of living in an aversive environment is conditioned· by the characteristics of individuals and other features of their social environment. For example, individuals in poor family environments are less likely to become delinquent if they are high in self-control or if they have been able to establish a positive relationship with a teacher at school (see Smith et al. 1995).

So the effect of a life domain on crime is conditioned by the levels of the other life domains. Or, to say the same thing, the life domains *interact* with one another in their effect on crime. I do not discuss all of the interactions between the life domains in this chapter (the interactions between the self and family domains, the self and school domains, the family and work domains, etc.), which would be time consuming and repetitive. Rather, in the first part of the chapter I advance a general principle that describes how the life domains interact in affecting crime. You can then use this principle to predict how any two or more of the life domains will interact. The second part of the chapter illustrates this principle by describing certain interactions that have been the subject of some research. The third part of the chapter applies this principle to the effects of the life domains on one another. I argue that the life domains not only interact in their effect on crime, but also in their effect on one another. For example, the effect of irritability/low self-control on school experiences depends on or is conditioned by parenting practices.

General Principle: A Cause Is More Likely to Lead to Crime When Other Causes Are Present

If we apply this principle to the life domains, it means that a life domain is more likely to lead to crime when the other life domains are conducive to crime.[1] For example, poor parenting is more likely to lead to crime when peer delinquency is high (and less likely when peer delinquency is low). This general principle, then, allows us to predict how the different life domains will interact with one another in affecting crime. Irritability/low self-control, for example, should be more likely to lead to crime when individuals experience poor parenting, school problems, peer delinquency, and/or work problems. (Note: Just as a cause is more likely to *increase* crime when other causes are present, a "crime stopper" is more likely to *reduce* crime when causes are present. For example, good parenting is more likely to reduce crime when juveniles associate with delinquent peers.)

To understand the basis for this general principle, you must remember that the variables in each life domain affect both the constraints against and the motivations for crime. For example, individuals who experience poor parenting are lower in external control, have a lower stake in conformity, experience more strain, have lower levels of social support, are more often exposed to aggressive models and beliefs, and are more likely to be reinforced for aggressive behavior (see Chapter 3). The same is more or less true for the other life domains. Given these facts, a cause is more likely to increase crime when other causes are present because the individual is: (1) freer to engage in crime (because their constraints against crime are lower), (2) more likely to cope with strains in a criminal manner (because they are experiencing other strains, are lower in conventional social supports, have fewer coping skills and resources, etc.), and (3) more likely to view crime as a desirable or appropriate response (because of their exposure to criminal models, beliefs favorable to crime, and reinforcements for crime).

Let us consider an example. Much research suggests that delinquent peer association is more likely to lead to crime among juveniles who experience poor parenting. Why might this be the case? Imagine juveniles with delinquent friends. These juveniles are sometimes exposed to delinquent models, beliefs favorable to delinquency, and provocations of various sorts. Will they respond to such things by engaging in delinquency themselves? That depends. One thing it depends on is whether they are experiencing poor parenting. Juveniles who are experiencing poor parenting are more likely to respond with delinquency for several reasons. They are "freer" to respond with delinquency because their parents are less likely to discover and sanction their delinquency (low external control). They are also freer to respond with delinquency because they do not care about their parents (low stake in conformity). Further, they are more disposed to respond with delinquency because they experience a lot of strain at home and receive little social support from parents. Finally, they are more disposed to respond with delinquency because they have learned from their parents that delinquency is an appropriate response in certain circumstances (e.g., via modeling, beliefs, and reinforcements).

By contrast, consider juveniles who experience good parenting. These juveniles are much *less* likely to respond to delinquent friends with delinquency. Such juveniles are well-supervised and strongly bonded to parents, which makes them hesitant to respond with delinquency. Such juveniles are treated well by parents and provided with social support when necessary. As such, they are better equipped to respond to provocations from peers and other strains in a legal manner. Finally, such juveniles have been taught that delinquency is never an appropriate response.

So, delinquent peer association is much more likely to lead to crime among those who experience poor rather than good parenting. Good parenting reduces or mutes the effect of delinquent peer association on crime, while poor parenting does little to reduce the effect and much to increase the effect of delinquent peer association on crime. Similar arguments can be used to account for the interactions between the other life domains.

Prior Theory and Research on Interaction Effects

Despite the importance of examining interactions, only a few theories and a small amount of research focus on interaction effects. Strain theorists have devoted the most attention to interaction effects, perhaps because it has long been apparent that only a minority of individuals respond to strain with crime. This has put strain theorists under much pressure to describe the factors that influence or condition the effect of strain on crime. Strain theorists argue that strain is more likely to lead to crime when individuals have poor coping skills and resources, are low in conventional social support, are low in social and self-control, and associate with delinquent peers, among other things (see especially Agnew 1992; 1997; Cullen 1984). The evidence for these conditioning or interaction effects is mixed, but recent research suggests that certain of these factors do condition the effect of strain on crime (Agnew et al. 2002; Luster and Small 1997; Mazerolle and Maahs 2000). Most other crime theorists and theories, however, devote little attention to interaction effects (for prominent exceptions, see Agnew 2003b; Gold 1963; Nagin and Paternoster 1994; Raine et al. 1997; Rankin and Wells 1990; Sheley 1983; Sherman 2000; Sherman et al. 1992; Tittle 1995).

Likewise, there has not been much research on interaction effects. The limited research that has been conducted, however, tends to support the general principle stated above. When researchers find interaction effects, it is usually the case that a cause has a larger effect on crime when other causes are present. Strain measures, for example, usually have a greater effect on crime when other causes of crime are present. Additional support for the general principle is presented below (also see Agnew 2003b; Bachman et al. 1992; Farrington 1994c, 384–386; Jessor et al. 1995; Mears et al. 1998; Raine 2002b; Raine et al. 1997; Rutter et al. 1998, 206–212; Wright et al. 2001). I should also note that the general principle is compatible with the research on prevention and rehabilitation programs (see Agnew 2005; Andrews and Bonta 2003; Cullen and Gendreau 2000 for overviews). The more successful of these programs address the causes of crime in the five life domains; for example, they try to improve parenting practices. Data suggest that these programs are most effective among those already inclined to engage in crime (that is, "crime stoppers" are most likely to reduce crime when the causes of crime are present).

Some research, however, fails to find evidence for interaction effects (see Agnew 2003b; Farrington 1994c; Rankin and Wells 1990; Sherman et al. 1992). This may be due to the fact that methodological problems make it very difficult to detect interaction effects with survey data (see McClelland and Judd 1993 for a discussion of these problems). Because most crime research relies on survey data, many significant interaction effects have probably been missed. Certain other research suggests that a cause may be more likely to increase crime when other causes are *absent* (e.g., Farrington 1994c; Raine et al. 1997; Sherman 2000). Most research, however, supports the general principle. Nevertheless, it is important to note that not all research is supportive and that more research and theorizing are needed in this area (see Note 2 in Chapter 11).

Some Illustrative Interactions

The general theory predicts that each life domain will interact with every other in its effect on crime. While it is not possible to discuss all of the interactions between the life domains in this short book, I do want to focus on certain interactions that have been the subject of some research. I first focus on the interactions between irritability/low self-control and the other life domains. These interactions are particularly important because they allow us to more fully integrate psychological theories of crime, which focus on individual traits, with sociological theories of crime, which focus on the social environment. It is typically argued that crime is most likely when people with traits conducive to crime are in social environments conducive to crime. I then focus on the interaction between the family and peer domains, which appears to be especially important, at least during the adolescent years. While I do not discuss the remaining interactions between the life domains, I should note that the strongest interactions should occur between those domains that have the strongest effects on the constraints against and the motivations for crime (see Chapter 3; keep in mind that effect sizes change over the life course).[2]

Interactions Involving Irritability/Low Self-Control and the Other Life Domains

Sheldon and Eleanor Glueck, two prominent criminologists, pointed to a major gap in crime theories in their classic 1950 book *Unraveling Juvenile Delinquency.* They noted that the leading crime theories of the day said that individuals engage in crime because they are in social environments conducive to crime, like troubled families or disorganized neighborhoods. The Gluecks acknowledged that such environments do increase the likelihood of crime, but they stated that most individuals in these environments are not criminals. The Gluecks criticized existing theories for failing to explain why this was so. They then went on to argue that a full explanation of crime must consider not only the characteristics of the individual's social environment, but also the characteristics or traits of the individual. In particular, they argued that some individuals are more likely than others to respond to aversive social environments with crime. The Gluecks, then, predicted that individual traits would condition the effect of the social environment on crime.

This prediction is now at the heart of efforts to integrate psychological and sociological theories of crime (see Moffitt 1993; Raine et al. 1997; Wright et al. 2001). As indicated, psychological theories tend to focus on those individual traits that contribute to crime, like irritability and low self-control, while sociological theories focus on those features of the social environment that contribute to crime. A number of criminologists, however, now argue that we must consider both individual traits and the social environment if we want to fully explain crime. In particular, they argue that traits interact with features of the social environment to produce crime. Individuals with traits conducive to crime are most likely to engage in crime when they are in aversive social environments, like troubled families. (Conversely, individuals in aversive social environments are most likely to engage in crime when they possess traits conducive to crime.)

As indicated in Chapter 3, irritability and low self-control are the two super-traits most strongly linked to crime. Like all traits, they influence how people experience and respond to their environment. Evidence increasingly suggests that individuals with these traits are much more likely to respond to aversive social environments with crime. This is easy to understand when you consider the characteristics of people with these traits. Among other things, they are easily upset, they tend to respond in an aggressive manner when upset, they like exciting and risky activities, they tend to act without thinking, and they show little concern for conventional rules or the feelings of others. As indicated earlier, they are "mean" and "out of control." Given these characteristics, it seems reasonable to suppose that they will be more likely to respond to things like harsh parenting, poor teacher relations, and peer delinquency with crime. They are more easily provoked and tempted to engage crime. And they are more likely to respond to provocations and temptations with crime, given their aggressive and impulsive nature, their limited coping skills, and their lack of concern for others.

Wright et al. (2001) found much support for these arguments. Individuals who were irritable and low in self-control were more likely to engage in crime when they were in family, school, peer, and work environments conducive to crime (e.g., they were weakly bonded to parents and spouses, had limited educations, associated with delinquent peers, and were unemployed). Likewise, Agnew et al. (2002) found that such individuals were more likely to respond to various forms of strain with crime, including strains involving the family, school, and peer domains. So there is good reason to believe that the traits of irritability and low self-control interact with the family, school, peer, and work domains in affecting crime.

Interactions Involving the Family and Peer Domains

There is also good reason to believe that the family and peer domains interact with one another, with peer delinquency being more likely to cause crime among individuals who experience poor parenting (and poor parenting being more likely to cause crime among individuals high in peer delinquency). As indicated above, poor parenting practices provide the freedom to follow delinquent peers by reducing constraints (external control, stake in conformity). They also provide some incentive to follow delinquent peers by increasing strain and fostering the social learning of crime. Good parenting practices, however, have the opposite effect. While researchers have not examined all of the components of peer delinquency, several studies indicate that association with delinquent peers is more likely to increase crime among individuals who experience poor parenting (and that poor parenting is more likely to increase crime among individuals who associate with delinquent peers). (See Agnew 2003b for an overview.)

The Life Domains Interact in Affecting One Another

The life domains not only affect crime, they also affect one another, with problems in one domain increasing the likelihood of problems in the other domains (see Chapter 4). But problems in one domain do not always lead to problems in the other domains. For example, irritability and low self-control increase negative school experiences for some people, but not for others. The explanation for this parallels that given above: The effect of one life domain on another is influenced or conditioned by the remaining life domains, so the life domains interact in affecting one another. For example, irritability/low self-control is more likely to lead to negative school experiences among those who experience poor parenting.

The life domains interact in affecting one another for largely the same reasons that they interact in affecting crime. For example, irritability and low self-control are more likely to lead to negative school experiences when parenting is poor for several reasons. When parenting is poor, children who are irritable and low in self-control are *freer* to neglect their schoolwork and misbehave at school (because they are lower in external control and have a lower stake in conformity). Further, such children are *more inclined* to neglect their schoolwork and misbehave because they are higher in family strain, receive little social support at home, and have not been taught the skills and attitudes necessary for success at school. By contrast, when parenting is good such children find it more difficult to neglect their schoolwork and misbehave. Their parents closely supervise them and they are more eager to please their parents, given their strong bonds to parents. Such children are also better able to cope with school strain in a legal manner, as they are well-treated by parents and receive much social support from them. Further, their parents have made an effort to teach them the skills and attitudes necessary to do well in school. So good parenting reduces or mutes the effect of irritability/low self-control on negative school experiences, while poor parenting enhances the effect. Similar arguments can be used to explain why the other life domains interact in affecting one another.

Summary

We can now add another key proposition to the general theory of crime: The life domains interact in affecting crime and one another. A given life domain is more likely to increase crime or negatively affect another life domain when the remaining life domains are conducive to crime. This proposition substantially improves the ability of the theory to explain crime. In particular, it allows the theory to better explain why a life domain increases crime or negatively affects another life domain among some people but not others.

This proposition also helps integrate psychological and sociological theories of crime. The integration of these theories began in Chapters 2 and 3, where I argued that both individual traits and the social environment cause crime. It continued in Chapter 4, where I argued that individual traits affect the social environment, while the social environment affects individual traits. This chapter comes close to completing the integration, with the argument that individual traits and environmental variables interact in their effect on crime.

The presentation of the core part of the general theory is now almost complete. I finish this presentation in the next chapter with a discussion of the timing and form of causal effects.

Notes

1. It is assumed that the interactions between the life domains are symmetric (e.g., poor parenting increases the effect of peer delinquency on crime, peer delinquency increases the effect of poor parenting on crime). It is further assumed that the interactions are roughly linear (e.g., as parenting becomes progressively worse, the effect of peer delinquency on crime becomes progressively larger). The theory and research on interaction effects, however, are rather rudimentary, and additional work may well challenge these assumptions (for fuller discussions, see Aiken and West 1991; Tittle 1995; Note 2 in Chapter 11).

2. Another factor affecting the strength of interactions is the extent to which experiences in one life domain *directly* enhance or mute the crime-producing experiences in another domain. For example, do delinquent peers remind juveniles of the ways in which their parents have mistreated them and encourage them to respond in a criminal manner? If so, delinquent peers will be even more likely to condition the effect of poor parenting on crime. This effect is distinct from the effect of delinquent peers on parenting practices, in that delinquent peers may enhance the crime-producing effects of poor parenting without affecting parenting practices. In practice, however, delinquent peers likely do both.

Discussion and Study Questions

1. List the key propositions of the general theory of crime (through the end of this chapter).

2. What is meant by an "interaction" or "conditioning" effect? Give an example using the life domains and crime.

3. Why is it important to study interaction effects?

4. Why do I predict that a specific life domain is more likely to increase crime when the other life domains are conducive to crime?

5. The general theory would predict that "bad jobs" are more likely to lead to crime among unmarried individuals or individuals in "bad" marriages (as opposed to individuals in "good" marriages). Why might this be the case?

6. Give an example where the life domains interact in affecting one another (other than the example used in the text). Describe why the life domains interact as they do in your example.

7. Psychological theories of crime focus on individual traits like irritability and low self-control, while sociological theories focus on the social environment, like the nature of family, school, peer, and work life. Drawing on the general theory, describe how individual traits and the social environment affect one another and work together to affect crime. ✦

Chapter 7

The Causes Tend to Have Contemporaneous and Nonlinear Effects on Crime and One Another

The general theory makes a number of causal assertions: The life domains affect crime, the life domains affect one another, crime affects the life domains, and prior crime affects subsequent crime. But very little has been said about the timing and form of these effects. Do the causes have an immediate effect on crime and one another or do they have a delayed effect? For example, does poor parenting have an immediate effect on crime or does it take some time before poor parenting leads to crime? Also, do the causes have a linear or a nonlinear effect on crime and one another? A linear effect is one where a given increase in a causal variable always leads to the same amount of change in a dependent variable like crime. For example, a one-unit increase in irritability always leads to two additional crimes per year on average. Linear effects can be plotted on a graph with a straight line, as shown in Figure 7-1 (also see Figure 1-1). Nonlinear effects cannot be plotted with a straight line; rather, they must be plotted with a curved or zig-zagged line. For example, it might be the case that as irritability increases it has an *increasingly larger* effect on crime, as shown in Figure 7-2.

Criminologists have not devoted much attention to the timing and form of causal effects (see the discussion in Tittle 1995, 35–43). Most criminologists implicitly assume that effects are delayed, with about a one-year period between cause and effect. They assume this mostly as a matter of convenience. Longitudinal surveys usually in-

121

Figure 7-1
The Effect of Irritability on Crime: Linear Effect

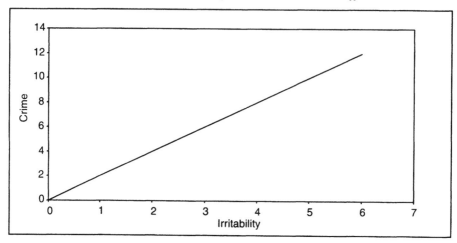

Figure 7-2
The Effect of Irritability on Crime: Nonlinear Effect

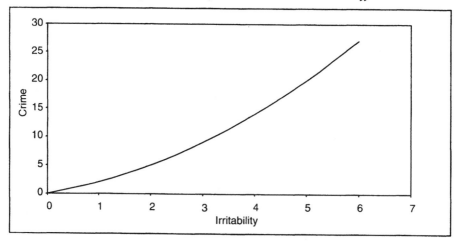

terview respondents every year, so criminologists end up determining whether causes measured in one year affect crime measured the following year. Most criminologists also implicitly assume that effects are linear. This assumption is frequently made out of convenience as well; most of the commonly used statistical techniques for estimating effect sizes assume that effects are linear. There are, however, good reasons to question the assumptions that effects are delayed and linear (see Tittle 1995).

In the first part of this chapter, I argue that the causes tend to have relatively immediate or contemporaneous effects on crime and one another, although each cause has a large delayed or lagged effect on itself (e.g., poor parenting at Time 1 has a large effect on poor parenting at Time 2). In the second part of this chapter, I argue that effects tend to be nonlinear, such that as the causes increase in size they have increasingly larger effects on crime and one another (the type of effect shown in Figure 7-2).

These arguments, if correct, will allow us to better explain and predict crime. For example, if we assume that a cause has a linear effect on crime when it in fact has a nonlinear effect, our predictions of future crime will be less accurate. We might predict that someone high in irritability will commit 14 crimes per year, when the actual number is 28 (see Figure 7-2). Agnew and Thaxton (2002) provide a real-life example of this. They examined the effects of negative parental and teacher bonding on crime, with one set of analyses assuming that the effects were linear and another set assuming that they were nonlinear. They found that the effects were, in fact, nonlinear; as negative parental and teacher bonding increased they had an increasingly larger effect on crime (a nonlinear effect of the type shown in Figure 7-2). Further, taking account of these nonlinear effects allowed for the much more accurate prediction of crime. Likewise, certain research suggests that our ability to explain and predict crime is often much improved when we assume that the causes have contemporaneous rather than lagged effects on crime (more below).

Effects Are Largely Contemporaneous in Nature, Although Each Cause Has a Large, Lagged Effect on Itself

The causes have largely contemporaneous effects on crime and one another, although each cause also has a large, lagged effect on itself. "Contemporaneous effects" refer to effects that occur within a relatively short period of time. In certain cases, a cause may have an immediate effect on crime, as when provocation by peers leads to immediate retaliation. In other cases, it may take somewhat longer for a cause to affect crime. For example, poor parental supervision may not immediately result in crime, but may lead to an increase in crime over the course of several weeks. While there is no precise definition of "contemporaneous," I somewhat arbitrarily define contemporaneous effects as those that occur within a few months' time (see Chapter 10 for a fuller discussion).

The Largely Contemporaneous Effects of the Life Domains on Crime

Why do the life domains have largely contemporaneous effects on crime? Each life domain, you will recall, measures the constraints against and the motivations for crime (i.e., it measures the individual's external control, stake in conformity, internal control, level of strain, and reinforcements/models/beliefs favorable to crime). The life domains have largely contemporaneous effects on crime because crime is largely a function of *current* constraints and motivations rather than those experienced in the past. Individuals, in particular, are most responsive to the controls, strains, and reinforcements they are currently experiencing. When contemplating crime, for example, individuals consider the likelihood of being caught and punished at that time, not the likelihood that existed a year ago, or they take account of their current beliefs regarding crime, not their beliefs a year ago.[1]

Several literatures support this argument. The literature on deterring crime suggests that individuals are primarily responsive to current probabilities of punishment rather than past probabilities, although it may take a short time to realize that probabilities have changed (Nagin 1998). The strain/stress literature suggests that current stressors have a much greater impact than prior stressors on psychological states and behavior (Agnew 1992). One recent study, for example, found that abuse suffered in *childhood* had little effect on adolescent crime, while abuse suffered in *adolescence* had a large effect on adolescent crime (Ireland et al. 2002). The social learning literature suggests that current reinforcement and punishment contingencies have a much greater impact on behavior than prior contingencies, although it may again take a short time to realize that contingencies have changed (Akers 1998). Further, the few studies in criminology that have explored lagged and contemporaneous effects on crime generally find that contemporaneous effects are larger than lagged effects, with lagged effects often being insignificant (e.g., Agnew 1991b; Brezina 1999; Burkett and Warren 1987; Ireland et al. 2002; Lauritsen et al. 1991; Liska et al. 1984; Liska and Reed 1985; Thornberry 1996; Thornberry et al. 1994).

The Largely Contemporaneous Effects of the Causes on One Another

The causes not only have largely contemporaneous effects on crime, but on one another as well. For example, our current experiences in school are more strongly affected by our current traits and environmental experiences than by our past traits and experiences. The same applies to the effects of crime on the life domains. For example, parenting practices are more strongly influenced by our current levels of crime than by our prior levels (although crime that results in official sanction may sometimes have lasting effects [see Chapter 11]).

But Each Life Domain Has a Large Lagged Effect on Itself

While effects are largely contemporaneous in nature, each cause has a large lagged effect on itself. For example, poor parenting at Time 1 has a strong effect on poor parenting at Time 2. The life domains, then, are self-perpetuating to some extent. There are several reasons for this, certain of which parallel the reasons given for the effect of prior crime on subsequent crime. The first reason has to do with the force of habit. As Tittle (1995, 209) states, "much human behavior is patterned and habitual, involving actions undertaken without forethought or critical reflection. The more often an individual does a particular thing in a specific way, the more proficient the person becomes at it, the more comfortable the person becomes at it, and the easier it is to do without thinking." So, for example, parents tend to engage in the same parenting practices over time partly out of habit.

The second reason that each life domain has a large lagged effect on itself is that the traits and patterns of interaction embodied in the life domains often result in reinforcement for the individual. For example, impulsive behavior often allows for the immediate satisfaction of desires, which increases the likelihood of further impulsive behavior. A third reason for the large lagged effects is that these traits and patterns of interaction often close off opportunities for change. For example, poor academic performance at Time 1 makes it difficult to master academic material at Time 2. The strain associated with poor parenting practices at Time 1 makes family members reluctant to treat one another in a more positive manner at Time 2.

So the traits and patterns of interaction that comprise the life domains tend to perpetuate themselves because they become habitual, they frequently result in reinforcement, and they close off opportunities for change.[2] Much data suggest that variables associated with the life domains have strong lagged effects on themselves (e.g., Agnew 1991b; Matsueda and Anderson 1998; Thornberry et al. 1991; Zhang et al. 1997).

I should note, however, that the lagged effect of a life domain on itself is conditioned by crime and the other life domains. For example, the effect of Time 1 negative school experiences on Time 2 negative school experiences is conditioned by Time 1 crime and the other Time 1 life domains. Time 1 negative school experiences are more likely to lead to Time 2 negative school experiences among individuals who experience poor parenting, are irritable and low in self-control, are high in peer delinquency, and are high in crime. Among other things, such individuals lack the motivation and ability to change their school behavior. Further, such individuals are more likely to be neglected or treated in a negative manner by teachers.

Don't Forget About *Indirect* Lagged Effects, Which May Be Very Important

As indicated, the causes have largely contemporaneous effects on crime and one another, and each cause has a *large lagged effect on itself*. The causes *do not have large lagged effects on crime and one another*. These arguments are illustrated in Figure 7-3, which for the sake of simplicity focuses on irritability/low self-control, poor parenting, and crime. As can be seen, Time 1 poor parenting has a large contemporaneous effect on Time 1 irritability/low self-control and Time 1 crime. Time 1 poor parenting also has a large lagged effect on Time 2 poor parenting. Time 1 poor parenting, however, does *not* have a large lagged effect on Time 2 irritability/low self-control or Time 2 crime.

Based on this figure, one might conclude that Time 1 poor parenting is not very relevant to the explanation of Time 2 irritability/low self-control or Time 2 crime. But this would be a mistake. While Time 1 poor parenting does not have a large *direct* effect on Time 2 irritability/low self-control, it has a large *indirect* effect. It has an indirect effect partly through its effect on Time 1 irritability/low self-control and partly through its effect on Time 2 poor parenting. Likewise, Time 1 poor parenting has a large *indirect* effect on Time 2

Figure 7-3
*An Illustration of the Contemporaneous and Lagged
Effects Predicted by the General Theory*

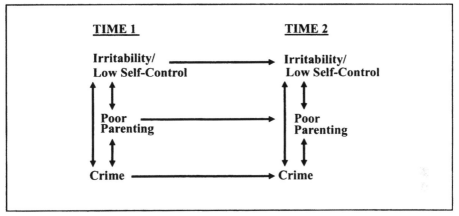

crime, through its effect on Time 1 crime and Time 2 poor parenting. You can trace these effects out in the figure. Similar arguments can be made regarding the effect of Time 1 irritability/low self-control on Time 2 poor parenting and Time 2 crime. Time 1 irritability/low self-control does not have a large *direct* effect on these variables, but it does have a large *indirect* effect. So even though early parenting experiences and early levels of irritability/low self-control may not have a large *direct* effect on later variables, they are still quite important, having large *indirect* effects on these variables. Similar arguments can often be made for the other life domains. This is an important point. While the general theory tends to emphasize contemporaneous effects, one should not take that to mean that the past is unimportant.

An Example

These arguments regarding the timing of causal effects might seem a little confusing, but the core points are easily understood with an example. Take the case of Bob. Whether Bob engages in crime is largely a function of his current traits and his current family, school, and peer experiences, not his past traits or experiences. For example, whether Bob engages in crime is largely determined by his current level of self-control, not his level of self-control a year ago. Likewise, his crime is largely determined by how much external control his parents exercise over him now, not how much control they exercised a year ago. But that is *not* to say that Bob's past is unimportant. For example, Bob's current family experiences are in large measure a function of his previous family experiences and (indirectly) traits. Further, his previous family experiences had a large effect on his previous level of crime, which in turn has a large effect on his current level of crime (prior crime has a large effect on subsequent crime).

Effects Are Nonlinear

As indicated, most research in criminology implicitly assumes that causes have a linear effect on crime. That is, it assumes that a given increase in a causal variable always results in the same amount of change in crime. But as was the case with lagged effects, there is reason to question this assumption. Tittle (1995, 35–43), for example, persuasively argues that several of the key causal variables in criminology may have nonlinear effects on crime, and certain strain theorists argue that strains or stressors may have a nonlinear effect on crime, with strains causing crime only after a certain threshold point or level of strain is reached (Agnew 1992; also see Paternoster and Mazerolle 1994). I expand on these arguments, and claim that all of the major causes have a nonlinear effect on crime and one another.

A Positive, Concave Upward Effect

I predict a particular type of nonlinear effect, one that assumes the shape of a positive, concave upward curve, as depicted in Figure 7-4 (and Figure 7-2). Let me describe this effect with an example. Suppose we measure parenting practices on a six-point scale, ranging from 1 (very good) to 6 (very bad). If parenting practices have a linear effect on crime, each one-unit increase in this scale (going from good to bad parenting) should result in the same increase in crime. Each one-unit increase, for example, may result in two additional crimes per year on average. But if parenting practices have a nonlinear effect of the type I describe, things get a bit more complicated (see Figure 7-4). Each one-unit increase in the parenting scale has an increasingly larger effect on crime. For example, people who score "3" on the parenting scale may commit one more crime per year on average than people who score "2." People who score "6," however, may commit eight more crimes per year on average than people who score "5." While this example is hypothetical, Agnew and Thaxton (2002) obtained similar results when they examined the effects of parental and teacher bonding on delinquency (also see

Figure 7-4
The Effect of Poor Parenting on Crime: Nonlinear Effect

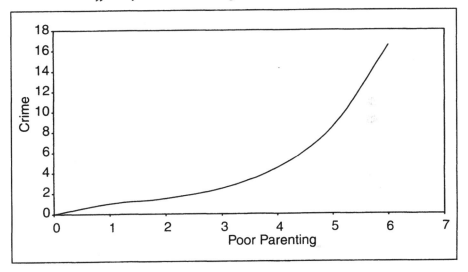

Farrington and Hawkins 1991).

Haynie (2001) also found a nonlinear effect of this type when she examined the effect of peer delinquency in close-knit friendship groups on the respondent's own delinquency. She measured peer delinquency in terms of the average number of delinquent acts committed by one's friends. As this average increased, so did the respondent's own delinquency. But increases in this average had an *increasingly larger effect* on the respondent's delinquency. For example, when the average number of delinquent acts committed by friends increased from 5 to 6, the respondent's own delinquency increased by a small amount. But when the average number of delinquent acts committed by friends increased from 25 to 26, the respondent's own delinquency increased by a much larger amount.

Reasons for Such a Nonlinear Effect

As a cause increases it has an increasingly larger effect on crime, because most causes must pass a certain threshold point before they start to have a meaningful effect on crime. The logic behind this threshold effect is most easily illustrated with respect to strains or stressors. Moving from a state of no strain to one of mild or moderate strain will not cause most people to engage in crime. Mild strains do not produce much anger and they are easily ignored or dealt with through legal coping methods. After a certain threshold point is reached, however, strains begin to generate some anger, they are less easily ignored, and they begin to tax legal coping efforts. It is at this point when strains become more likely to generate crime. The further one moves beyond the threshold point, the more likely strains are to generate crime—including frequent and serious crime. Cairns and Cairns (1994:74) provide an example of the nonlinear effect of strain, based on their study of violent incidents between juveniles. They discovered that about half of all violent incidents were precipitated by prior negative acts (or strains). But in their words, "not all instances of unkindness are likely to bring about [violence]. . . . [W]e find that children and adolescents ignored or otherwise tolerated insults and rudeness, up to a point . . . but when a given threshold is reached, negative acts beget more negative acts" (1994, 74).

A similar argument can be made with respect to the major social learning variables. Occasional exposure to criminal models or beliefs favorable to crime does not cause most people to engage in crime. This occasional exposure is more than offset by regular exposure to conventional models and beliefs. At a certain threshold point, however, the individual's exposure to criminal models and beliefs begins to counterbalance his or her exposure to conventional models and beliefs. It is at this point that crime becomes especially likely. The same may be true of reinforcements for crime: The occasional reinforcement of crime may have little impact on criminal behavior, but at a certain threshold point the likelihood of being reinforced for crime exceeds the likelihood of being reinforced for conventional behavior. Once again, it is at this point that crime becomes especially likely (although see Conger and Simons 1997, on the matching principle).[3]

Likewise, the same sort of argument can be made with respect to control variables. A mild to moderate decrease in external control does not have much of an impact on crime because individuals still feel there is a good chance that their crime will be detected and sanctioned. After a certain threshold point, however, individuals may feel that the odds of getting away with crime have shifted in their favor and crime becomes more likely. Similarly, a mild to moderate decrease in one's stake in conformity may have little effect on crime because individuals may feel that they still have much to lose by engaging in crime. But at a certain point, individuals may begin to feel that they have little to lose and crime again becomes more likely. The same logic applies to internal control.[4]

So the causes are more likely to affect crime after a certain threshold point is reached, contributing to a nonlinear effect of the type shown in Figures 7-2 and 7-4.[5]

The Effect of the Life Domains on One Another and the Effect of Crime on the Life Domains

The focus up to this point has been on the effect of the life domains on crime. One can also use the above arguments to claim that as the level of the life domains increase they have increasingly larger effects on one another. For example, mild to moderate levels of irritability may not be sufficient to cause parents to dislike their children and treat them harshly. Levels of irritability may have to pass a certain threshold point before this happens. Likewise, one can use these arguments to claim that as crime increases in frequency and seriousness it has an increasingly larger effect on the life domains. For example, minor levels of crime may not cause conventional peers to reject the juvenile. Crime may have to pass a certain threshold point before peer rejection occurs.

Another Reason for the Nonlinear Effect of the Life Domains on Crime and One Another

There is a second reason to expect nonlinear effects of the type shown in Figures 7-2 and 7-4. Each life domain is comprised of several more specific causes of crime. Poor parenting practices, for example, include negative parent/juvenile bonding, poor supervision/discipline, family conflict and child abuse, the absence of positive parenting, and criminal parents/siblings. Each of these causes increases crime in its own right. Further, these causes often interact with one another in their effect on crime. Negative bonding, for example, has a larger effect on crime when supervision is poor (for reasons indicated in Chapter 6). So each cause has a larger effect on crime when the other causes are high. The overall measure of poor parenting is simply the sum of these more specific causes. So as the overall measure increases in size, the specific causes are more likely to be high and to interact with one another in the manner just described. As a consequence of such interactions, increases in the overall measure have an increasingly larger effect on crime.

Conclusion

This discussion of the timing and form of causal effects completes my presentation of the core part of the general theory of crime. Once more, it may be useful to pause and summarize the major points made so far:

1. Crime is caused by five clusters of variables, organized into the life domains of self (irritability/low self-control), family (poor parenting practices, no/bad marriages), school (negative school experiences, limited education), peers (peer delinquency), and work (unemployment, bad jobs). The effect of the life domains on crime often varies over the life course.

2. The variables in each domain increase crime by reducing the constraints against crime and increasing the motivations for crime. The constraints against crime include external control, stake in conformity, and internal control. The motivations for crime include strain, reinforcements for crime, exposure to successful criminal models, and beliefs favorable to crime.

3. Each life domain affects the other domains, although some effects are stronger than others and effect sizes often change over the life course. These effects are such that problems in one domain contribute to problems in another; for example, irritability/low self-control contributes to poor parenting, which in turn contributes to irritability/low self-control. Problems in the domains, then, tend to mutually reinforce one another (the "web of crime"), and each domain has both a direct effect on crime and an indirect effect through the other domains.

4. Prior crime has a direct effect on subsequent crime and an indirect effect through the life domains. These effects are conditioned or influenced by the individual's standing on the life domains. Prior crime is most likely to lead to further

crime when the individual is high in irritability, low in self-control, and in social environments conducive to crime.

5. The life domains interact in affecting crime and one another. A given life domain is more likely to increase crime or negatively affect another life domain when the remaining life domains are conducive to crime.

6. The life domains have nonlinear and largely contemporaneous effects on crime and one another, although each life domain has a large lagged effect on itself. Likewise, crime has a nonlinear and largely contemporaneous effect on the life domains.

The general theory of crime up to this point is summarized in Figure 7-5, which departs from previous figures in that I do not include a causal arrow for each of the many effects in the theory; if I did so, the figure would be a jumble of arrows. Rather, I employ certain simplifying devices. The left side of the model lists the five life domains and crime in a box (measured over the same period of time). The arrows going up and down the sides of the box refer to the fact that the life domains and crime have contemporaneous effects on one another; that is, the five life domains affect crime, the five domains affect one another, and crime affects the five domains. The zig-zagged sides of the box refer to the fact that these effects are nonlinear. The x's within the box refer to the fact that the life domains and crime interact with one another in their effects. The box on the right side of the figure can be interpreted in the same way, except that the life domains and crime in this box are measured at a later period of time. The heavy lines from the first box to the second refer to the fact that crime and each life domain has a strong lagged effect on itself, although this effect is conditioned by the other life domains and crime (as indicated by the x's at the start of each arrow).

This model may appear complex on one level, positing many different effects and making a number of claims about the form and timing of these effects. But on another level, it is quite simple. As indicated above, a few simple arguments are sufficient to generate the model in Figure 7-5.

It is, however, important to note that this is a "bare bones" model. I do not attempt to list the reasons why the causes affect

Figure 7-5
The General Theory of Crime: Core Model

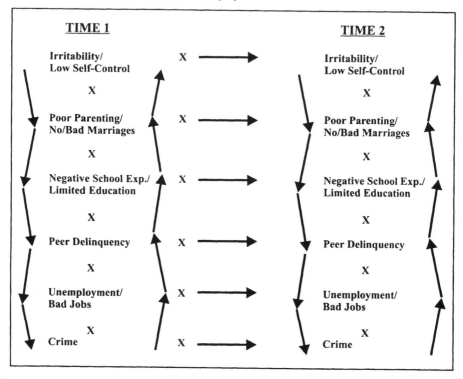

crime and one another. Such reasons, however, are easily described: The causes affect crime by impacting the constraints against and the motivations for crime listed in Chapter 2. And the causes affect one another for similar reasons. The model also does not describe differences in effect sizes. These differences change over the life course, so separate models for childhood, adolescence, and adulthood would be necessary to properly describe differences in effect sizes. Again, however, it is easy to describe the major features of such models.

The Childhood Period

Irritability/low self-control and poor parenting practices have relatively large effects on one other, the other life domains, and crime. School and peer factors have relatively small to moderate effects on one another, the other life domains, and crime. Work/bad jobs is irrelevant during this time. Crime has a relatively large effect on the life domains and further crime.

The Adolescent Period

Irritability/low self-control and peer delinquency have large effects on crime, with poor parenting practices and negative school experiences having moderate effects. Work experiences have a minor effect on crime. Irritability/low self-control has a large effect on the other life domains. Poor parenting practices have a small to moderate effect on irritability/low self-control and a large effect on negative school experiences and peer delinquency. Negative school experiences have a small to moderate effect on irritability/low self-control and parenting practices and a large effect on peer delinquency. Peer delinquency has a small to moderate effect on irritability/low self-control and poor parenting practices, but a large effect on negative school experiences. Crime has a large effect on the life domains and further crime.

The Adult Period

Irritability/low self-control, peer delinquency, no/bad marriages, and unemployment/bad jobs have large effects on crime, with education having a small to moderate effect. Parenting practices have a small effect on adult crime. Irritability/low self-control has a large effect on the other life domains. No/bad marriages has a small to moderate effect on irritability/low self-control, education, and unemployment/bad jobs, but a large effect on peer delinquency. Unemployment/bad jobs has a small to moderate effect on irritability/low self-control, but a large effect on peer delinquency and no/bad marriages. Education has a small to moderate effect on irritability/low self-control and no/bad marriages, but a large effect on peer delinquency and unemployment/bad jobs. Finally, peer delinquency has a small to moderate effect on irritability/low self-control and a large effect on the other life domains.

Notes

1. While the causes have largely contemporaneous effects on crime, they also have smaller delayed or lagged effects as well. For example, poor parenting at Time 1 has a small lagged effect on crime at Time 2. This lagged effect reflects the fact that past experiences sometimes have a direct effect on current behavior. For example, juveniles may remember the strong bond they once had with parents, which may restrain them from engaging in crime even if current relations with parents are

poor (you may have heard the expression "for old time's sake"). Or juveniles may remember that they were abused by peers in the past and the memory may motivate crime in the present. Similar arguments apply to the other life domains. These effects, however, are not predicted to be strong and they obviously fade with time.

2. The life domains exhibit some stability over time not only because each life domain has a large lagged effect on itself (e.g., Time 1 poor parenting causes Time 2 poor parenting), but also because the factors that cause each life domain are somewhat stable over time. For example, poor parenting is somewhat stable over time because the factors that cause poor parenting—like the irritability/low self-control of children, parental stress, and parental ignorance of good parenting practices—are somewhat stable over time.

3. Sutherland et al. (1992, 89) make a similar point when they state that "a person becomes criminal because of an excess of definitions favorable to violation of law over definitions unfavorable to violation of law."

4. Some criminologists have argued that there may be "ceiling effects," points beyond which further increases in the causes have little additional effect on crime. For example, some individuals may be under such tremendous strain that any further increase in strain has little effect on crime, or may even reduce crime by immobilizing the individual. Or some individuals may have such a low stake in conformity that any further reduction in their stake in conformity has little effect on crime. While plausible, I tend to reject this argument based on the assumption that few people reach such extreme positions. Nevertheless, this argument should certainly be explored (see Yu and Liska 1993).

5. Where is this threshold point? It differs across individuals. For example, some individuals are angered and overwhelmed by strains that have little effect on others. Some individuals are tempted to engage in crime by levels of external control that deter others, and some are attracted to crime by rewards that have little effect on others. The location of the threshold point is influenced by the traits of individuals, especially their levels of irritability and self-control. Irritable individuals, for example, are more easily upset by strains. The threshold point is also influenced by the social environment of individuals. Individuals with a low stake in conformity, for example, may be tempted to engage in crime at levels of external control that would deter others. These sorts of effects are captured by the interactions described in Chapter 6. For example, poor parenting has a greater effect on crime among individuals who are irritable and low in self-control partly because such people are more sensitive to the strains associated with poor parenting, are more likely to respond to lax parental super-

vision with crime, etc. So the location of the threshold point varies from person to person. But overall, the threshold point tends to occur at *relatively* low levels of control, high levels of strain, and high levels of exposure to criminal models, beliefs, and reinforcements. That is why the causes have an effect on crime like that shown in Figures 7-2 and 7-4.

Discussion and Study Questions

1. Define linear and nonlinear effects. Give an example of a linear and a nonlinear effect that involves crime. Give an example of a nonlinear effect that assumes a different form than that shown in Figure 7-2.

2. Define contemporaneous and lagged effects. Give an example of a contemporaneous and lagged effect that involves crime.

3. Why do I argue that the life domains have a largely contemporaneous effect on crime?

4. Why do I argue that each life domain has a large lagged effect on itself?

5. Even though most effects in the general theory are contemporaneous in nature, I state that "one should not take this to mean that the past is unimportant." Why is this the case?

6. Draw a positive, concave upward curve.

7. Why do I argue that nonlinear effects assume the shape of a positive, concave upward curve?

8. I argue that the specific causes of crime in a life domain often interact with one another in affecting crime. Describe the nature of these interactions. How do these interactions contribute to the nonlinear effect of the life domain as a whole on crime?

9. List the major propositions or arguments of the general theory.

10. Describe the key points of the causal model in Figure 7-5. Be sure to describe what the arrows, x's, and zig-zagged lines mean. ✦

Chapter 8

The Life Domains Are Influenced by a Range of Outside Factors, Including Biological and Environmental Factors

The core part of the general theory of crime has now been presented. At the heart of the theory are five clusters of variables: (1) irritability/low self-control, (2) poor parenting and no/bad marriages, (3) negative school experiences and limited education, (4) peer delinquency, and (5) unemployment/bad jobs. These clusters constitute the major direct causes of crime and, as such, they allow us to explain why some individuals are more likely to engage in crime than others. But the general theory is not yet complete. One key ingredient is missing: What determines an individual's standing on these clusters or life domains? For example, what determines whether an individual experiences poor parenting or is irritable and low in self-control? Part of the answer to this question was presented in Chapters 4 and 5: The variables in each cluster affect one another and are affected by the individual's crime. Poor parenting practices, for example, are affected by irritability/low self-control, negative school experiences, and peer delinquency, as well as the juvenile's criminal behavior. The discussions in Chapters 4 and 5, however, only present part of the story. The variables in each cluster or life domain are also influenced by outside factors, including biological factors and features of the social environment.

This chapter lists those outside factors that directly affect the life domains. Certain of these outside factors only affect one of the life domains. For example, biological factors affect irritability/low self-control, but have little direct effect on the other life domains. Other factors affect all or most of the life domains. This is true of the "sociodemographic" characteristics of the individual, including the individual's age, sex/gender, race/ethnicity, the socioeconomic status (SES) of the individual's parents, and the characteristics of the community in which the individual lives, especially whether the individual lives in a very poor inner-city community.[1] Partly for this reason, the general theory focuses on these sociodemographic characteristics. It is possible to list additional outside factors that affect the life domains, particularly factors having to do with the larger social and cultural environment. For example, economic conditions in the United States have a large effect on the life domains. A full discussion of these larger factors is beyond the scope of this book, but I briefly discuss how these factors might affect the life domains.

It is of course important to describe the outside factors that affect the life domains. Doing so dramatically expands our knowledge of the causes of crime by pointing to those factors that *indirectly* affect crime through their effect on the five life domains. We learn, for example, that factors like genetic inheritance and brain injury indirectly affect crime through their effect on irritability/low self-control, and that age, sex/gender, race/ethnicity, parental SES, and community SES indirectly affect crime through their effect on all or most of the life domains. Further, describing how outside factors affect the life domains allows us to better explain group differences in *crime rates*.[2] For example, knowing that males are more likely than females to be irritable and low in self-control helps us explain why males have higher crime rates than females (see especially Moffitt et al. 2001). This topic is explored further in Chapter 9, where I use the general theory to explain group differences in crime rates. Finally, describing these outside factors allows us to better control crime. As I argue in Chapter 11, the best way to control crime is to alter the direct causes of crime, but this is difficult to do without addressing at least certain of these outside factors. For example, efforts to improve parenting practices will be more successful to the extent that they address the causes of poor parenting, like parental stress and limited knowledge of good parenting practices.

This discussion of the outside factors that affect the life domains will complete my presentation of the general theory of crime, and I conclude this chapter by presenting an overview of the full theory.

Outside Factors That Affect the Life Domains

While I describe the outside factors that affect all of the life domains, I focus on the factors that affect irritability/low self-control and poor parenting practices, given the central role they play in the general theory.

Outside Factors That Affect Irritability/Low Self-Control

Data suggest that irritability and low self-control are caused by biological factors and the social environment, including environmental factors that extend beyond the family, school, peer, and work domains.

Biological Influences. Biological factors of a genetic and nongenetic nature influence these traits (see Agnew 2005; Caspi 1998; Caspi et al. 1994; Ellis and Walsh 2000; Fishbein 2001; Moffitt 1990; Raine 1993; 2002a; 2002b; Raine et al. 1997; Rowe 2002; Rutter et al. 1998; Walsh 2000). Data suggest that these traits are inherited to some extent, so individuals are more likely to develop these traits if their natural parents possess them (even if we take account of parenting practices). Also, biological factors of a nongenetic nature increase the likelihood of developing these traits. Such factors involve a range of "biological harms," like the mother's poor health habits during pregnancy (e.g., poor nutrition, alcohol and drug use), certain types of delivery complications, head injuries, and exposure to toxic substances like lead.

These genetic and nongenetic factors likely influence individual traits through their impact on the nervous system, including the structure and functioning of the brain. The precise nature of these influences is still being investigated, however. One popular theory with some support is that these factors result in reduced levels of serotonin in the brain. Serotonin is a neurotransmitter, allowing for communication between brain cells. Reduced serotonin may lower one's inhibitions and thereby contribute to impulsive behavior, a key ingredient of low self-control. It may also contribute to aggressiveness, a key ingredient of irritability. Another popular theory with some support is that these factors affect the autonomic nervous system, which influences our emotional reaction to stimuli. Some individuals show less emotional response to stimuli. These individuals may be less fearful of punishment, which contributes to impulsive behavior. They may also have a greater need for thrills and excitement, since it takes more to stimulate or arouse them (see Raine 2002a; 2002b).

I should note that while biological factors have some independent effect on the development of irritability/low self-control, evidence suggests that they are most likely to lead to these traits when individuals are also in aversive social environments, like troubled families (see especially Raine et al. 1997; Raine 2002b). That is, biological and environmental factors may interact in their effect on traits.

Sociodemographic Influences (Age, Sex, Race/Ethnicity, Parents' SES, and Community Characteristics). One's levels of irritability and self-control are also influenced by such factors as sex, age, parents' SES, community SES, and, possibly, race/ethnicity. In particular, data indicate that males are higher in irritability and lower in self-control than females (Moffitt et al. 2001). Part of the reason for this may have to do with biological differences between males and females; males may be more likely to inherit these traits and they may be more likely to experience certain biological harms that contribute to these traits, like head injury. Part of the reason may have to do with differences in how males and females are treated in our society. Much data, in particular, suggest that females are more likely to be taught to exercise self-restraint, show empathy for others, avoid risky activities, and refrain from aggressive behavior (Steffensmeir and Allan 2000).

There is also some evidence that age affects irritability and low self-control, with levels of irritability/low self-control peaking in adolescence.[3] Again, this may be partly due to biological factors, like hormonal surges during puberty and differences in brain functioning during adolescence (see Agnew 2003a; Caspi 1998; Raine 2002b; Walsh 2000 for overviews). It may also be due to social factors, like reduced levels of supervision and increased levels of strain during adolescence (see Chapter 9; Agnew 2003a).

Further, parental SES may influence irritability/low self-control. SES is typically measured in terms of income, education, and occupational prestige. Individuals from low-SES families may be more likely to inherit these traits, as these traits may be more common among low-SES individuals (see Caspi 1998; Jarjoura et al. 2002). Individuals from low-SES families are also more likely to suffer certain biological harms which contribute to these traits, like poor prenatal health care, birth complications, head injury, and exposure to toxic substances like lead (e.g., Denno 1990; Ellis and Walsh 2000; Rutter et al. 1998; Walsh 2000). And individuals from low-SES families are more likely to experience certain strains or stressors, like economic hardship, which may contribute to irritability. (Parental SES may also have an indirect effect on these traits through its influence on parenting practices; see below.)

In addition, individuals from poor inner-city communities may be more likely to have these traits (Caspi and Moffitt 1995; Wikstrom and Loeber 2000), partly because they are more likely to suffer biological harms and partly for social reasons. Bernard (1990), for example, argues that individuals in very poor communities regularly confront a range of stressors or strains, which increase their level of irritability. Observational studies of low-income communities provide some support for this argument (Anderson 1999).

It is unclear whether race/ethnicity influences these traits *after we take account of race/ethnic differences in parental and community SES.* Race/ethnicity is strongly correlated with parental and community-level SES in the United States, due to the effects of past and present discrimination. For example, African Americans are more likely to be poor and live in high-poverty communities than are whites, although most African Americans are not poor. Much of the effect of race/ethnicity on the life domains and crime is explained by this correlation. For example, data suggest that the association between race and crime is substantially reduced when we take account of race differences in individual *and* community-level SES (see Agnew 2005). It is possible, however, that race/ethnicity may influence irritability/low self-control even after we take account of parental and community-level SES. For example, African Americans at all SES levels are more likely than whites to experience certain strains, like race-based discrimination, and this may contribute to higher levels of irritability (see Hughes and Thomas 1998; Simons et al. 2002).

Outside Factors That Affect Parenting Practices and the Likelihood and Quality of Marriage

Parenting practices and marital experiences are also influenced by factors that extend beyond those listed in the life domains. Much data, in particular, suggest that parenting practices are strongly influenced by the characteristics and experiences of parents, as well as the sociodemographic factors listed above. A similar set of factors affect marital experiences.

Characteristics and Experiences of Parents. Some parents lack the knowledge and traits necessary to be good parents. Parents who were exposed to poor parenting when they were children are more likely to be poor parents themselves, suggesting that one must be taught good parenting skills (Patterson et al. 1992). Also, many parents possess traits like irritability and low self-control that reduce their motivation and ability to engage in good parenting. Such parents care less about their children, are less willing to invest the time and effort necessary for good parenting, and are more prone to engage in harsh, abusive parenting practices.

Further, some parents are exposed to a range of strains that undermine their ability and motivation to engage in good parenting. These strains include economic hardship; family conflict, including family violence; drug and alcohol use; large family size; teenage motherhood; divorce or separation; work-related stressors, including the poor conditions associated with work in "bad jobs"; housing problems; neighborhood problems, including the problems associated with living in high-poverty communities; and a range of stressful life events and "daily life hassles" (Agnew et al. 2000; Conger et al. 1995; Lempers et al. 1989; Patterson et al. 1989; 1992; Peterson and Hann 1999; Rutter et al. 1998; Sampson 1987; Stern and Smith 1995).

Poor parenting is especially likely when all of these factors come together. Imagine, for example, parents who have little knowledge of good parenting practices, are irritable and low in self-control, and face a variety of strains (e.g., they are single parents trying to raise a large family on a small salary). The odds against good parenting are clearly strong. Further, imagine that these parents are trying to raise children who are irritable and low in self-control. Unfortunately, these factors do come together in many families. Parents who are irritable and low in self-control are more likely to lack knowledge of good parenting practices and face a variety of strains. They are also more likely to have children who are irritable and low in self-control, partly because of their poor parenting practices and partly for biologically based reasons (the children of such parents are more likely to inherit these traits and experience biological harms that contribute to these traits).

Sociodemographic Influences. As was the case with irritability/low self-control, poor parenting practices are influenced by age, sex, parents' SES, community SES, and, possibly, race/ethnicity. The age of the child has a large effect on parenting practices; adolescents, for example, are less closely supervised by and receive less social support from parents than do children (see Chapter 9; Agnew 2003a). Likewise, the sex of the child has a large effect on parenting practices; for example, males are more likely to experience poor supervision and harsh discipline than females (Agnew 2005; LaGrange and Silverman 1999; Lanctot and LeBlanc 2002; Moffitt et al. 2001; Rutter et al. 1998). Low parental SES and residence in poor communities also contribute to a variety of poor parenting practices, both directly and through their effect on factors like divorce and teenage parenthood (see Agnew et al. 2000; Bellair and Roscigno 2000; Colvin 2000; Conger et al. 1994; Elder and Caspi 1988; Lempers et al. 1989; Patterson et al. 1992; Thornberry et al. 2003b; Wadsworth 2000; Wikstrom and Loeber 2000). Once more, it is unclear whether race/ethnicity affects poor parenting practices after we take account of parental and community SES. The fact that race/ethnicity has an independent effect on the experience of certain strains, like racial discrimination, may lead to such an effect.

Marital Experiences. A similar set of outside factors influence the likelihood and quality of marriage. Some individuals have poor marriages and divorce because they marry people who lack the knowledge and traits necessary for successful marriages. This may partly explain why divorce is more common among those who marry as teenagers, have less education, have divorced parents, and have criminal records (Faust and McKibben 1999; Simons et al. 2002). Also, a variety of strains affect the likelihood of being married and the quality of one's marriage, with such strains including economic hardship and residence in poor, inner-city communities (Faust and McKibben 1999; Haas 1999).

Outside Factors That Affect School, Peer, and Work Experiences

Negative School Experiences. School experiences are affected by several factors beyond those in the life domains, including one's cognitive abilities and a range of factors related to the school environment. Juveniles are more likely to have negative school experiences when they are assigned to noncollege-prep tracks, they are in large classes and large schools, their teachers spend little time on academic tasks, there are infrequent evaluations of student performance, other students in the school discourage academic pursuits, the school sets low academic goals for its students, school disciplinary practices are poor, and there is little community involvement in the school (see Agnew 2005; Colvin 2000; Gottfredson 2001; Riordan 1997).

Sociodemographic factors also influence school experiences. Most notably, individuals from low-SES families and poor communities are more likely to be placed in noncollege tracks and attend inferior schools. The same seems to be true for the members of certain racial and ethnic groups, even after we take account of SES (see Bellair and Roscigno 2000; Riordan 1997; Wadsworth 2000; Welsh et al. 2000). Age also influences school experiences in that the nature of school changes as students move from elementary to secondary school; among other things, teachers grade in a more rigorous manner and create a more competitive environment through practices like normative grading and public evaluations of student performance. These and other changes contribute to a decrease in grades and an increase in dissatisfaction with school (see Chapter 9). The effect of sex on school experiences is more complicated; females generally outperform males in school through puberty, when levels of school performance become more similar—although males outperform females in math and science (Riordan 1997).

Peer Delinquency. Peer delinquency, including association with delinquent peers or gang members, is influenced by certain school factors, especially track placement and the prevalence of delinquent peer groups/gangs in one's school. It is also influenced by age, sex, race/ethnicity, parent's SES, and community characteristics. Adolescents are much more likely than children and adults to be members of delinquent peer groups; to spend unsupervised, unstructured time with peers; and to experience peer abuse (see Chapter 9;

Warr 2002). Males are much higher in peer delinquency than females (see Chapter 9; Warr 2002). African Americans and members of certain other race/ethnic groups are more likely to experience certain types of peer abuse, like discriminatory treatment. And individuals in low-SES families and communities are higher in peer delinquency (Agnew 2001a; Colvin 2000; Gottfredson et al. 1991; Wikstrom and Loeber 2000).

Unemployment/Bad Jobs. Age, sex, race/ethnicity, parental SES, and community characteristics also influence the likelihood of being unemployed and working at bad jobs. Young adults are more likely than older adults to be unemployed and work in bad jobs. Women are more likely to be unemployed and work in "bad jobs," although there are no sex differences in job satisfaction (England et al. 2001; Ferber and O'Farrell 1991; Jacobs 2001; Mueller and Wallace 1996; Reskin and Padavic 1999). African Americans and members of certain other racial and ethnic groups are more likely to be unemployed and work in bad jobs, with evidence suggesting that race/ethnicity often has a direct impact on employment and type of work (Kaufman 2001; Reskin and Padavic 1999). Individuals with low-SES parents are more likely to be unemployed and work in bad jobs, partly because low-SES parents lack job connections and are less able to set their children up in business. Individuals living in poor, inner-city communities are also more likely to be unemployed and work in bad jobs. Decent jobs are more scarce in such communities, residents are less able to assist one another in finding decent jobs, and the residents of such communities are less likely to learn the attitudes and skills necessary to secure such jobs (see Wilson 1987; 1996).

Incorporating Outside Factors Into the General Theory

It would be difficult to incorporate all of the above outside factors into the general theory without seriously threatening the simplicity or parsimony of the theory. For that reason, the general theory focuses on the effects of age, sex, race/ethnicity, parents' SES, and community characteristics. These key variables have large direct effects on all or most of the life domains. They also influence or are strongly correlated with those factors that affect specific life domains. In particular, these sociodemographic characteristics influence or are correlated with those biological factors that impact irritability/low self-control, with the characteristics and experiences of parents, with track placement and the characteristics of the individual's school, and with the characteristics of marital partners. Focusing on these sociodemographic characteristics, then, should not seriously compromise our efforts to explain why some individuals are more likely to engage in crime than others.

It is, however, important to keep in mind the reasons why these sociodemographic characteristics affect the life domains. For example, it is important to know that parental SES affects parenting practices because it affects or is correlated with such things as the parent's irritability/low self-control, knowledge of good parenting practices, and experience of strains. This information not only increases our understanding of why parental SES is important, but it has important policy implications as well. It may not always be possible to alter parental SES, but it may be possible to alter some of the intervening mechanisms by which parental SES affects parenting practices. For example, one might provide instruction in good parenting practices or reduce certain of the strains that low-SES parents face, like housing, work, and childcare problems.

A Note on Larger Social and Cultural Influences

The above discussion lists the more immediate outside influences on the five life domains. It is also important to take account of how larger social and cultural forces directly and indirectly affect the life domains. Such forces include cultural values and beliefs (e.g., beliefs about how males and females should behave); the nature and operation of the major institutions in the society, including economic and political institutions; and demographic processes like the size and composition of the population.

These larger forces *affect the more immediate outside influences listed above*, and thereby have an indirect effect on the life domains. Most notably, economic and other forces influence the socioeconomic status of families and the nature of the communities in which individuals live. To give one prominent example, economic and social trends over the past few decades have lead to an increase in the number of people living in very poor inner-city communities. Such trends include a dramatic decrease in the number of manufacturing jobs in inner-city areas, which has made it increasingly difficult for inner-city residents with limited education to get decent work. They include the migration of working- and middle-class African Americans to the suburbs, leaving the poor behind, and they include government housing policies that concentrate public housing in poor inner-city communities (see Agnew 2005; Sampson and Wilson 1995).

These larger forces also *condition the effect of the more immediate outside factors on the life domains.* For example, cultural beliefs regarding males and females condition the effect of sex on parenting practices. Sex is more likely to affect parenting practices in societies where males and females are viewed as very different. To give another example, the degree to which societies are industrialized conditions the effect of age on peer delinquency. In less industrialized societies, teenagers work on their parents' farms or work full time in "regular" jobs. As a consequence, they regularly interact with adults and peer delinquency is less common. But in industrialized societies like our own, few families engage in farming and teenagers are largely excluded from full-time work, partly because of the educational requirements of most jobs. Instead, teenagers are segregated from adults in age-graded schools, where they spend most of their time interacting with one another. This does much to encourage peer delinquency. Age, then, is more likely to be related to peer delinquency in industrialized societies (see Felson 1998; Warr 2002, 18–22 for fuller discussions).

Further, these larger forces sometimes have a *direct effect on the life domains.* For example, economic conditions have a direct effect on the likelihood of being unemployed or working in a bad job. Also, these forces sometimes *condition the effect of the life domains on crime.* For example, poor parental supervision may have a larger effect on crime in highly affluent, urbanized societies than in less affluent, rural societies. As Felson (1998) and others point out, there are more opportunities for crime in affluent, urbanized societies. Among other things, there are more "attractive targets" for crime (e.g., lightweight, expensive goods) which are more often unprotected (e.g., homes are left empty during the day because the occupants are at school and work, merchandise is displayed on open shelves in large stores). As a result, poorly supervised juveniles are more readily tempted to commit crimes in societies like the United States. To give another example, the generosity of a society's social welfare programs may condition the effect of unemployment/bad jobs on crime. Generous welfare and unemployment programs may partially insulate people from the negative effects of unemployment and bad jobs, thus reducing the impact of these factors on crime (see DeFronzo 1997; Savolainen 2000).

So larger social and cultural forces indirectly and sometimes directly affect the life domains. It is beyond the scope of this book to fully discuss such effects, but excellent discussions of the larger forces that affect crime can be found in a number of works (e.g., Colvin 2000; Cullen and Agnew 2003; Currie 1998; Felson 1998; Hagan 1994; LaFree 1998; Lynch and Stretesky 2001; Messner and Rosenfeld 2001; Sampson and Wilson 1995). These works, however, often fail to consider the ways in which these larger forces work through the life domains to affect crime. A major task, then, is to integrate such work with the general theory of crime presented in this book. On the one hand, such an integration will place the general theory in broader context, allowing us to better understand the enormous effect that larger social and cultural forces have on the life domains. On the other hand, such an integration will allow us to better understand the ways in which these larger social and cultural forces influence criminal offending.[4]

An Overview of the General Theory of Crime

My presentation of the general theory of crime and delinquency is now complete. The general theory is easily summarized in a few simple propositions, most of which have already been presented.

1. Crime is caused by five clusters of variables, organized into the life domains of self (irritability/low self-control), family (poor parenting practices, no/bad marriages), school (negative school experiences, limited education), peers (peer delinquency), and work (unemployment, bad jobs). The effect of the life domains on crime often varies over the life course.

2. The variables in each domain increase crime by reducing the constraints against crime and increasing the motivations for crime. The constraints against crime include external control, stake in conformity, and internal control. The motivations for crime include strain, reinforcements for crime, exposure to successful criminal models, and beliefs favorable to crime.

3. Each life domain affects the other domains, although some effects are stronger than others and effect sizes often change over the life course. These effects are such that problems in one domain contribute to problems in another; for example, irritability/low self-control contributes to poor parenting, which in turn contributes to irritability/low self-control. Problems in the domains, then, tend to mutually reinforce one another (the "web of crime"), and each domain has both a direct effect on crime and an indirect effect through the other domains.

4. Prior crime has both a direct effect on subsequent crime and an indirect effect through the life domains. These effects are conditioned or influenced by the individual's standing on the life domains. Prior crime is most likely to lead to further crime when the individual is high in irritability, low in self-control, and in social environments conducive to crime.

5. The life domains interact in affecting crime and one another. A given life domain is more likely to increase crime or negatively affect another life domain when the remaining life domains are conducive to crime.

6. The life domains have nonlinear and largely contemporaneous effects on crime and one another, although each life domain has a large lagged effect on itself. Likewise, crime has a nonlinear and largely contemporaneous effect on the life domains.

7. As described in this chapter, age, sex, race/ethnicity, parents' SES, and community characteristics (especially whether the respondent lives in a poor inner-city community) are key outside factors that affect the level of the life domains. In particular, the life domains are more likely to be conducive to crime when individuals are in the adolescent years, are male (with the exception of work/unemployment), are African American or members of certain other race/ethnic groups, have parents who are low in SES, and reside in poor, inner-city communities. (The effects of age and sex are discussed further in Chapter 9.)

Notes

1. The individual's own socioeconomic status is encompassed by the life domains. As indicated in Chapter 3, the "school" domain includes the individual's education and the "work" domain includes the type of work done by the individual and the benefits associated with this work, including income.

2. The crime rate usually refers to the number of crimes committed per 1,000 group members. For example, it might be the case that there are 74 crimes committed per 1,000 males versus 22 crimes committed per 1,000 females.

3. It is important to note that while the individual's level of irritability/ low self-control *relative to others* may show much stability over the life course, the individual's *absolute* level of irritability/low self-control may vary a fair amount over the life course. The discussion here refers to absolute levels.

4. Taking account of the effects of larger social and cultural forces on the life domains may also lead to modifications in the general theory, particularly if we extend the theory to other societies. As indicated, such forces not only influence the level of the life domains (e.g., the level of poor parenting), but also the impact of the life domains on crime. In certain societies, it may be necessary to add new life domains to the model (e.g., religion), delete certain domains because of their limited impact on crime, or redefine the content of certain life domains (e.g., the components of poor parenting).

Discussion and Study Questions

1. Why is it important to examine the outside factors that affect the life domains?

2. Give an example of an outside factor that has a direct effect on only one of the life domains. Give an example of an outside factor that directly affects all of the life domains.

3. What factors are included under the sociodemographic characteristics of individuals? Why does this chapter focus on such sociodemographic characteristics?

4. Describe those biological factors that may affect irritability/ low self-control and discuss why they may do so.

5. What do I mean when I state that "biological and environmental factors may interact in their effect on traits" (like irritability and low self-control)?

6. Pick one sociodemographic characteristic and describe its effect on the life domains.

7. Why are some parents more likely to engage in poor parenting than others?

8. List three school characteristics that increase the likelihood that students will have negative school experiences.

9. What do I mean when I state that much of the effect of race/ethnicity on the life domains is probably indirect, due to the correlation of race/ethnicity with parental and community SES?

10. Describe some of the "larger social and cultural forces" that may impact the life domains. These larger forces directly and indirectly affect the individual's standing on the life domains. They also condition the effect of the more immediate outside factors on the life domains and the effect of the life domains themselves on crime. Give examples of these direct, indirect, and conditioning effects.

11. Describe the general theory of crime and delinquency in your own words. ✦

Chapter 9

Using the General Theory to Explain Group Differences in Crime and Patterns of Offending Over the Life Course

The general theory is designed to explain why some individuals are more likely to engage in crime than others. But with some elaboration, it can also explain why certain groups have higher crime rates than others. I begin this chapter by describing how the general theory might accomplish this task, and then use it to explain why males have higher crime rates than females and why adolescents have higher crime rates than children and adults. I focus on sex and age because these are the two group characteristics most strongly associated with crime.

I conclude the chapter by using the general theory to address an issue that is attracting much attention among criminologists. There is a small group of individuals who offend at high rates over much of their lives. These individuals make up about 5 to 10 percent of the population and are sometimes referred to as "life-course persistent" offenders (see Moffitt 1993). There is also a much larger group of individuals who tend to limit their offending to the adolescent years; they are sometimes referred to as "adolescence-limited" offenders. Criminologists have recently asked how we might explain the offending behavior of these groups, with some criminologists arguing that separate theories are needed to explain the behavior of "life-course persistent" and "adolescence-limited" offenders. I describe how the general theory explains the offending patterns of both these groups, and in doing so, I briefly discuss the relationship between socioeconomic status (SES), race/ethnicity, and crime.

How Might the General Theory Explain Group Differences in Crime Rates

Groups Differ in Their Standing on the Life Domains

The general theory explains group differences in crime rates primarily by the fact that groups differ in their standing on the life domains. That is, members of some groups are more likely than members of other groups to have traits conducive to crime, experience family problems, have negative school experiences, be high in peer delinquency, and/or have work problems. These group differences are the major reason why some groups have higher crime rates than other groups. For example, males are more likely than females to be irritable and low in self-control, experience poor parental supervision and harsh discipline, have weak family ties as adults, and be high in peer delinquency (see below). This is the major reason why males have higher crime rates than females.

Group Differences in the Effect of the Life Domains on Crime

There are other ways to explain group differences in crime rates.[1] Most notably, it can be argued that the life domains have larger effects on crime among some groups than others; that is, there are group differences in effect sizes. For example, poor parenting may be more likely to cause crime among lower-SES individuals than among higher-SES individuals. Lower-SES individuals, then, may have higher crime rates not only because they are more likely to experience poor parenting, but also because their poor parenting is more likely to lead to crime.

Why might a life domain have a larger effect on crime in one group than another? Why, for example, might poor parenting have a larger effect on crime among members of Group A than among members of Group B? There are two possible reasons. First, poor parenting may be more likely to lead to crime among members of Group A because their constraints against crime are lower and their motivations for crime are higher. For example, members of Group A may be more likely to respond to poor parenting with crime because they are higher in peer delinquency (see the discussion of interaction effects in Chapter 6). Second, poor parenting may be more likely to lead to crime among members of Group A because parents *occupy a more central place in their lives.* In particular, their parents have more responsibility for their socialization and meeting their needs;[2] their parents face less competition from other groups in these tasks; and members of Group A are more likely to have traits, interests, and abilities that make them dependent on their parents (see the discussion of the relative importance of the life domains in Chapter 3).

So there are two major reasons why the life domains might have larger effects on crime in some groups than in others. The general theory takes account of the first reason. In particular, the theory takes account of the fact that the effect of each life domain on crime is conditioned by the major constraints against and motivations for crime. These constraints and motivations are embodied in the life domains, and the general theory states that the effect of each life domain on crime is conditioned by the other life domains (e.g., the effect of poor parenting on crime is conditioned by one's level of peer delinquency). A full test of the general theory, then, would take account of the interactions between the life domains (e.g., the interaction between poor parenting and peer delinquency). In doing so, such a test would reduce the likelihood that we will find group differences in effect sizes. For example, it would reduce the likelihood that we will find that poor parenting has a larger effect on crime among members of Group A than Group B. That is because we "control" for one of the reasons why poor parenting might have a larger effect on crime among members of Group A (i.e., we control for the interaction between poor parenting and peer delinquency).

The general theory also takes *some* account of the second reason for group differences in effect sizes. In particular, the theory recognizes that the roles of family, school, peers, and work change dramatically over the life course. Parents, for example, play a central role in the lives of young children but a marginal role in the lives of adult children. That is why the general theory explicitly states that the effects of the life domains on crime and one another change over the life course. It is less clear whether the life domains play different roles in the lives of males versus females, lower- versus higher-SES groups, and different race and ethnic groups (not to mention groups distinguished by age, sex/gender, SES, *and* race/ethnicity). Numerous arguments have been made in these areas, but the empirical research is often scant, flawed, and mixed in its findings. It is certainly possible, however, that the life domains sometimes play different roles in the lives of different groups, and as a consequence, group differences in the effects of the life domains on crime may sometimes emerge. Indeed, I predict certain differences in effect sizes when discussing the relationship between sex/gender and crime below.

Overall, however, the general theory explains group differences in crime primarily by group differences in standing on the life domains. The emerging evidence tends to support this position (e.g., Fleming et al. 2002; Moffitt et al. 2001; Rowe et al. 1994; 1995), with certain possible exceptions, some of which are discussed below.

Explaining Age Differences in Crime

Crime rates peak during the adolescent years and decline rapidly thereafter. Data suggest that the adolescent peak in offending is due largely to the appearance of new offenders during adolescence ("adolescence-limited" offenders), although existing offenders also increase their levels of offending during adolescence (see Agnew 2003a). A central question for criminologists, then, is how can we explain the fact that adolescents are more likely to offend than children and adults.

Age-Related Differences in Standing on the Life Domains

Drawing on the general theory, I would argue that the adolescent peak in offending is largely explained by adolescents' standing on the life domains. That is, adolescents are more likely than children and adults to be irritable and low in self-control, experience family problems, have negative school experiences, and be high in peer delinquency. I briefly discuss some of the evidence for these age effects below, along with the reasons for these age effects (see Agnew 1997; 2003a for fuller discussions).

The Nature of Adolescence. Adolescence affects the life domains as it does largely because of the social changes associated with adolescence in industrialized societies. Adolescence is a period of transition from childhood to adulthood, with adolescents preparing for adult family and work roles. Reflecting this fact, adolescents are given *some, but not all* of the privileges and responsibilities of adulthood. For example, they are given more autonomy and material resources than children (although less than adults). They are also expected to assume greater responsibility for their behavior, devote more effort to their schoolwork, and expand their social relationships, including romantic relationships. It is felt that adolescents are better prepared to handle such privileges and responsibilities than children and that doing so will help prepare them for adult roles. The ways in which these and others changes associated with adolescence affect the life domains are described below.

Irritability/Low Self-Control. Some data suggest that adolescents have higher levels of irritability and lower levels of self-control than children and adults. In particular, adolescents are more sensitive to stressors, more likely to blame others for their problems, less concerned about the rights and welfare of others, more accepting of beliefs conducive to crime, and more impulsive and sensation seeking than children and/or adults (see Agnew 2003a; Caspi 1998; Turner and Piquero 2003). The reasons for this may be in part biologically based; for example, these traits may be influenced by hormonal surges during puberty and differences in brain functioning during adolescence (Raine 2002b; Walsh 2000). Also, adolescents may be more likely to possess these traits because of the social changes associated with adolescence. For example, the reduction in supervision associated with adolescence may contribute to impulsivity, and the increase in association with delinquent peers (see below) may contribute to beliefs favorable to crime and sensation seeking.[3]

Poor Parenting Practices. Adolescents are also more likely to experience parenting practices that are conducive to crime. First, they are *less well supervised* than children. Parents relax the rules they impose on adolescents; for example, adolescents are allowed to stay out later and exercise more choice over their friends. Parents also engage in less direct monitoring of adolescents, partly because adolescents spend much less time with parents than do children. Second, adolescents receive *less social support* from parents. Adolescents are more often expected to cope on their own. Also, adolescents are often reluctant to seek support from parents, partly because they feel that they should be able to cope on their own. Finally, adolescents are more likely to get into *conflicts with parents*, with many of these conflicts having to do with the privileges and responsibilities of adolescence—like how much autonomy adolescents should have and how much effort should be devoted to schoolwork. So several dimensions of parenting suffer during the transition from childhood to adolescence, which helps explain the increase in offending during adolescence.

Parents, of course, become much less relevant to the explanation of crime as individuals make the transition from adolescence to *adulthood.* Parents are typically replaced with spouses during this time. Most adolescent offenders get involved in "good marriages," which helps explain the reduction in offending that occurs during adulthood. Those offenders who fail to marry or who get involved in "bad" marriages, however, may continue to offend well into the adult years.

Negative School Experiences. The transition from elementary school to secondary school is often associated with an increase in negative school experiences. Adolescents are expected to devote more attention to their educational and occupational futures. School becomes more demanding as a consequence; secondary-school teachers grade in a more rigorous manner and create a more competitive environment through practices like normative grading and public evaluations of student performance. Partly as a result, school performance and satisfaction suffer. There is reason to believe that school supervision and social support decline as well. While secondary schools often place more emphasis on discipline, teachers supervise many more students and spend much less time with each student, which likely undermines their efforts to monitor and support students. So negative school experiences may increase during the transition from childhood to adolescence, and this too helps explain the increase in offending during adolescence.

Individuals usually finish their schooling sometime during the transition from adolescence to adulthood. Most adolescent offenders then develop some commitment to their jobs, which partly explains the reduction in offending during adulthood. Those offenders who are unable to get jobs or who work at "bad jobs," however, may continue to offend into the adult years.

Peer Delinquency. Adolescents spend much more time with peers than children, partly as a result of reduced levels of supervision. Adolescents also encounter a more diverse group of peers, partly because they attend larger, more diverse schools and can travel farther given their access to automobiles. Further, adolescents find *delinquent* peers more attractive, partly because they are somewhat alienated from parents and school and partly because such peers have obtained the autonomy and adult privileges they desire. As a consequence, adolescents are more likely to associate with delinquent peers; to spend time in unstructured, unsupervised activities with peers; and to suffer peer abuse. The transition from childhood to adolescence, then, is marked by a major increase in peer delinquency, and certain data suggest that this increase accounts for much of the surge in crime during this period (Warr 2002; Osgood et al. 1996).

The transition from adolescence to adulthood, however, is marked by a major decrease in peer delinquency. Work and family responsibilities reduce the amount of time adults have for peer associations and reduce the motivation for associating with delinquent peers.

In sum, there is reason to believe that adolescents are more likely than children and adults to be irritable and low in self-control, experience family problems, have negative school experiences, and be high in peer delinquency. These facts largely explain the adolescent peak in offending.

Age-Related Differences in the Effect of the Life Domains on Crime

The adolescent peak in offending *may* also be due to the fact that the effect of the life domains on crime varies with age. This argument assumes that effect sizes are *generally* larger during adolescence. However, while the effect of certain of the life domains on crime is larger during adolescence, the effect of other life domains is not. In particular, peer delinquency and negative school experiences may have larger effects on crime during adolescence, but the other life domains do not (see Chapter 3).[4] On balance, I suspect that age-related differences in effect sizes make a *small* contribution to the adolescent peak in offending. Most notably, age differences in the effect of peer delinquency on crime may contribute to the adolescent peak. Peer delinquency may have a larger effect on crime during adolescence and this increased effect, in combination with much higher levels of peer delinquency during adolescence, may offset the fact that certain of the other life domains have a weaker effect on crime during adolescence.

The major reason for the peak in adolescent offending, then, is that adolescents are more likely than children and adults to be irritable/low in self-control, have family problems, have negative school experiences, and—especially—be high in peer delinquency.

Explaining Sex Differences in Crime[5]

Males are much more likely to engage in crime than females, with sex differences in offending being greatest for serious crimes (Agnew 2005; Chesney-Lind and Shelden 2004; Moffitt et al. 2001; Rutter et al. 1998; Steffensmeir and Allan 2000). For example, 10 percent of all arrests for robbery are females, and 37 percent of all arrests for larceny-theft are females (Federal Bureau of Investigation 2003). A major question for criminologists is why are males more likely to engage in crime than females.

Sex Differences in Standing on the Life Domains

As was the case with age differences, sex differences in offending are explained largely by the fact that males and females differ in their standing on the life domains. Most notably, males are more likely than females to be high in irritability and low in self-control, to be poorly supervised and harshly disciplined by parents, to have weaker family ties as adults, and to be high in peer delinquency.

These differences partly stem from biological differences between males and females, which are discussed below. They also stem from differences in the socialization and social position of males and females. Parents, peers, teachers, and others are more likely to teach males to be assertive, risk-taking, independent, and competitive; and they are more likely to teach females to be submissive, cautious, dependent, and concerned with the welfare of others. These differences in socialization are reinforced by differences in the social position of males and females. Females, for example, are less likely to work or earn as much money as males if they do work, which reinforces their dependence on and concern for others; and females are more subject to sexual victimization, which reinforces their more cautious orientation (for fuller discussions, see Chesney-Lind and Shelden 2004; Coltrane 1998; Cullen and Agnew 2003; England et al. 2001; Hagan et al. 1979; Heimer 1995; Lanctot and LeBlanc 2002; Messerschmidt 1993; Steffensmeier and Allan 1996;

2000). The ways in which these factors affect the life domains are discussed below.

Irritability/Low Self-Control. Males are much more likely than females to be irritable and low in self-control, which explains much of the sex difference in crime, especially serious crime (Burton et al. 1998; LaGrange and Silverman 1999; Moffitt et al. 2001). The reasons for the sex difference in irritability/low self-control may be partly biological. Males may be more likely to inherit these traits than females. In particular, certain evolutionary theorists argue that it is adaptative for males to be aggressive and competitive because it increases their chances of reproducing with many females and thereby passing their genes on to others, while it is adaptive for females to show concern for others because they are directly involved in gestating offspring (see Ellis and Walsh 1997; Fishbein 2001; Rowe 2002 for fuller discussions). It has also been argued that males are more likely to be exposed to certain biological harms that might contribute to these traits, like birth complications and head injuries (see Archer 1995; Moffitt et al. 2001; Rutter et al. 1998; Tibbetts and Piquero 1999). The specific biological mechanisms contributing to these traits are unclear, although sex differences in brain functioning and testosterone levels have been mentioned (Fishbein 2001). Sex differences in irritability and low self-control are also socially produced, reflecting sex differences in the socialization and social position of males and females. Males, for example, are more likely to receive encouragement for risk-taking behavior and to be in situations where risk-taking is reinforced.[6]

Parenting Practices. It has also been argued that males are more likely than females to engage in crime because they are more often subject to poor parenting practices. In particular, there is good reason to believe that males are less closely supervised than females, are less likely to be punished for aggressive behavior, and are somewhat more likely to receive harsh punishments when they are sanctioned (Agnew 2005; Bottcher 2001; Chesney-Lind and Shelden 1998; Lanctot and LeBlanc 2002; Moffitt et al. 2001). These differences in parenting practices are manifestations of the sex differences in socialization noted above. They may also reflect the different personality traits possessed by males and females; for example, parents may be more likely to treat boys harshly because boys are more irritable and lower in self-control.[7] (It is, however, important to note that girls are more likely to be sexually abused than boys, and such sexual abuse may play an important role in much female crime [see Chesney-Lind and Sheldon 1998; Lanctot and LeBlanc 2002; Siegel and Williams 2003]).

Adult Family Ties. The lives of adult females are also more closely controlled than the lives of males. Females are more likely than males to be tied to the household—that is, to assume greater responsibility for household tasks and childcare—even if they work outside the home (Coltrane 1998; Ferber and O'Farrell 1991). As a consequence, they face more constraints against crime because they spend less time in public and feel more responsibility for other family members. Their stronger ties to the family, however, are conducive to certain types of crime, like family violence and minor forms of theft tied to family roles, like shoplifting. It is in these areas where sex differences in the extent of crime are smallest (see Moffitt et al. 2001; Steffensmeier and Allan 1996; 2000).

Peer Delinquency. Males are more likely than females to associate with delinquent peers/gang members; spend unstructured, unsupervised time with peers; and experience peer abuse, especially criminal victimization (Bottcher 2001; Lanctot and LeBlanc 2002; Mears et al. 1998; Miller 2001; Morash 1986; Moffitt et al. 2001; Moore and Hagedorn 2001; Osgood et al. 1996; Warr 2002, 114–117). These differences stem partly from sex differences in personality traits and levels of parental supervision. Nevertheless, the higher peer delinquency of males makes some independent contribution to the explanation of sex differences in crime.

A Note on Work. Females are more likely than males to be unemployed and work at bad jobs, although females do not express more job dissatisfaction than males (Mueller and Wallace 1996). But as argued below, negative work experiences may have a lower effect on crime among females than males.

Sex differences in crime, then, are largely a function of sex differences in standing on the life domains, with certain data suggesting that sex differences in irritability/low self-control are especially important (see Moffitt et al. 2001).

Sex Differences in the Effect of the Life Domains on Crime

There is some debate over whether there are sex differences in the effect of the life domains on crime. For example, it has been argued that peer delinquency has a larger effect on crime among males than females (Mears et al. 1998; also see Miller 2001). A number of studies have examined whether there are sex differences in effect sizes; the results of such studies are somewhat mixed, but most find that the life domains have similar effects on crime among males and females (see Fleming et al. 2002; Giordano et al. 2002; Lanctot and LeBlanc 2002; Moffitt et al. 2001; Rowe et al. 1995; Rutter et al. 1998; Smith and Paternoster 1987). And to the extent that sex differences in effect sizes exist, I believe that they are largely explained by the fact that males and females differ in irritability/low self-control and their standing on many of the other life domains. For example, males may be more likely than females to respond to peer delinquency with crime because they are higher in irritability, lower in self-control, and more poorly supervised than females. Once the interactions between these variables and peer delinquency are taken into account, sex differences in effect sizes should largely disappear. There are, however, two areas in which sex differences in effect sizes may remain: Adult family factors may have a larger effect on crime among females and work factors may have a larger effect on crime among males.

I make these predictions because the family occupies a more central place in the lives of adult women, while work occupies a more central place in the lives of adult men. Despite substantial changes in the relationship between sex, work roles, and family roles over the last few decades, women are still more committed to and affected by their family life than men, and men are still more committed to and affected by their work life than women (Coltrane 1998; Ferber and O'Farrell 1991; Giordano et al. 2002; Simons et al. 2002). This disparity reflects differences in socialization and social position. People are socialized to believe that women should assume primary responsibility for household maintenance and childcare while men should play the role of "breadwinner." Women spend more time than men on household tasks and childcare. And although women have become more involved in the labor force, men still provide the major source of financial support in most families (reflecting to some extent the fact that there is still much gender discrimination in the work world).

I therefore predict that marital status and quality will have a stronger effect on crime among females than males. In particular, being involved in a good marriage should be more likely to reduce crime among females than males (conversely, being involved in a bad marriage or being unmarried should be more likely to increase crime among females). Also, having children should be more likely to reduce crime among women than men. I further predict that work experiences will have a larger effect on crime among males than females. While there has not been much research in these areas, Simons et al. (2002) recently found support for certain of these predictions. They followed a sample of 236 adults and their romantic partners over time. Having a romantic partner with a criminal history and being in a poor-quality relationship were more likely to cause crime among females than males, and job dissatisfaction was more likely to cause crime among males (also see Giordano et al. 2002; Laub and Sampson 2001; Moffitt et al. 2001, 190–193; Thornberry et al. 2000).[8]

In sum, there may be sex differences in the effect of certain of the life domains on crime, reflecting the fact that family life is more central to females and work life is more central to males. Overall, however, sex differences in crime are largely due to sex differences in standing on the life domains.

Explaining 'Life-Course Persistent' and 'Adolescence-Limited' Offending

The general theory is designed to explain why some *individuals* have higher rates of offending than others, that is, to explain *between-individual* differences in offending. But as illustrated above, the general theory can—with some elaboration—be used to explain why some *groups* have higher offending rates than other groups. Further, the general theory can be used to explain *within-individual* patterns of offending over the life course, that is, to explain why offenders increase, decrease, or maintain their levels of offending over time.

Not all offenders are alike; they differ in such things as the frequency, seriousness, and duration of their offending. Criminologists have recently made much progress in identifying the major types of offenders, with two types standing out. There is a small group of offenders who offend at high rates over much of their lives. These "life-course" persistent offenders account for a large share of all serious crime, although they also commit much nonserious crime as well. There is also a much larger group of "adolescence-limited" offenders who offend at high rates largely during the adolescent years. In addition, some research has identified other types of offenders, most notably (1) low-rate life-course persistent offenders, who offend at low to moderate rates over much of their lives; and (2) low-rate adolescence-limited offenders, who offend at low to moderate rates largely during the adolescent years (see Chung et al. 2002; D'Unger et al. 1998; Fergusson et al. 2000).

Criminologists have recently asked how we might explain the offending patterns of these different types of offenders. I next use the general theory to address this issue, drawing heavily on the work of Moffitt (1993), Patterson (1989), and Thornberry and Krohn (2001). I begin with life-course persistent offenders.

Life-Course Persistent Offenders. Some individuals develop high levels of irritability/low self-control and experience poor parenting early in life, partly for biological reasons and partly for social reasons (see Chapter 8). This sets the stage for *high rates* of offending *over the life course* (see Fergusson et al. 2000; Moffitt and Harrington 1996; Moffitt et al. 2001; Patterson et al. 1998; Wright et al. 1999).

Let me first focus on why irritability/low self-control and poor parenting lead to *high rates* of offending. High levels of irritability/low self-control and poor parenting directly contribute to high rates of offending (recall that the life domains have a nonlinear effect on crime, so that *high* levels of irritability/low self-control and poor parenting have especially large effects on crime [see Chapter 7]). Also, irritability/low self-control and poor parenting greatly increase the likelihood of negative school experiences, peer delinquency, no/bad marriages, and work problems (see Chapter 4). These factors also directly contribute to high rates of offending. In addition, all of these factors interact with one another in their effect on crime, further increasing rates of offending (recall from Chapter 6 that the life domains interact in their effect on crime, such that a domain is more likely to cause crime when the other life domains are conducive to crime).

Let me next focus on why irritability/low self-control and poor parenting lead to high rates of offending *over the life course*. First, individuals who have relatively high levels of irritability/low self-control and poor parenting as children tend to have relatively high levels as adolescents and adults. As a consequence, they tend to offend at high rates over much of their lives. The stability of irritability/low self-control and poor parenting is partly due to the fact that these factors have large lagged effects on themselves; for example, poor parenting at Time 1 directly increases the likelihood of poor parenting at Time 2 (see Chapter 7). The stability is also due to the fact that irritability/low self-control and poor parenting affect the other life domains and crime in ways that contribute to further irritability/low self-control and poor parenting. For example, irritability/low self-control increases the likelihood of family, school, peer, and work problems, all of which contribute to further irritability/low self-control (see Chapter 4). Further, the stability is due to the fact that some of the outside factors that cause irritability/low self-control and poor parenting are stable over the life course. For example, one's genetic predisposition to irritability/low self-control may be stable over the life course (see Chapter 8).

Second, irritability/low self-control and poor parenting lead to high rates of offending *over the life course* because they contribute to negative school and peer experiences during adolescence and to poor marital and work experiences during adulthood (see Chapter 4). These effects, in turn, directly increase the likelihood of offending over the life course. In sum, individuals who possess high levels of irritability/low-self and experience poor parenting during childhood become enmeshed in a web of crime from which escape is difficult (although not impossible; see Giordano et al. 2002; Laub and Sampson 2001; Shover 1996).[9]

One of the factors that influences whether individuals develop irritability/low self-control and experience poor parenting is their parent's socioeconomic status. As indicated in Chapter 8, individuals with low-SES parents are more likely to develop irritability/low self-control and experience poor parenting for a range of biologically and socially based reasons. Another factor is sex, with males being more likely to develop irritability/low self-control and experience poor parenting. As such, it should come as no surprise that males and the children of low-SES parents are much more likely to be high-rate, life-course persistent offenders (Chung et al. 2002; D'Unger et al. 2002; Moffitt et al. 2001; Patterson et al. 1998; Tibbetts and Piquero 1999). Race/ethnicity is also related to life-course persistent offending, with data suggesting that African Americans are more likely than whites to be high-rate offenders and continue offending into the adult years (Chung et al. 2002; Elliott 1994; Elliott and Ageton 1980). I believe that this relationship stems largely from the fact that African Americans are more likely than whites to be poor and live in high-poverty communities in the United States. Once this relationship between race and SES is taken into account, the relationship between race and life-course persistent offending should largely disappear (see Agnew 2005).

Adolescence-Limited Offenders. Adolescence-limited offenders tend to limit their offending to the adolescent years. This suggests that they have do *not* have high levels of irritability/low self-control and poor parenting when they are children, and research indicates that this is the case (Aguilar et al. 2000; Fergusson et al. 2000; Moffitt et al. 2001). Why, then, do they offend during adolescence? As indicated in the above discussion of age and crime, the social and biological changes associated with adolescence often affect the life domains in ways that increase the likelihood of crime. These changes include hormonal surges and problems in brain functioning during puberty (which may contribute to irritability and low self-control), reduced supervision by parents and teachers, reduced social support by parents and teachers, increased demands at school, and increased association with delinquent peers. Data support this argument, suggesting that adolescence-limited offenders are more likely than non-offenders to experience certain personality, family, school, and especially peer problems during adolescence (Aguilar et al. 2000; Fergusson et al. 2000; Moffitt et al. 2001; Simons et al. 1994).[10] Adolescence-limited offenders, however, do not experience these problems to the same degree as life-course persistent offenders (Fergusson et al. 2000).

Since the experience of these problems is strongly tied to the biological and social changes associated with adolescence, most adolescence-limited offenders substantially reduce their levels of offending as they become adults. In particular, the biological and social changes associated with adulthood increase their constraints against and reduce their motivations for crime. Most notably, adolescence-limited offenders come to increase their level of self-control, reduce their level of irritability, form strong marital ties, develop strong commitments to good jobs, and substantially reduce their association with delinquent peers. (The problems of life-course persistent offenders are more deeply rooted and extreme, so they are more likely to remain irritable and low in self-control and they have more trouble forming strong marital and work ties. As a consequence, they are much more likely to continue engaging in crime [see Cernkovich and Giordano 2001; Moffitt et al. 2001;

Piquero et al. 2002; Sampson and Laub 1993; Simons et al. 2002; Wright et al. 2001]).

The changes that contribute to adolescence-limited offending affect both males and females and individuals in all SES groups, although they may be somewhat more likely to affect males and lower-SES individuals. In any event, SES and sex differences in adolescence-limited offending should be much smaller than those in life-course persistent offending, and data tend to suggest that this is the case (Moffitt et al. 2001).

In sum, the general theory is able to explain both life-course persistent and adolescence-limited offending. Biological and parenting problems early in life set the stage for life-course persistent offending, with these problems ensnaring individuals in a web of crime from which escape is difficult. The biological and social changes associated with adolescence set the stage for adolescence-limited offending, with these changes temporarily altering the life domains in ways conducive to crime.

Conclusion

The general theory can easily explain group differences in crime rates, with such differences being largely due to group differences in standing on the major life domains. That is, groups differ in crime rates primarily because the members of some groups are more likely than the members of other groups to be high in irritability/low self-control, poor parenting, negative school experiences, peer delinquency, no/bad marriages, and/or no/bad jobs. This chapter provided a few illustrations of this fact, with the general theory being used to explain differences in offending between males and females and between adolescents and other age groups. In principle, the general theory can be applied to the explanation of numerous other group differences in crime in the United States. Doing so, however, requires that we build on the general theory by describing how particular group characteristics affect the life domains and why they have such effects.

The general theory is also able to explain within-individual patterns of offending over the life course. In particular, the individual's standing on the life domains over the life course influences their pattern of offending over the life course. Once more, however, it is necessary to build on the general theory by more fully describing those factors that affect the individual's standing on the life domains over time.

Notes

1. Such explanations include the following: the direct causes of crime differ across groups, interaction effects differ across groups, and the timing and form of effects differ across groups.

2. This includes the role that parents are *supposed to play* and the role that they *actually play* in socializing and meeting the needs of the individual. In particular, parenting practices will have a larger effect if parents are supposed to be the major socializing agents for the individual, even if they do not play this role. For example, the failure to supervise children has a major effect on them, because parents are primarily responsible for their supervision. Further, parenting practices will have a larger effect if parents do act as the major socialization agents for the individual. For example, poor bonding will have a larger effect on children if parents spend much time with their children and make an active effort to influence/control them. Similar factors are operative when considering the role of the other domains in the life of the individual, although there are some differences across domains. For example, when considering the role of marriage and parenthood for adults we must ask not only about the role that spouses and children play in socializing and meeting the needs of the individual, but also about the role of the individual in socializing and meeting the needs of others in the family.

3. The lower levels of impulsivity that characterize adults are reflected in the responses that adult ex-criminals give when asked why they stopped committing crimes. They typically state that crime is no longer exciting/thrilling or that they are worried about the sanctions they might receive (Shover 1996; Shover and Thompson 1992).

4. See Britt (1997), Jang (1999), and Tittle and Ward (1993) for limited research on the relative effects of selected variables on crime over segments of the life course.

5. The phrase "sex differences" is sometimes used to refer to the biological/physical differences between males and females, while the phrase "gender differences" is used to refer to the socially produced differences between males and females. I refer to both biologically and socially produced differences, so neither term is fully appropriate. I use "sex differences" because I think it is less likely to create confusion among students.

6. However, gender differences in socialization and social position may in part stem from biologically based differences between males and females. For example, parents may more often encourage risk taking on the part of males because males seem more "disposed" to engage in risk taking.

7. Parenting practices and traits, of course, have reciprocal effects on one another, so not only do traits influence parenting practices, but parenting practices influence traits.

8. It is important to emphasize that adult work and family life interact with one another in their effect on crime. Unemployment/bad jobs should be more likely to cause crime among those who are unmarried or involved in bad marriages, and this should be true of women as well as men. Reflecting this fact, researchers have noted that women are especially likely to engage in crime when they are unmarried and unemployed/employed in bad jobs (although not as likely as men in this situation). It is unclear whether the presence of children further increases the likelihood of crime in such circumstances. I suspect that it does not; while the presence of children may create much financial and other strain, children also act as a constraint against crime, tying women to home and increasing the fear of punishment (see Giordano et al. 2002; Laub and Sampson 2001).

9. As indicated, there also appear to be a group of offenders that offends at low to moderate rates across the life course. The general theory can explain the offending of these individuals by arguing that they develop *moderate* levels of irritability/low self-control and experience *moderately* poor parenting during childhood. Such traits and parenting directly contribute to moderate levels of offending. They also contribute to moderate problems in the major life domains over the life course. Fergusson et al. (2000) provide some support for this argument; they find that low-rate life-course persistent offenders experience more problems in the life domains than nonoffenders, but far fewer problems than high-rate life-course persistent offenders. There is, however, the question of why the low-rate life-course persistent offenders do not experience a large increase in offending during adolescence. Data suggest that the reason for this is that they do not experience a large increase in peer delinquency (see Fergusson et al. 2000; Patterson et al. 1998). And data from Nagin and Land (1993) provide a hint as to why this might be the case: They have much lower intelligence levels. More generally, it may be the case that they suffer from social disabilities that limit their association with other peers, including delinquent peers, which helps keep their offending at a low to moderate level.

10. Not all adolescents experience these changes. Some adolescents are in families that maintain high levels of supervision, some adolescents have the skills and support to avoid negative school experiences, and some are able to avoid delinquent peers, perhaps because they are shy or are in environments where delinquent peers are less common, like all-female schools (e.g., Caspi et al. 1993; Moffitt and Harrington 1996).

Discussion and Study Questions

1. What is the major way in which the general theory explains group differences in crime rates? What are some additional ways in which the general theory might explain such differences? (See Note 1.)

2. I argue that the life domains might have larger effects on crime in some groups than others. How can we explain such group differences in effect sizes? Give an example of such a group difference.

3. Why are adolescents more likely than children and adults to be high in irritability/low self-control, experience family problems, have negative school experiences, and be high in peer delinquency?

4. Why are there sex differences in standing on the life domains?

5. Describe the offending patterns of life-course persistent and adolescence-limited offenders. How does the general theory explain these offending patterns?

6. SES, sex, and race/ethnicity are more strongly related to life-course persistent offending than to adolescence-limited offending. How might we explain this?

7. What questions should you ask if you want to explain why one group has a higher crime rate than another group?

8. Apply the general theory to the explanation of other groups differences in offending (e.g., use it to explain the fact that crime rates are higher in very poor, inner-city communities versus wealthier and suburban communities). ✦

Chapter 10

Testing the General Theory

As described in prior chapters, there is much indirect support for the general theory. For example, data suggest that many of the specific variables that comprise the life domains are related to crime. Such indirect support is not surprising, because the general theory is partly designed to integrate the major research on the causes of crime. The core propositions of the theory, however, have not been tested. This chapter provides general guidelines for testing each of these propositions.

I do not expect that tests will fully support the general theory, but they should be largely supportive if the theory is to be retained in some form. That is, we should find evidence for most of the predicted effects, including reciprocal, interactive, and nonlinear effects, and we should find that most effect sizes are as predicted by the theory. Empirical tests, however, will surely result in some modification of the theory.

Testing the Core Propositions of the General Theory

A. Crime Is Caused by Five Clusters of Variables, Organized Into the Life Domains of Self (Irritability/Low Self-Control), Family (Poor Parenting Practices, No/Bad Marriages), School (Negative School Experiences, Limited Education), Peers (Peer Delinquency), and Work (Unemployment/Bad Jobs). The Effect of Certain of These Clusters on Crime Varies Over the Life Course

This broad proposition should be tested in several steps:

1. List the Variables in Each Domain and Estimate Their Effect on Crime. The key variables in each domain are listed in Chapter 3. The effect of most of these variables on crime is reasonably well-established (although see Note 2, Chapter 3), but the effect of some variables is less certain. In particular, there is not much research on whether crime is affected by positive parenting, spouse/partner supervision and social support, school supervision/discipline, positive teaching, peer conflict/abuse, bonding to work, work performance, work supervision/discipline, working conditions, and criminal coworkers (see Chapter 3 for descriptions of these variables). If the general theory is correct, each of the variables listed in Chapter 3 should have a significant direct effect on crime with the other variables controlled. Researchers, however, should conduct separate analyses for children, adolescents, and adults, as the effect of these variables on crime likely changes over the life course (see point 4 below). If certain variables do not affect crime they can be excluded from further analysis and the general theory should be modified accordingly. (It is also possible that research will identify new variables for inclusion in the general theory.)

2. *Factor Analyze All Variables to Determine Whether They Cluster by Life Domain.* Factor analysis is a technique that examines the correlations between variables in order to determine which variables "hang together" (see Kim and Mueller 1978). Variables that hang together are taken as indicators of an underlying factor or construct. For example, we might find that measures of poor parental supervision, negative parental bonding, and harsh discipline hang together, and these measures might be said to reflect the underlying factor of "poor parenting practices."

All of those variables found to have a significant direct effect on crime in step 1 should be factor analyzed, with separate factor analyses being conducted for children, adolescents, and adults. If the general theory is correct, variables should load on factors reflecting the five life domains (i.e., a personality trait factor, family factor, school factor, peer factor, and work factor). It is possible that more than one factor will emerge in a given life domain, particularly if there are multiple measures for certain variables in that domain (e.g., multiple items or scales measuring aspects of parental supervision). In such cases, a second-order factor analysis may be performed to further reduce the data.[1] If there is still more than one factor in a life domain, it may be necessary to subdivide the domain, and the general theory should be modified accordingly.

3. *Combine the Variables Indexing Each Life Domain Into Scales.* Those variables that hang together or load on particular life

domains should be combined into scales, with these scales constituting the measures of the life domains. For example, suppose measures of negative parental bonding, poor parental supervision, harsh discipline, family conflict, the absence of positive parenting, and criminal parents/siblings load on a single "family" factor. These variables should be combined to create a scale measuring "poor parenting practices." Data suggest that combining variables in this manner does not diminish our ability to predict crime, although it may be useful to weight variables by effect size if some variables have a much larger effect on crime than others (see Agnew and White 1992; Wiatrowski et al. 1981).[2] Further, combining variables in this manner allows us to better measure the life domains, because we take account of the major dimensions of each domain and the fact that these dimensions may interact in their effect on crime (as captured in the nonlinear effect of each domain on crime—see Chapter 7). This approach is quite different from that taken in most studies, where researchers only examine one or a few dimensions of each life domain and fail to consider interactions between these dimensions.

4. Examine the Effect of the Life Domain Scales on Crime Across the Life Course. If the general theory is correct, each scale should have a direct effect on crime with the other scales controlled. Further, the relative effect of the life domains on crime should vary across the life course as predicted in Chapter 3. (Irritability/low self-control should have a relatively large effect on crime at all ages. Poor parenting practices should have a large effect during childhood, a small/moderate effect during adolescence, and a small effect during adulthood. No/bad marriages should have a large effect during adulthood. Negative school experiences/ limited education should have a small to moderate effect at all ages. Peer delinquency should have a large effect during adolescence and adulthood and a small to moderate effect during childhood. And unemployment/ bad jobs should have a large effect during adulthood.)

Does the Theory Apply to All Types of Crime, Including White-Collar Crime? The general theory should apply to those crimes that are generally condemned and carry a significant risk of state sanction if detected. Street crimes such as assault, robbery, and burglary clearly fall into this category. The status of white-collar crimes committed by middle- and upper-class individuals is less certain, because many such crimes are weakly condemned and carry little risk of state sanction (facts readily explained by conflict theories; see Cullen and Agnew 2003). Nevertheless, the general theory has some applicability to these "upper-level" white-collar crimes.

It is true that the middle- and upper-class individuals who commit white-collar offenses do not possess many of the causes of crime described in this book. Such individuals are reasonably high in self-control, have good educations, and work in what appear to be "good jobs" (Benson and Moore 1992; Shover and Wright 2001). Nevertheless, the general theory would predict that their crime is at least partly a function of the constraints and motivations described in earlier chapters. While such individuals may possess some level of self-control, they possess beliefs favorable to certain types of white-collar crime and they often have a preference for risky activities. Further, they tend to work in jobs where the likelihood that white-collar crimes will be detected and sanctioned is low. They are often surrounded by coworkers who model, reinforce, and present beliefs favorable to white-collar crime. And while their working conditions are generally good, they often face personal and business strains that create much pressure to engage in white-collar crime. For example, they may work for corporations that face strong competitive pressures to engage in certain types of criminal activities if they are to survive and prosper (for a fuller discussion, see Shover and Wright 2001). So the general theory not only explains "street crimes," but can also shed some light on the origin of white-collar crimes by middle- and upper-class offenders.

5. *(Optional): Analyze the Variables Within Each Scale.* Although not a key part of testing the general theory, researchers might conduct certain analyses with the specific variables in each life-domain scale. While combining these variables into more general scales greatly simplifies the general theory, it does result in the loss of certain information. Most notably, we lose information on the relative effects of the specific variables on one another. For example, it may be the case that association with delinquent peers has a relatively large effect on peer abuse and time spent in unstructured, unsupervised activities with peers. Knowing that certain variables have relatively large effects on others is useful to policy makers, because this information can help them target key variables in prevention and rehabilitation programs.[3]

B. The Variables in Each Domain Increase Crime by Reducing the Constraints Against Crime *and* Increasing the Motivations for Crime

This proposition focuses on the reasons *why* the variables in the life domains increase crime. Such reasons are seldom examined by researchers, although it is important to do so. Examining why variables cause crime not only increases our understanding of crime, but has important policy implications as well (Agnew 1995b; Brezina 1998). We may reduce crime not only by altering the variables that cause it (e.g., reducing poor parenting), but also by altering the mechanisms by which these variables cause crime (e.g., reducing anger).

The general theory is distinguished by its claim that the variables in each life domain affect both the constraints against and the motivations for crime. It is possible to *roughly* test this proposition by constructing measures of the major constraints and motivations and then determining the extent to which these measures mediate the effect of the major variables on crime. This strategy is illustrated in Figure 10-1 and in the work of Agnew (1993; 1995b) and Brezina (1998).

Drawing on Chapter 2 and Agnew (1995b), the constraints against crime might be measured by asking individuals about (1) the likelihood that others—including parents, teachers, and friends—will detect their crime; (2) the likelihood of negative reactions from these others, with such reactions ranging from mild disapproval to severe violence; (3) their own reactions to committing criminal acts, ranging from self-condemnation and negative affect (e.g., guilt, shame) to self-approval and positive affect (e.g., pride, excitement); (4) how much they care about these effects; and (5) how much satisfaction they gain from their conventional life and pursuits. Several studies have already examined certain of these factors, particularly studies on deterrence, rational choice, and social learning theories (see Agnew 1995b; Farrington 1993).

We can measure the motivations for crime partly by asking individuals about the extent to which they experience negative emotions like anger, frustration, and depression. An effort should be made to measure both long-term emotional traits (e.g., chronic anger) and the frequency of short-term emotions (e.g., angry episodes). We can also ask individuals about their ability to cope with

Figure 10-1
The Variables in Each Life Domain Increase Crime by Reducing the
Constraints Against Crime and Increasing the Motivations for Crime

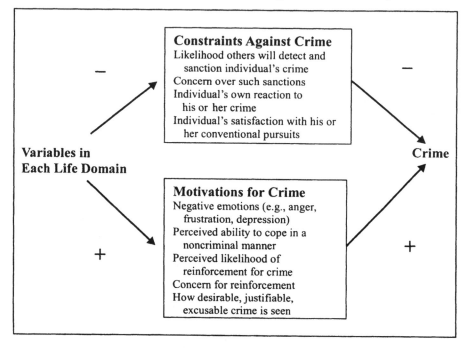

strain and negative emotions in a noncriminal manner. Strain theorists sometimes employ measures in both these areas (e.g., Agnew 1985; Agnew and White 1992; Brezina 1998; Mazerolle and Piquero 1998). Further, we can ask individuals about the likelihood that their crime will result in reinforcements of various types and how much they care about these reinforcements. Finally, we can ask how desirable, justifiable, or excusable crime is in certain situations. Social learning and rational choice theorists sometimes employ measures in these two areas (see Agnew 1995b; Farrington 1993; Teevan and Dryburgh 2000).[4]

Measures of this sort have their problems. Individuals may not be able to provide accurate information in certain of the above areas (see Farrington 1993). As noted in Chapter 2, for example, individuals are sometimes not even conscious of the reinforcements and punishments that affect their behavior. In such cases, it may sometimes be possible to measure constraints and motivations in alternative ways; for example, researchers may observe the reinforcements and punishments that individuals receive or they may manipulate reinforcements and punishments in an experiment. Another problem is that it is sometimes difficult to distinguish the variables that we are examining from the constraints and motivations they allegedly affect. For example, the trait of irritability is said to increase crime partly because it increases the likelihood that individuals will experience negative emotions like anger. Irritability, however, is often measured by asking individuals how often they get angry. The measure of irritability, then, is confounded with one of the motivations for crime. It is possible to minimize this problem with carefully constructed questions, and it may eventually be possible to develop alternative measures of irritability based on physiological measures (i.e., bodily indicators of how one responds to stressors and other stimuli).

It is possible, then, to at least roughly examine the extent to which the key variables in the life domains increase crime by affecting the major constraints against and motivations for crime. If the general theory is correct, most variables should affect several of the constraints *and* motivations listed above. That is why the variables listed in Chapter 3 constitute the leading direct causes of crime: they have far-ranging effects, both reducing the constraints against and increasing the motivations for crime.

C. Each Life Domain Affects the Other Life Domains, Although Some Effects Are Stronger Than Others and Effect Sizes Change Over the Life Course. Each Domain Therefore Has Both a Direct Effect on Crime and an Indirect Effect Through the Other Life Domains

Chapter 4 describes the effects of the life domains on one another, making a distinction between large versus small/moderate effects and noting how effect sizes sometimes change over the life course. The arguments in Chapter 4 are summarized in Figures 4-2 through 4-4, with separate figures for the childhood, adolescent, and adult years. At the most basic level, the general theory predicts that the life domains have reciprocal effects on one another (e.g., poor parenting causes peer delinquency and peer delinquency causes poor parenting).

Testing this proposition requires longitudinal or over-time data. Cross-sectional data or data from one point in time allow us to determine whether the life domains are associated with one another, but do not allow us to determine the reasons for this association. For example, cross-sectional data may reveal that poor parenting and peer delinquency are strongly associated, but these data do not allow us to determine the extent to which this association is due to the effect of poor parenting on peer delinquency, the effect of peer delinquency on poor parenting, or the reciprocal effects of poor parenting and peer delinquency on one another.

Testing this proposition also requires data from the childhood, adolescent, and adult years, as the general theory predicts that effects vary over the life course. For example, poor parenting is said to have a large effect on the other life domains during childhood, but a weak effect during adulthood.

If the theory is correct, the life domains will have reciprocal effects on one another and effect sizes will roughly conform to those described in Chapter 4 and shown in Figures 4-2 through 4-4. As illustrated in Figure 4-2, for example, the effect of poor parenting on negative school experiences should be larger than the effect of school experiences on poor parenting. A few researchers, most notably Thornberry and associates (Thornberry 1996; Thornberry et al. 2003b), have looked at certain reciprocal effects. Evidence for such effects is mixed, but researchers often examine narrowly defined variables (e.g., parental attachment instead of "poor parenting" as defined in this book). I suspect that researchers will be more likely to find reciprocal effects if they examine the more broadly defined variables in the general theory (e.g., poor parenting, negative school experiences, peer delinquency). Such variables better capture the full range of family, school, peer, and work experiences relevant to crime.

D. Prior Crime Has a Direct Effect on Subsequent Crime, and an Indirect Effect Through the Life Domains. These Effects Are Conditioned by the Individual's Standing on the Life Domains: Prior Crime Is Most Likely to Lead to Further Crime When the Individual Is High in Irritability, Low in Self-Control, and in Social Environments Conducive to Crime

Testing this proposition also requires longitudinal data, since we must estimate the effect of prior crime on subsequent crime. Further, we must determine whether crime and the life domains have reciprocal effects on one another (e.g., crime causes poor parenting and poor parenting causes crime). If the general theory is correct, prior crime will have a significant effect on subsequent crime with controls for the life domains. Also, crime will have a significant effect on the life domains (as well as being affected by the life domains).

The effect of crime on the life domains and subsequent crime, however, is said to be conditioned by the individual's standing on the life domains. For example, prior crime is more likely to cause subsequent crime among individuals who are irritable and low in self-control, experience poor parenting, have negative school experiences, and are high in peer delinquency. Aiken and West (1991) provide an excellent discussion of how to test for such interactions. Tests using survey data, however, often fail to detect significant interactions for reasons indicated in McClelland and Judd (1993). There is as of yet no good solution to this problem, although in some cases it may be possible to test for interactions using experimental, quasi-experimental, vignette, and observational data (see the discussion in Agnew 2003b).

E. The Life Domains Interact in Affecting Crime and One Another. A Given Life Domain Is More Likely to Increase Crime or Negatively Affect Another Life Domain When the Remaining Life Domains Are Conducive to Crime

The above comments on testing interactions apply here.

F. The Life Domains Have Nonlinear and Largely Contemporaneous Effects on Crime and One Another, Although Each Life Domain Has a Large Lagged Effect on Itself. Likewise, Crime Has a Nonlinear and Largely Contemporaneous Effect on the Life Domains

Chapter 7 describes the nature of the nonlinear effects that are expected. As the level of each life domain increases, it should have an increasingly larger effect on crime and the other life domains. The same is true of the effect of crime on the life domains. The nonlinear effects, then, should resemble a positive, concave upward curve, as illustrated in Figure 7-5. There are several methods for determining whether the life domains and crime have this type of nonlinear effect. Agnew and Thaxton (2002) describe some of these methods and discuss their advantages and disadvantages.

The effects of the life domains on one another and crime should also be largely contemporaneous in nature. The same is true for the effect of crime on the life domains. Each life domain, however, should have a large lagged effect on itself. Estimating contemporaneous and lagged effects requires longitudinal data, and researchers should give careful thought about how such data are collected. As indicated in Chapter 7, contemporaneous effects are defined as those that occur within a few months' time. Given that longitudinal data are required, researchers might measure the individual's crime and standing on the life domains during the January to June period, and then again during the July to December period. These arguments are illustrated in Figure 10-2.

Figure 10-2
Measuring the Life Domains and Crime Over Time

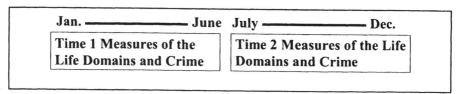

Contemporaneous and then lagged effects can be estimated using the procedures described in Finkel (1995; see Agnew 1991b for examples). If the general theory is correct, the contemporaneous effects should be significantly larger than the lagged effects, although each life domain should have a large lagged effect on itself. However, it is not possible to estimate *both* contemporaneous and lagged effects at the same time with two waves of data. Rather, one must estimate contemporaneous and lagged effects separately, which may bias the estimates that are obtained. Finkel (1995) discusses ways to deal with this problem (also see Agnew 1991b). It is possible to estimate both contemporaneous and lagged effects at the same time with three waves of data, although the data must meet a rather stringent set of conditions (see Greenberg and Kessler 1982; Finkel 1995).

G. Age, Sex, Race/Ethnicity, Parents' SES, and Community SES Affect Standing on the Life Domains, Such That the Life Domains Are More Likely to Be Conducive to Crime Among Adolescents, Males (With the Exception of Work/Unemployment), the Members of Certain Race and Ethnic Groups, Those With Low-SES Parents, and Those Who Live in Low-SES Inner-City Communities

Testing this proposition is relatively straightforward, although certain problems do present themselves (e.g., see Jang 1999 on distinguishing age from cohort effects; also see O'Brien et al. 1999). If the general theory is correct, the sociodemographic characteristics listed above should affect the life domains as indicated. Further, the effect of the sociodemographic characteristics on crime should be largely explained by the life domains, because the life domains are the leading *direct* causes of crime.

Summary

The core propositions of the general theory are for the most part amenable to testing. At present, however, there are few data sets that allow for anything close to a full test. Also, a full test would impose large demands on the data and computational programs, as a large number of effects require estimation, including reciprocal, nonlinear, and interactional effects. Given these facts, the general theory is probably best tested in bits and pieces at this time. Researchers, for example, might test one or a few propositions (or portions of propositions) with data from adolescent samples. Tests of this sort can shed important light on the status of the general theory and contribute to the crime literature more generally.

Notes

1. One might also employ the following strategy if there are a large number of measures for selected variables, like irritability, parental bonding, or bad jobs. First, factor the items in a single life domain, like the self or family or work domains. Use these factor results to create scales measuring the major variables in each domain. Then do a second factor analysis with the scales from all of the life domains. This approach reduces the problems that sometimes result when a large number of items are factor analyzed.

2. Combining variables also reduces the problem of multicollinearity, because highly correlated variables will likely be part of the same domain.

3. Researchers may also want to determine whether the effects of specific variables on crime vary across groups and types of crime. Large differences in effect sizes *may* mean that the life domains have to be defined somewhat differently across groups and/or types of crime. For example, suppose that family conflict has a much larger effect on violent

crime than on property crime. This suggests that the family life domain may have to be defined somewhat differently when explaining violent versus property crime (with more weight being given to family conflict when explaining violent crime). I do not expect this to happen often (e.g., Fleming et al. 2002).

4. These measures of constraint and motivation likely interact in their effect on crime, and researchers may want to create product terms reflecting such interactions (see Aiken and West 1991).

Discussion and Study Questions

1. Describe the major steps in testing the first proposition of the general theory.

2. What does "factor analysis" do?

3. What do I mean when I state that "it may be useful to weight variables by effect size if some variables have a much larger effect on crime than others"?

4. How would the general theory explain white-collar crimes committed by middle- and upper-class individuals?

5. The second proposition of the general theory states that the variables in each life domain increase crime by reducing the constraints against *and* increasing the motivations for crime. Develop a short questionnaire with questions that measure the leading constraints against and motivations for crime.

6. Describe how we might examine the effect of a cause of crime on one of the constraints/motivations by doing an experiment, an observational study, or a "vignette" study (a study where you describe certain situations to people and ask how they might react).

7. Why are longitudinal or over-time data required to test many of the propositions in the general theory?

8. Describe at least one empirical finding or test result that would challenge or refute each proposition of the general theory (e.g., finding that adolescents do *not* score higher on the life domains would challenge the seventh proposition of the general theory). ✦

Chapter 11

Recommendations for Controlling Crime

This chapter draws on the general theory to make recommendations for controlling crime. I begin by evaluating what is now the dominant method of controlling crime: arresting and officially sanctioning offenders, often by placing them in prison. I argue that this strategy has a limited impact on crime, largely because it fails to address the causes of crime and often makes them worse. I then offer suggestions for improving this strategy. Finally, I discuss an alternative strategy for controlling crime, one that relies on rehabilitation and prevention programs that address the causes of crime embodied in the life domains. Brief descriptions of these programs are provided and I draw on the general theory to offer some guidelines for their effective use.

Arrest and Official Sanction

The major strategy for controlling crime and delinquency in the United States right now involves "getting tough" with offenders—that is, increasing the likelihood that they will be punished and increasing the severity of their punishment. This strategy has been implemented by putting more police on the street, improving the ability of the police to detect crime through new policing strategies, increasing the likelihood that the police will make arrests when they catch suspected offenders (at least in some jurisdictions), and increasing the severity of the sanctions administered to convicted offenders (see Blumstein 2002; Cullen 1995; Sherman 2002). The increasing severity of sanctions is illustrated by the "three strikes and you're out" laws passed in most states. These laws impose severe penalties—often life imprisonment—on offenders upon their third conviction for certain crimes. The increasing severity is also illustrated by the recent wave of state laws making it easier to try certain juvenile offenders in adult criminal court, where they are subject to more severe penalties.

As a result of all these changes, rates of imprisonment in the United States have increased about fivefold since the early 1970s (Blumstein 2002). Over 1,400,000 people are now in state and federal prison, with over 600,000 in jail (awaiting trial or serving sentences of less than one year) (Bureau of Justice Statistics 2003, see http://www.ojp.usdoj.gov/bjs/), and the United States now has the highest rate of imprisonment in the world. There has also been a dramatic increase in the number of offenders being supervised in the community. Many of these offenders are subject to a range of new "intermediate" sanctions, designed to provide more control and punishment than regular probation, but less than imprisonment. These sanctions include electronic home confinement and brief stays in boot camps. This increased use of sanctions has had an especially large impact on certain segments of the population, with more than one out of every three young African-American men under the supervision of the criminal justice system (in prison or jail, or on probation or parole).

This get-tough movement is partly designed to deter individuals from offending, including both those who are punished and those in the general population. Punished individuals should become more fearful of committing crime as a result of their punishment, and those in the general population should become more fearful of committing crime as they see that the certainty and severity of punishment have increased. This movement is also designed to control crime by locking up or "incapacitating" offenders so they cannot commit crimes on the street. Whether incapacitated offenders are fearful of further punishment is immaterial, because they cannot commit crimes against the general public as long as they are behind bars (although most are eventually released). Arrest and official sanction, then, represent a particular type of external control: external control by the state. Legislatures make rules that prohibit crime, the police monitor behavior, and the courts sanction rule violations. But how effective is this strategy?

How Effective is the 'Get Tough' Approach to Controlling Crime?

The Deterrent Effect of Arrest and Sanction on Those Who Are Punished

Does arresting and sanctioning individuals deter them from committing further crime? A number of studies have been done in this area. Most try to determine if offenders who receive *more severe* sanctions are less likely to reoffend than comparable offenders who receive *less severe* sanctions. For example, are individuals who serve long prison sentences less likely to reoffend than those who serve short sentences? A few studies try to determine if offenders who have been punished in some manner are less likely to reoffend than comparable offenders who have *not* been punished. When we examine the studies in these areas, we find that some suggest that punishment (or more severe punishment) does reduce offending, but most suggest that punishment does not reduce offending and may sometimes increase it (e.g., Andrews and Bonta 2003; Cullen and Gendreau 2000; Farrington 1995; Huizinga et al. 2003; Sampson and Laub 1993; Sherman et al. 2002; Smith and Gartin 1989). There are three major reasons why arrest and sanction generally do not reduce crime among punished individuals.

First, arrest and official sanction usually do not meet the criteria for effective external control described in Chapter 2. Arrest and sanction are inconsistently applied; in fact, the vast majority of delinquent and criminal acts do not result in arrest or official sanction. Elliott (1995), for example, estimates that only about two out of every 100 serious violent acts committed by juveniles result in arrest. Further, the arrest and sanctioning process is often experienced as unfair and overly harsh. Police officers sometimes discriminate and are frequently quite gruff when dealing with suspected offenders. The same is true of the court system, and certain sanctions—like jail and imprisonment—are quite brutal. When Decker and Van Winkle (1996, 205) asked a gang member how his gang got along with the police, the gang member replied "I hate the motherfuckers. They be fucking with us, shaking us down all the time and shit. . . ." Based on his study of gang members, Padilla (1992, 90) states that: "Youngsters come to believe that, as long as the police are protected by their status as officials, a system of harassment and dehumanization will persist. And, of course, the deep frustrations youngsters experience in their encounters with police involve much more than physical fear, lost time, and inconvenience; they are damaging to their human integrity." Rather than functioning as a type of external control, arrest and official sanction more often function as sources of strain (see especially Sherman 1993).

Second, arrest and official sanction do little to address the other causes of crime. Arrest and sanction constitute *one type* of external control. There are other types of *external* control, including control by family members, friends, school officials, and employers. There are other types of control besides external control, including stake in conformity and internal control, and there are a range of motivations for crime. Arrest and sanction sometimes affect these other causes in positive ways; for example, arrest may prompt parents to increase the level of external control they exercise. Overall, however, arrest and sanction generally do little to address these other causes—and so the effect of arrest and sanction on crime is limited.

Third, arrest and official sanction sometimes impact these other causes in ways that increase the likelihood of further crime. Arrest and sanction often increase irritability. In particular, experiences with the police, courts, and prisons are said to leave many offenders angry and bitter (see Sherman 1993; 2000). Arrest and sanction often disrupt relations with parents and break up or prevent marriages (Stewart et al. 2000; 2002b). Arrest and sanction often interrupt schooling (De Li 1999; Tanner et al. 1999). Arrest and sanction often increase the likelihood of association with criminal peers. In particular, incarcerated offenders are isolated from conventional others and confined with other criminals, and offenders in the larger community often find that conventional others are reluctant to associate with them, so they associate with other criminals. Finally, arrest and sanction often make it difficult for individuals to keep or obtain decent jobs (Fagan and Freeman 1999; De Li 1999; Sampson and Laub 1993; 1997; Tanner et al. 1999). These effects are described in some detail by labeling theorists (see Cullen and Agnew 2003, Part VIII; Sampson and Laub 1997).

But the Effect of Arrest and Official Sanction Depends on the Nature of the Arrest and Sanctioning Process and the Reaction It Calls Forth From Others. While arrest and official sanction *usually* fail to deter punished offenders from further crime, arrest and sanction *sometimes* have a deterrent effect. This occurs when the certainty of arrest and sanction is perceived as high, when arrest and sanction are administered in a just manner and are not overly harsh, and when arrest and sanction do not lead to rejection and harsh treatment by others, like family members, school officials, peers, and employers. Whether arrest and sanction have these characteristics is partly a function of the individual's standing on the life domains and prior level of crime (at the time of arrest and sanction).

Take individuals who are (a) low in irritability, (b) high in self-control, (c) in social environments opposed to crime, and (d) low in prior crime. These individuals are more likely to be sanctioned in ways that deter further crime. In particular, they are more likely to believe that the certainty of punishment is high, partly because they have little prior experience with crime. They are more likely to be treated in a fair manner by the police and other sanctioning agents, because they do not fit the stereotype of a "criminal" and they have the resources to resist negative treatment. They are also less likely to be rejected and treated harshly by others as a result of their arrest and sanction. Again, they do not fit the criminal stereotype and they have the resources to resist negative treatment. Further, they have close ties to others like family members, and these others tend to treat them in a more positive manner as a result.

However, the opposite is true of individuals who are (a) irritable, (b) low in self-control, (c) in social environments conducive to crime, and (d) high in prior crime. Such individuals are more likely to believe that the certainty of punishment is low (partly because they have "gotten away with" or seen others get away with crime in the past). They are more likely to be treated in an unfair and harsh manner by the police and other sanctioning agents, and they are more likely to be rejected and treated harshly by others (or subject to the other reactions that increase crime, like the "failure to respond to the crime" and the "approving/supportive of the crime" responses described in Chapter 5). As a consequence, arrest and sanction are more likely to lead to further crime among such individuals.[1] Some data provide support for this prediction, suggesting that arrest and sanction are more likely to increase crime among individuals who are low in self-control or have low stakes in conformity (see Nagin and Paternoster 1993; Nagin and Pogarsky 2001; Piquero and Pogarsky 2002; Piquero and Tibbetts 2002; Sherman 2000; Sherman et al. 1992).[2]

Summary. Arrest and sanction usually do not deter crime among those who are punished. However, the effect of arrest and sanction on crime depends on the nature of the arrest and sanctioning process. Arrest and sanction lead to further crime when the perceived likelihood of arrest is low, the arrest and sanctioning process is unfair and overly harsh, and arrest and sanction call forth negative reactions from others. Arrest and sanction are most likely to have these characteristics when individuals are irritable, low in self-control, in social environments conducive to crime, and high in prior crime. Arrest and sanction, however, may be applied in a more effective manner (high certainty of arrest and sanction, applied in a fair manner and not overly harsh, applied in a way that does not call forth negative reactions from others). When this occurs, arrest and official sanction should deter further crime.

The Deterrent Effect of Arrest and Sanction Among Those in the General Population

While arrest and sanction generally do not reduce levels of offending *among those who are punished,* they do reduce levels of offending by a small to moderate amount *among those in the general population*—most of whom have not personally experienced punishment (Agnew 2005; Nagin 1998). In particular, increases in the certainty or likelihood of punishment lead to small to moderate reductions in crime among the general public. Increases in the severity of punishment have less effect, although some studies suggest that increases in severity reduce crime if the certainty of punishment is high (i.e., threatening people with severe punishments reduces crime *if* the likelihood of punishment is high).

It may seem odd that arrest and sanction do not reduce offending among most punished individuals, but do reduce offending in the general population. Part of the reason for this is that most people in the general population do not experience the negative effects of arrest and sanction described above (because they do not experience arrest and sanction). So increasing the certainty of punishment (and possibly the severity, if certainty is high) leads to a small to moderate reduction in crime among those in the general population. It does not lead to a large reduction in crime, because threatening individuals with official sanction does little to address all of the other causes of crime.

The 'Incapacitation Effect'

While arrest and sanction may not deter punished offenders from committing crime, there is little doubt that incapacitating or "locking up" offenders prevents them from committing crimes on the street. There is some uncertainty, however, over how much crime it prevents. Initial estimates of the incapacitation effect appear to have been exaggerated, because they failed to take account of such things as the fact that some incarcerated offenders are replaced by other criminals (e.g., imprisoned drug sellers are replaced by other drug sellers). The most recent and best estimates suggest that locking up offenders reduces crime by a moderate amount. For example, it is estimated that California's fourfold increase in the number of prisoners during the 1980s reduced the number of offenses that otherwise would have been committed by about 15 percent (Zimring and Hawkins 1995; also see Blumstein and Wallman 2000). Further, this strategy carries heavy financial and social costs (Visher 2000).

How to Make Arrest and Official Sanction More Effective

Drawing on the above discussion, there are several things we can do to increase the effectiveness of arrest and official sanction. First, we should increase the certainty of arrest and official sanction so as to make it a more effective form of external control. New methods of policing have been developed to do just that. Certain of these methods involve improving the ties between the police and community residents and better involving community residents in crime-control activities like surveillance efforts. Such efforts increase the likelihood that residents will report crimes to police and otherwise assist them (Greene 2000). Certain other methods involve focusing police resources on those places where crime is most likely to occur and on those individuals most likely to engage in crime. A large share of all crime occurs in a small number of places or "hot spots." In particular, over half of all crimes occur at less than 3 percent of the addresses in a city, with these crimes being most likely during certain days of the week and times of the day. New methods of computer tracking are able to identify these hot spots on an ongoing basis. Further, most serious crimes are committed by a small group of high-rate offenders, and it is possible to identify many of these offenders. Focusing police resources on these hot spots and offenders is one way to increase the probability that crimes will be sanctioned, and strategies like the increased patrol of hot spots and the increased monitoring of high-rate offenders have been shown to reduce the level of crime (Sherman 2002; Sherman and Eck 2002).

Second, we should change police practices, court procedures, and the nature of sanctions so they do not generate as much strain. This involves creating closer ties between the police and community residents, increasing the responsiveness of the police to community concerns, and having the police treat suspected offenders in a more polite or respectful manner. Limited data suggest that such changes—which are part of the "community policing" movement— may contribute to lower levels of crime (Greene 2000; Paternoster et al. 1997; Sherman 2000; 2002; Sherman and Eck 2002). It also involves changing how offenders are processed by the court system. This can be accomplished through those practices that are part of the "restorative justice" approach, which is reshaping the justice systems in certain states and countries (Bazemore 2000; Braithwaite 2002). Under this approach, there is a "conference" or meeting involving the offender, victim, family members of the offender and victim, and selected community residents. The offender learns firsthand of the harm that he or she has caused. And everyone—including the offender—develops a plan to repair that harm, often through restitution to the victim and community service. The involvement of the offender in this process is critical, for it increases the likelihood that the offender will view the process as fair or just, thus reducing strain. It also increases the likelihood that the sanctions will be seen as appropriate, especially because they focus on repairing the harm done by the offender.

Further, the strain created by the criminal justice system can be minimized by reducing the use of imprisonment, since much data suggest that prisons are inherently brutal institutions (see Colvin 2000). Rather than imprisonment, we should place offenders who do not pose a high risk to others in community programs. Reducing the use of imprisonment means that we may not prevent as much crime through incapacitation, but this effect should be minimal if we reserve community programs for lower-risk offenders and take care to properly supervise these offenders. Finally, strain can be minimized by making prisons less coercive for those offenders who must be confined (see Colvin 2000, 169–172).

Third, we should minimize the negative effects of arrest and official sanction on the life domains. In countries like the United States, offenders are often incarcerated for long periods, where they are isolated from conventional others and forced to associate with other criminals. And offenders are usually not forgiven for their crimes when their punishment is complete; rather, they are viewed and treated as criminals for much of their lives. Family members and conventional others in the community do not want to associate with them, employers refuse to hire them, and only other criminals are willing to associate with them. As a consequence, they experience the family, school, peer, and work problems noted above. Once again, the restorative approach provides some suggestions for minimizing these negative effects. In particular, this approach seeks to minimize the stigma and rejection that often result from arrest and punishment.

Victims, family members, and community residents are encouraged to forgive the offender after he or she has repaired the harm caused by the crime, and are urged to help restore the offender's ties to the community. For example, efforts may be made to secure legitimate work for the offender, and the offender may eventually become involved in crime-control programs in the community, like mentoring programs. Studies on the effectiveness of this approach are encouraging (Andrews and Bonta 2003; Braithwaite 2002; Sherman et al. 2000). That is not to say that the restorative justice approach can work for all offenders; some very serious offenders need to be confined, with their confinement preventing much crime. But the approach, or elements of it, can reduce the negative consequences of crime for large numbers of offenders.

Fourth, we should better address the other factors that cause individuals to engage in crime. The restorative justice approach does this to some extent. It strengthens the bonds between offenders and conventional others; it makes offenders more aware of the harm they have caused, which may increase their empathy for others and challenge their beliefs favorable to crime; and it sometimes addresses other problems of offenders, like difficulty obtaining legitimate work. But more emphasis needs to be placed on rehabilitation or treatment programs that target those causes of crime embodied in the life domains. We also need to make greater use of prevention programs, which address these causes before they result in crime. Such changes are critical because arrest and sanction—if carried out in an effective manner—only increase one type of external control. They do not address all of the other causes of crime and, as such, their ability to control crime is limited. The types of rehabilitation and prevention programs that can reduce crime are described next.

Rehabilitation and Prevention Programs

The best way to control crime is to address the direct causes of crime embodied in the five life domains. That is, reduce irritability/ low self-control, improve parenting practices and marital relations, improve school experiences, reduce peer delinquency, and help people obtain decent jobs. Doing these things should help rehabilitate offenders so that they are less likely to engage in further crime, and it should help prevent crime, so that individuals are less likely to become offenders in the first place. A variety of programs have been developed to address the direct causes of crime, and data suggest that the best of these programs can substantially reduce levels of offending (Cullen 2002; Cullen and Gendreau 2000). I provide brief descriptions of these programs below and then conclude the chapter by offering some guidelines for their use (the descriptions and guidelines that follow draw heavily from Agnew 2005; Andrews and Bonta 2003; Catalano et al. 1998; Colvin 2000; Cullen 2002; Cullen and Gendreau 2000; Gottfredson 2001; Howell 2003; Sherman et al. 2002; Thornton et al. 2002; Tolan 2002; U.S. Department of Health and Human Services 2001; Wasserman and Miller 1998).

Programs Addressing the Causes of Crime Embodied in the Life Domains

A large number of programs try to address the individual, family, school, peer, and work problems that contribute to crime. Rather than describing specific programs, I list what I see as the essential features of the more effective programs in each area. But before describing these features, I should note that the most effective programs tend to share certain features in common. Most notably, they are intensive in nature. You do not change someone's personality traits or parenting practices by giving them a pamphlet to read or making a speech. It takes great effort to alter the causes, and the most effective programs usually last for months or years and employ a variety of strategies. For example, parents may be taught how to employ better parenting techniques through the following strategies: parents are told about good parenting techniques; they are given reading materials on these techniques; they are exposed to role-playing situations where instructors demonstrate these techniques; parents engage in role-playing situations where they are asked to demonstrate these techniques, and they receive feedback and reinforcement when appropriate; parents apply these techniques to real-life problems, again receiving feedback and reinforcement when appropriate; parents are periodically visited to check on their progress; and parents occasionally take refresher courses. Poor parenting, however, is not simply a matter of a lack of knowledge, and so an effort may also be made to address the other factors that contribute to poor parenting, like housing problems, work problems, and family violence.

Programs Focusing on Irritability/Low Self-Control. Certain programs target the specific traits that comprise irritability and low self-control. These include anger-management programs and programs that teach social and problem-solving skills. These programs are sometimes offered to offenders, sometimes to "at-risk" juveniles—like those nominated by teachers—and sometimes to broader groups. Anger-management programs try to help individuals better understand the causes and negative consequences of their anger. Individuals are then taught to recognize the early warning signs of their anger (e.g., tensed muscles, negative thoughts) and to better control their anger. Individuals may experiment with a range of anger-control techniques, like counting backwards, imaging peaceful scenes, and deep breathing.

Social-skills training teaches individuals the skills necessary to effectively and peacefully interact with others, including basic social skills (e.g., maintaining eye contact when talking to others) and more advanced skills (e.g., recognizing and showing sensitivity to the feelings of others). Individuals are also taught how to deal with certain problems in a noncriminal manner, including problems like teasing by peers and being stopped and questioned by the police. Problem-solving training provides more general instruction in problem-solving techniques. Such techniques typically include pausing before you act, analyzing the situation, thinking of possible responses to the problem, and considering the likely consequences of these responses. Problem-solving training, then, strongly discourages impulsive behavior. Taken together, anger-management, social-skills, and problem-solving training address most of the specific traits that fall under irritability and low self-control.

Still other programs address the major causes of irritability and low self-control. Some programs attempt to alter parenting practices in ways that reduce irritability and increase self-control, with these programs being described below. Others attempt to reduce the likelihood of experiencing those "biological harms" that contribute to irritability and low self-control. Such harms include the mother's poor health habits during pregnancy, birth complications, exposure to toxic substances like lead, and head injuries. Certain of these programs begin before the birth of the child. They often target pregnant women who are at risk for experiencing problems with their pregnancy; for example, they might target teenagers or poor women without health insurance. These programs provide medical care to the pregnant women and discourage alcohol and drug use during pregnancy. Many programs also provide medical care to the children of these women after they give birth. Further, parents may be provided with health and safety training so they can better care for their children, and a nurse, social worker or other trained person may visit the family on a regular basis, to monitor conditions, offer advice, and provide assistance in dealing with a range of problems, like housing, financial, and medical problems. This home visitor makes an effort to establish a close relationship with the family, functioning as a friend or ally (rather than as an "outsider" who "talks down" to them).

Programs That Address Poor Parenting Practices. Parent training programs are sometimes offered to the families of delinquents; to families that are at high risk for poor parenting, like teenage parents; and to broader groups. Such programs typically teach parents how to better supervise and discipline their children; that is, how to set clear rules, properly monitor behavior, and consistently sanction rule violations in a meaningful, but not overly harsh manner. Older children are often given a role in developing disciplinary programs; for example, they may work with parents and a counselor to develop rules about how they should behave (e.g., how late they should stay out) and decide on the punishments for rule violations. Such programs also try to increase the bonds between parents and children. Parents are encouraged to make greater use of praise and other positive reinforcers and to engage in pleasurable activities with their children, and family members are taught how to resolve conflicts in a peaceful manner. Further, such programs often try to address additional causes of poor parenting. For example, efforts may be made to reduce parental stressors like housing and childcare problems and to teach parents to better cope with those stressors that cannot be eliminated. Similar programs have been developed to help adults improve the quality of their marriages (Wesley and Waring 1996).

Programs That Address Negative School Experiences. Programs designed to improve school experiences often begin before the child has entered school. Preschool enrichment programs, like Project Headstart, better prepare children for school and thereby improve their academic performance and other school experiences. Such programs focus on children in disadvantaged areas and attempt to equip them with the knowledge, skills, and attitudes necessary to do well in school. They also encourage parents to become more involved in their child's schoolwork. A range of in-school programs also attempt to reduce negative school experiences. Some programs provide students who are having problems with tutoring or other services. Others help teachers better manage their classrooms and more effectively instruct their students. Teachers, in particular, are taught how to clearly state rules for classroom behavior, monitor behavior, reinforce rule compliance, effectively sanction rule violations, and minimize the impact of disruptive behavior. They also learn innovative instructional techniques, like the use of cooperative learning groups in which small groups of students help one another master class materials. Still other programs attempt to alter the entire school environment in ways that improve academic performance, increase bonding to school, and improve discipline.

Programs That Address Peer Delinquency. Some programs try to break up or change the nature of delinquent peer groups and gangs, although such programs have not been very successful. Other programs try to discourage juveniles from joining gangs or delinquent peer groups and to equip them with the skills to resist negative peer influences; such programs have been more successful. These programs often focus on the negative consequences of gang membership, describe how gangs try to recruit members, and discuss methods of resisting recruitment efforts. Former gang members may be involved in such programs, because they have better rapport with juveniles. Still other programs try to reduce peer abuse, with anti-bullying programs in the school system showing much success. These programs try to make teachers and parents more aware of the extent and negative consequences of bullying. School officials then establish clear rules against bullying, better monitor student behavior, consistently sanction bullying in an appropriate manner, and support and protect victims. Finally, certain programs try to reduce the likelihood that juveniles spend unsupervised, unstructured time together. After-school recreational programs are the best example. Carefully constructed programs that make an effort to aggressively recruit and retain youth have shown some success at reducing delinquency.

Programs That Address Work Problems. A number of programs try to provide offenders and others, like school dropouts, with the educational and job skills they need to obtain better employment. Job Corps is one example of such a program. The most successful programs not only teach jobs skills but also try to deal with the other problems that individuals might be facing, like drug problems (see Cullen 2002; Currie 1998).

Some General Guidelines for Rehabilitation and Treatment Programs

The types of programs listed above have shown some success at reducing crime, but it is possible to enhance that success by following the guidelines below.

Focus on Individuals Who Score Very High on One or More of the Life Domains. Treatment and prevention programs should focus on individuals with serious problems in one or more of the life domains, because they are the most likely to offend (recall that the domains may have a nonlinear effect on crime). The greatest amount of crime can therefore be prevented by focusing on such individuals. Further, such individuals are often easy to identify because they frequently stand out to school, social welfare, and criminal justice officials. Focusing on individuals who do not have problems in the life domains will not prevent much crime, as these individuals are unlikely to offend regardless of whether they participate in treatment or prevention programs. Data tend to support this argument, suggesting that the most effective programs are those which focus on individuals at high risk for offending (Andrews and Bonta 2003; Cullen and Gendreau 2000).

Target Most or All of the Life Domains if Necessary. Programs should screen offenders and at-risk individuals to determine their standing on the life domains and then target all or most of those domains where problems are evident. (Some consideration should be given to the age of the offender when targeting the life domains, as the effect of the domains on crime varies somewhat over the life course.) It is important to target all or most of the "problematic" life domains because the domains mutually reinforce one another. Therefore, altering one domain without targeting the others will be difficult. For example, altering peer delinquency without targeting irritability/low self-control, poor parenting practices, and negative school experiences will be difficult, because these latter factors play a major role in maintaining peer delinquency. Targeting several domains, however, greatly increases the likelihood of reducing crime, as improvements in one domain contribute to improvements in the others. Further, the domains interact with one another in their effect on crime, so improvements in one domain reduce the effect of the others. Data support these arguments, suggesting that the most effective programs are those which target multiple causes of crime (Tolan 2002).

Emphasize Prevention Programs That Begin Early in Life. Many programs target older juveniles and adults who are already deeply embedded in the "web of crime." Such programs are important and can do much to reduce crime. But it makes even more sense to identify and treat such individuals before they become enmeshed in the web of crime. For example, efforts can be made to identify young children who show signs of irritability/low self-control or who are in troubled families. Treating such children will prevent much crime and it should be easier to treat such children before their traits and family problems lead to school, peer, and work problems. Limited data support this argument, suggesting that it is easier to prevent further crime when interventions begin at an early age (Agnew 2005).

Address the Larger Causes of Crime. As indicated in Chapter 8, the individual's standing on the life domains is influenced by certain biological factors and features of the larger social environment. Programs will be more effective to the extent that they target these factors. As noted above, certain programs try to prevent those biological harms that contribute to irritability/low self-control. Likewise, certain programs try to alleviate those parental stressors that contribute to poor parenting and alter those school characteristics that contribute to negative school experiences. At the most general level, programs should target certain of the sociodemographic characteristics listed in Chapter 8, because these characteristics often have a large effect on all of the life domains.

In this area, certain programs help individuals raise their SES, such as welfare programs, job training programs, job creation programs like those that provide work in the public sector, and laws that require all jobs to pay a "living wage." Other programs reduce the negative consequences of low SES by creating a range of social support programs for families and children, including health care, housing assistance, child care, and food assistance. Still other programs try to increase the SES of communities; for example, they attempt to attract businesses to poor communities through a variety of economic incentives or they attempt to attract higher-SES individuals to poor communities through the construction of working and middle-class housing (see Colvin 2000; Currie 1998). Some criminologists, however, argue that meaningful change in these areas will not occur unless we make fundamental changes in the nature of our economic system (e.g., see Part IX in Cullen and Agnew 2003; Currie 1998; Messner and Rosenfeld 2001).

We cannot alter the individual's race/ethnicity, age, or sex. However, we can influence some of the reasons why race/ethnicity, age, and sex impact crime. For example, we might alter the effect of race/ethnicity on crime by making more of an effort to address the effects of current and past discrimination so as to reduce the association between race/ethnicity and SES. We might alter the effect of age on crime by teaching parents and school officials to better supervise adolescents. Further, adolescents can be given more assistance in meeting the increased academic and social demands they face (e.g., tutoring, improved methods of instruction, social skills training; see Agnew 2003a for a fuller discussion). We might alter the effect of sex on crime by attempting to influence sex differences in socialization and social position; for example, we might teach parents to better supervise their male children and train them to be less aggressive.

Conclusion

In sum, the best way to reduce crime is to address the causes of crime embodied in the life domains. Current efforts to control crime through arrest and sanction have little impact on the direct causes of crime and sometimes make them worse. As such, the effect of such efforts on crime is limited. The effectiveness of arrest and sanction, however, may be increased by increasing the certainty of arrest and sanction, reducing the strain associated with arrest and sanction, and minimizing the other negative effects associated with arrest and sanction. With these changes, arrest and sanction may come to function as a moderately effective form of external control. Much more emphasis, however, should be placed on targeting the life domains. A range of rehabilitation and prevention programs have shown some success at improving the individual's standing on the life domains, and thereby reducing crime. The most effective prevention and rehabilitation programs are intensive, target individuals who have serious problems in one or more of the life domains, attempt to alter all or most of those life domains contributing to crime, begin early in life, and address those biological factors and larger social forces that impact the life domains—as well as directly targeting the life domains.

Notes

1. These arguments draw heavily on Sherman (2000), and they parallel the discussion of the effect of prior crime on subsequent crime in Chapter 5, with prior crime being most likely to increase subsequent crime among individuals who are irritable, low in self-control, and in social environments conducive to crime.

2. As indicated, individuals who are irritable, low in self-control, in social environments conducive to crime, and high in prior crime are more likely to be officially sanctioned in ways that increase subsequent crime. But let us suppose that such individuals are subject to effective sanctions—sanctions that are consistently applied, are fair and not overly harsh, and do not call forth negative reactions from others. How would such individuals respond? Recall the "general principle" for interactions presented in Chapter 6. It states that a "crime stopper" is more likely to reduce crime among those who are irritable, low in self-control, and in social environments conducive to crime. In accord with this principle, I predict that *effective sanctions* will have a larger negative effect on crime among such individuals (versus individuals who are low in irritability, high in self-control, in environments opposed to crime, and low in prior crime). It is true that individuals who are irritable, low in self-control, etc. are harder to deter. They give little thought to the possibility of sanctions when engaging in crime, given their low self-control. They are often angered by the sanctions they experience, given their irritability. They have less to lose through arrest

and sanction, given their low stake in conformity. And they are sometimes under great pressure to engage in crime; for example, they have a desperate need for money or face strong pressure from peers to engage in crime. Certain deterrence and rational choice theorists make these same points (see Nagin and Paternoster 1993; Nagin and Pogarsky 2001; Piquero and Pogarsky 2002; Piquero and Tibbetts 2002; Sherman 1993; Sherman et al. 1992). Nevertheless, I believe that the "general principle" is still correct. While such individuals may be harder to deter, I predict that the application of *effective external controls* will have a greater negative effect on their subsequent crime. I make this prediction because such individuals are much more likely to engage in crime than those who are low in irritability, high in self-control, and in social environments opposed to crime. These latter individuals are unlikely to engage in subsequent crime, regardless of whether they are sanctioned (see Wright et al. 2001). Therefore, the application of external controls (and other "crime stoppers") should have less of an effect on them. More research, however, is needed in this critically important area (see Agnew 2003b for further discussion of this issue). One possibility, suggested by several deterrence theorists, is that arrest/sanction may interact with the causes of crime in a *nonlinear* manner. Sanctions may have little effect on individuals who are at *very high* risk for crime, as these individuals are impulsive, have little to lose from crime, have much to gain, and are under much pressure to engage in crime. Sanctions may have a relatively large effect on crime among individuals at *moderate* risk for crime, because they are somewhat more thoughtful, have something to lose from crime, etc. And sanctions may have little effect on individuals at *low risk* for crime, as they are unlikely to reoffend regardless of whether they are sanctioned or not.

Discussion and Study Questions

1. Describe recent efforts to "get tough" on crime (i.e., efforts to increase the certainty and/or severity of punishment).

2. How do I explain the fact that arrest and sanction do little to reduce offending *among those who are punished*?

3. I argue that the effect of arrest and sanction on crime depends on the nature of the arrest and sanctioning process. Describe my arguments in this area, being sure to note when arrest and sanction are most likely to deter crime and when they are most likely to increase crime.

4. I argue that the arrest and sanctioning process is least likely to deter crime among those who are irritable, low in self-control, in environments conducive to crime, and high in prior crime. Why?

5. Suppose an effective system of arrest and sanctioning were developed (high in certainty, administered in a fair manner, not overly harsh, and unlikely to call forth negative reactions from others). Do you think this system would prevent more crime among those high in irritability, low in self-control, in environments conducive to crime, and high in prior crime, or among those low in irritability, high in self-control, in environments opposed to crime, and low in prior crime? (Remember the "general principle" for interactions stated in Chapter 6 and see Note 2 in this chapter.)

6. Describe the effect of arrest and sanction on people in the general population.

7. What is meant by an "incapacitation effect"?

8. What should we do to improve the effectiveness of the arrest and sanctioning system? (Be sure to describe changes in policing, the court system, and the use of imprisonment.)

9. Why do I argue that even if we increase the effectiveness of arrest and sanction, they will still have a *limited* effect on crime?

10. How does prevention differ from rehabilitation?

11. Describe a prevention/rehabilitation program designed to improve the individual's standing on one of the life domains.

12. What general guidelines should be followed if we want to maximize the effectiveness of prevention and rehabilitation programs?

13. How would you respond if someone asked the following question: "what do you think we should do to reduce crime and delinquency"? ✦

Chapter 12

The General Theory as an Integrated Theory of Crime

This brief chapter describes how the general theory integrates previous theories and research on crime. In doing so, it presents a final summary of the theory and discusses the ways in which the theory differs from other integrated theories.

Considers a Broad Range of Variables

The general theory includes the leading direct causes of crime identified in most of the major crime theories and research. At the most general level, the theory includes a range of variables that measure both the constraints against and the motivations for crime, including both long-lasting and situational constraints and motivations. Certain of these variables refer to the individual's personality traits while others refer to the individual's social environment, including family, school, peer, and work environments. At a more specific level, the theory includes most of the major variables associated with the leading crime theories, including social control, self-control, social learning, strain, social support, and labeling theories. Further, the theory includes all of the variables found to have a meaningful direct effect on individual offending. It also includes several additional variables that may have meaningful effects but have not yet been the subject of much research. Such variables include "positive parenting" and "positive teaching," spouse/partner supervision and support, teacher supervision/discipline, peer conflict/abuse, and several of the work variables (see Chapter 3 for fuller descriptions).

The general theory is distinguished from other integrated theories by the broad range of variables it considers. Most integrated theories, for example, fail to include personality traits like irritability and low self-control (e.g., Elliott et al. 1979; 1985; Johnson 1979; Thornberry 1987—although see Thornberry and Krohn 2001). This is a major shortcoming because recent research suggests that such traits have a relatively large effect on crime and that they condition the effect of social variables on crime (e.g., Agnew et al. 2002; Wright et al. 2001). Likewise, most integrated theories fail to consider other key variables that may have important effects on crime, including measures of social support and types of strain like peer abuse (see Agnew 2005; Cullen 1994). I do not mean to criticize the authors of these integrated theories: They developed their theories before we became aware of the importance of these variables. The general theory of crime builds on their theories by taking account of recent developments in criminology.

Considers a Broad Range of Intervening Mechanisms

The general theory argues that the above variables affect crime for reasons related to all of the leading theories. In particular, these variables increase the likelihood of crime because they reduce one or more types of control, increase strain, and foster the social learning of crime. This argument is at odds with the position taken by most criminologists, who assume that each theory "owns" a particular set of variables that affect crime for reasons related to that theory. They assume, for example, that social learning theory owns the variable of "delinquent peer association" and that this variable affects crime through its effect on reinforcements, modeling, and beliefs. The general theory, however, argues that this variable also increases strain and reduces control, particularly the awareness of and concern for external sanctions. So the general theory not only incorporates all of the variables commonly associated with the leading crime theories, but also incorporates all of the intervening mechanisms associated with these theories, arguing that each variable affects crime through all or most of these intervening mechanisms. An integrated theory, however, is more than a collection of variables and intervening mechanisms. An integrated theory also describes the relationships among variables.

Groups the Specific Causes of Crime
Into Clusters Organized by Life Domain

The general theory argues that the specific variables that cause crime can be grouped into five clusters organized by life domain: self (irritability/low self-control), family (poor parenting practices, no/bad marriages), school (negative school experiences, limited education), peers (peer delinquency), and work (unemployment/bad jobs). A strategy for constructing each cluster is presented in Chapter 10. It is predicted that the following variables will fall into each cluster, although subsequent research may result in some modification of these variables.

Irritability/Low Self-Control: Easily upset, negative attributional bias (quick to blame others), intense emotional reactions to stressors, low empathy, impulsivity, sensation seeking, lack of motivation or perseverance, and beliefs favorable to crime.

Poor Parenting Practices: Negative parent/juvenile bonding, poor supervision/discipline, family conflict and child abuse, absence of positive parenting (instruction in social, academic, and problem-solving skills; provision of social support), and criminal parents/siblings.

No/Bad Marriages: Unmarried or, if married, negative bonding to spouse/partner, negative bonding to children, family conflict, poor spouse/partner supervision, criminal spouse/partner, and low social support.

Negative School Experiences/Limited Education: Negative bonding to teachers and school, poor academic performance, little time spent on homework, low educational and occupational goals, poor supervision/discipline, negative treatment by teachers, absence of positive teaching, and limited education (for adults out of school).

Peer Delinquency: Close friends engage in crime, peer conflict/abuse, and spend much time with peers in unstructured, unsupervised activities.

Unemployment/Bad Jobs: Long-term unemployment, poor supervision/discipline, negative bonding to work, poor work performance, poor working conditions, and criminal coworkers.

Grouping variables into clusters organized by life domain differs from the approach taken by most integrated theories. Such theories examine individual variables or group variables into clusters organized by theory (e.g., social control variables, strain variables, social learning variables). However, as argued in Chapter 1, there are now too many individual variables to examine separately. And as argued in Chapter 3, each variable affects crime for reasons related to all or most of the leading theories. Therefore, it does not make sense to group variables by theory. It does, however, make sense to group variables by life domain. In particular, the variables in a life domain have stronger effects on one another and are more likely to share common causes than the variables in a theoretical group. As a consequence, the variables in a life domain are more strongly associated with one another than the variables in a theoretical group (see Chapter 3).

Grouping variables together by life domain greatly simplifies the general theory and does not result in a loss in explanatory power (see Chapter 10). In fact, grouping variables in this manner may improve our ability to explain crime. Examining the impact of some specific variable on crime, with all related variables held constant, can produce misleading results. To illustrate, crime is not simply the product of some specific family variable (e.g., family conflict), but rather is the combined product of a range of family variables working together. These variables are often closely related, making it difficult to estimate their separate effects, and they often interact with one another in their effect on crime. Combining all of the key family variables together into a general scale allows us to better represent the family environment of the individual and better estimate the effect of this environment on crime. Similar arguments can be made for the other life domains.

Argues That the Life Domains Have Reciprocal Effects on One Another Which Vary Over the Life Course

The general theory argues that the life domains have reciprocal effects on one another, although some effects are stronger than others and effect sizes sometimes vary over the life course. For example, poor parenting has a large effect on peer delinquency, which in turn has a small/moderate effect on poor parenting, at least during the childhood and adolescent years. While the argument that the life domains affect one another complicates the general theory, there is a certain simplicity in this complexity. One simple rule is sufficient to describe the major relations between the life domains: The life domains mutually reinforce one another. Further, these mutual effects help explain why certain individuals offend at high rates over much of their lives: Such individuals become enmeshed in the "web of crime." Irritability/low self-control and poor parenting in childhood lead to school and peer problems, which in turn reinforce irritability/low self-control and poor parenting. And all of these factors increase the likelihood of bad marriages and bad jobs in adulthood.

Most integrated theories do not consider reciprocal effects or changes in effect sizes over the life course, with the prominent exception of Thornberry's interactional theory (1987). Thornberry's theory, however, only focuses on the adolescent years while the general theory examines the entire life course (although see Thornberry and Krohn 2001). Further, Thornberry's theory does not consider certain key variables mentioned above, like peer abuse. It also does not consider the full range of intervening mechanisms described above, particularly those associated with strain theory (see below for additional differences between the general theory and Thornberry's theory).

Argues That Crime Affects the Life Domains and That Prior Crime Affects Subsequent Crime

The general theory argues that crime affects the life domains and that prior crime has a direct effect on subsequent crime. The nature of these effects, however, is conditioned by the individual's standing on the life domains. Crime is more likely to negatively affect the life domains and lead to subsequent crime among individuals who are irritable, low in self-control, and in family, school, peer, and work environments that are conducive to crime. (A similar argument was made regarding the effect of arrest and official sanction on subsequent crime.) These arguments integrate recent work in labeling and deterrence theory, particularly Braithwaite's (1989) theory of reintegrative shaming and Sherman's (1993; 2000) work on defiance theory.

Drawing on Braithwaite, the general theory argues that the individual's social circumstances (and personality traits) determine how others respond to his or her crime. In particular, they determine whether others "firmly reject the crime, but accept the person," a response that discourages further crime (similar to "reintegrative shaming" in Braithwaite), or whether others respond in a manner that fosters further crime, including a "harsh/rejecting" response (similar to "disintegrative shaming"), an "approving/supportive of the crime" response, and a "failure to respond to the crime" response (see Chapter 5).

Drawing on Sherman and certain rational-choice theorists, the general theory also argues that the individual's traits and social circumstances determine how he or she responds to his or her own crime and to the reactions of others. Individuals who are irritable, low in self-control, and in social environments conducive to crime are less likely to be deterred by the negative consequences of their crime, are more likely to be angered by the negative reactions of others, and are more likely to find their crime reinforcing.

Argues That the Life Domains Interact in Affecting Crime and One Another

The general theory argues that the life domains interact in affecting crime and one another. For example, irritability and low self-control are more likely to lead to crime among individuals who experience poor parenting. Most integrated theories neglect interaction effects and thereby overlook a major way in which variables work together to affect crime (although see Raine et al. 1997; Tittle 1995). Any comprehensive integration of psychological and sociological theories, for example, must recognize that social factors like poor parenting practices are more likely to lead to crime among individuals who possess personality traits like irritability and low self-control (and vice versa). More generally, a consideration of interaction effects allows us to better explain why the leading causes only result in crime some of the time (e.g., why only some individuals who experience poor parenting turn to crime).

Argues That the Life Domains Have Nonlinear and Largely Contemporaneous Effects on Crime and One Another

The general theory argues that the life domains have nonlinear and largely contemporaneous effects on crime and one another, although each life domain has a large lagged effect on itself. The nonlinear effect is such that as the level of a life domain increases it has an increasingly larger effect on crime and the other domains. Likewise, crime has a nonlinear and largely contemporaneous effect on the life domains. Most integrated theories pay little attention to the form and timing of causal effects, implicitly assuming that most effects are linear and lagged (although see Tittle 1995). These assumptions, as argued in previous chapters, may substantially reduce the explanatory power of such theories.

Argues That Biological Factors and the Larger Social Environment Affect the Life Domains

Finally, the general theory states that biological factors and the larger social environment affect the life domains. The discussion of biological factors integrates research on the biological bases of crime with research on the psychological and social causes of crime. Among other things, I argue that biological factors have a direct effect on irritability/low self-control and an indirect effect on the other life domains through irritability/low self-control. (I also argue that social factors have an impact on biological factors, influencing the individual's exposure to biological harms like birth complications and head injuries.)

The discussion on the larger social environment paves the way for integrating the general theory with macro-level theories of crime. Macro-level theories, like conflict, feminist, and social disorganization theories, describe those larger social forces that influence the individual's standing on the life domains and sometimes condition the effect of the life domains on crime (e.g., gender conditions the effect of family factors on crime). The general theory, in turn, describes the mechanisms by which these larger social forces affect individual crime (and thereby affect crime rates). A full integration between the general theory and macro-level theories, however, must await another book.

Conclusion

I believe that the general theory provides a "reasonably complete" explanation of individual offending (see Chapter 1). In particular, the theory reflects the major crime research and captures the essential arguments of the major crime theories, including biological, psychological, social control, self-control, strain, social learning, social support, and labeling theories.[1] I further believe that the general theory organizes this research and these theories into a "unified whole." In particular, the general theory is much more than a patchwork of different theories. The general theory integrates the major theories and research on the causes of crime in the several ways indicated above—ways that go well beyond the common strategy of claiming that the variables associated with one theory cause the variables associated with another theory (e.g., poor parental supervision causes association with delinquent peers). As a result, each theory is entwined in multiple ways with every other theory. Finally, I believe that the general theory provides a "clear and concise" answer to the question of "why do they do it?"—although you, the reader, are the final judge.

Note

1. The reader should note that the general theory also incorporates certain of the key ideas of rational choice theory, the routine activities perspective, and the "chaotic" perspective (ideas like holism, nonlinear dynamics, and sensitivity to initial conditions; see Walters 1999). ✦

References

Agnew, Robert. 1984. "Autonomy and delinquency." *Sociological Perspectives* 27:219–240.

———. 1985. "A revised strain theory of delinquency." *Social Forces* 64:151–167.

———. 1990. "The origins of delinquent events: An examination of offender accounts." *Journal of Research in Crime and Delinquency* 27:267–294.

———. 1991a. "The interactive effect of peer variables on delinquency." *Criminology* 29:47–72.

———. 1991b. "A longitudinal test of social control theory and delinquency." *Journal of Research in Crime and Delinquency* 28:126–156.

———. 1992. "Foundation for a General Strain Theory of Crime and Delinquency." *Criminology* 30:47–87.

———. 1993. "Why do they do it? An examination of the intervening mechanisms between 'Social Control' variables and delinquency." *Journal of Research of Crime and Delinquency* 30:245–266.

———. 1994. "The techniques of neutralization and violence." *Criminology* 32:555–580.

———. 1995a. "Determinism, indeterminism, and crime: An empirical exploration." *Criminology* 33:83–109.

———. 1995b. "Testing the leading crime theories: An alternative strategy focusing on motivational processes." *Journal of Research in Crime and Delinquency* 32:363–398.

———. 1997. "Stability and change in crime over the life course : A strain theory explanation." Pp. 101–132 in *Developmental Theories of Crime and Delinquency*, ed. Terence P. Thornberry. New Brunswick, NJ: Transaction.

———. 2001. "Building on the foundation of general strain theory: Specifying the types of strain most likely to lead to crime and delinquency." *Journal of Research in Crime and Delinquency* 38:319–361.

——. 2002. "Experienced, vicarious, and anticipated strain: An exploratory study focusing on physical victimization and delinquency." *Justice Quarterly* 19:603–632.

——. 2003a. "An integrated theory of the adolescent peak in offending." *Youth & Society* 34:263–299.

——. 2003b. "The interactive effects of social control variables on delinquency." In *Control Theories of Crime and Delinquency, Advances in Criminological Theory,* Volume 12, eds. Chester Britt, and Michael R. Gottfredson. New Brunswick, NJ: Transaction.

——. 2005. *Juvenile Delinquency: Causes and Control.* Los Angeles: Roxbury.

Agnew, Robert, Timothy Brezina, John Paul Wright, and Francis T. Cullen. 2002. "Strain, personality traits, and delinquency: Extending general strain theory." *Criminology* 40:43–72.

Agnew, Robert, Cesar Rebellon, and Sherod Thaxton. 2000. "A general strain theory approach to families." In *Families, Crime and Criminal Justice,* ed. Greer Litton Fox, and Michael L. Benson. New York: JAI.

Agnew, Robert, and Sherod Thaxton. 2002. "The nonlinear effects of parental and teacher attachment on delinquency: Disentangling strain from social control explanations." Chicago: American Society of Criminology annual meeting.

Agnew, Robert, and Helene Raskin White. 1992. "An empirical test of general strain theory." *Criminology* 30:475–499.

Aguilar, Benjamin, Alan Sroufe, Byron Egeland, and Elizabeth Carlson. 2000. "Distinguishing the early-onset/persistent and adolescent-onset antisocial behavior types: From birth to 16 years." *Development and Psychopathology* 12:109–132.

Aiken, Leona S., and Stephen G. West. 1991. *Multiple Regression: Testing and Interpreting Interactions.* Newbury Park, CA: Sage.

Akers, Ronald L. 1985. *Deviant Behavior: A Social Learning Approach.* Belmont, CA: Wadsworth.

——. 1989. "A social behaviorist's perspective on integration of theories of crime and deviance." Pp. 23–36 in *Theoretical Integration in the Study of Deviance and Crime: Problems and Prospects,* eds. Steven F. Messner, Marvin D. Krohn, and Allen E. Liska. Albany: State University of New York Press.

——. 1998. *Social Learning and Social Structure: A General Theory of Crime and Deviance.* Boston: Northeastern University Press.

Akers, Ronald L., and Christine S. Sellers. 2004. *Criminological Theories.* Los Angeles: Roxbury.

Allan, Emily Anderson, and Darrell J. Steffensmeier. 1989. "Youth, unemployment, and property crime: Differential effects of job availability and job quality on juvenile and adult arrest rates." *American Sociological Review* 54:107–123.

Ambert, Ann Marie. 1999. "The effect of male delinquency on mothers and fathers: A heuristic study." *Sociological Inquiry* 69:621–640.

Anderson, Elijah. 1994. "Code of the streets." *Atlantic Monthly:* 81–94.

———. 1999. *Code of the Street.* New York: W. W. Norton.

Andrews, D.A, and James Bonta. 1998. *The Psychology of Criminal Conduct.* Cincinnati, Ohio: Anderson.

Archer, Dane, and Patricia McDaniel. 1995. "Violence and gender: Differences and similarities across societies." Pp. 63–88 in *Interpersonal Violent Behaviors,* eds. R. Barry Ruback and Neil Alan Weiner. New York: Springer.

Arneklev, Bruce J., Harold G. Grasmick, and Robert J. Bursik, Jr. 1999. "Evaluating the dimensionality and invariance of 'low self-control.' " *Journal of Quantitative Criminology* 15:307–331.

Aseltine, Robert H., Jr. 1995. "A reconsideration of parental and peer influences on deviance." *Journal of Health and Social Behavior* 36:103–121.

Asendorf, Jens B. 1998. "Personality effects on social relationships." *Journal of Personality & Social Psychology* 74:1531–1544.

Aulette, Judy Root, and Raymond Michalowski. 1993. "Fire in Hamlet: A case study of a state-corporate crime." Pp. 171–206 in *Political Crime in Contemporary America,* ed. Kenneth D. Tunnell. New York: Garland.

Bachman, Ronet, and Raymond Paternoster. 1997. *Statistical Methods for Criminology and Criminal Justice.* New York: McGraw-Hill.

Bachman, Ronet, Raymond Paternoster, and Sally Ward. 1992. "The rationality of sexual offending: Testing a deterrence/rational choice conception of sexual assault." *Law & Society Review* 26:343–372.

Baier, Colin J., and Bradley R. E. Wright. 2001. " 'If you love me, keep my commandments': A meta-analysis of the effect of religion on crime." *Journal of Research in Crime and Delinquency* 38:3–23.

Bankston, Carl L., III. 1999. "Schools." Pp. 1171–1178 in *Encyclopedia of Family Life,* ed. Carl L. Bankston, III. Pasadena, CA: Salem Press.

Barak, Gregg. 1998. *Integrating Criminologies.* Boston: Allyn and Bacon.

Baron, Stephen W., and Timothy F. Hartnagel. 1997. "Attributions, affect, and crime: Street youths reactions to unemployment." *Criminology* 35:409–434.

Barrick, Murray R., Michael K. Mount, and Timothy A. Judge. 2001. "Personality and performance at the beginning of the new millennium:

What do we know and where do we go next?" *International Journal of Selection and Assessment* 9:9–30.

Baskin, Deborah R., and Ira Sommers. 1999. "Women, work, and crime." Pp. 32–46 in *In Their Own Words*, ed. Paul Cromwell. Los Angeles: Roxbury.

Bazemore, Gordon. 2000. "Community justice and a vision of collective efficacy: The case of restorative conferencing." Pp. 225–297 in *Policies, Processes, and Decisions of the Criminal Justice System, Criminal Justice 2000*, Volume 3, ed. Julie Horney. Washington, DC: National Institute of Justice.

Bellair, Paul E., and Vincent J. Roscigno. 2000. "Local labor market opportunity and adolescent delinquency." *Social Forces* 78:1509–1538.

Belsky, Jay. 1990. "Parental and nonparental child care and children's socioemotional development: A decade in review." *Journal of Marriage and the Family* 52:885–903.

Benson, Michael L. 2002. *Crime and the Life Course*. Los Angeles: Roxbury.

Benson, Michael L., and Elizabeth Moore. 1992. "Are white-collar and common offenders the same? An empirical and theoretical critique of a recently proposed general theory of crime." *Journal of Research in Crime and Delinquency* 29:251–272.

Bernard, Thomas J. 1990. "Angry aggression among the 'truly disadvantaged.' " *Criminology* 28:73–96.

Bernard, Thomas J., and Jeffrey B. Snipes. 1996. "Theoretical integration in criminology." In *Crime and Justice*, ed. Michael Tonry. Chicago: University of Chicago Press.

Blumstein, Alfred. 2002. "Prisons: A policy challenge." Pp. 451–482 in *Crime*, eds. James Q. Wilson and Joan Petersilia. Oakland, CA: ICS Press.

Blumstein, Alfred, and Joel Wallman. 2000. *The Crime Drop in America*. Cambridge: Cambridge University Press.

Bottcher, Jean. 2001. "Social practices of gender: How gender relates to delinquency in the everyday lives of high risk youths." *Criminology* 39:893–932.

Bouffard, Jeffrey A. 2002. "The influence of emotion on rational decision making in sexual aggression." *Journal of Criminal Justice* 30:121–134.

Braithwaite, John. 1989. *Crime, Shame and Reintegration*. Cambridge, England: Cambridge University Press.

——. 2002. *Restorative Justice and Responsive Regulation*. New York: Oxford University Press.

Brezina, Timothy. 1996. "Adapting to strain: An examination of delinquent coping responses." *Journal of Research in Crime and Delinquency* 34:39–60.

———. 1998. "Adolescent maltreatment and delinquency: The question of intervening processes." *Journal of Research in Crime and Delinquency* 35:71–99.

———. 1999. "Teenage violence as an adaptive response to family strain: Evidence from a national sample of male adolescents." *Youth & Society* 30:416–44.

———. 2000. "Delinquent problem-solving: An interpretative framework for criminological theory and research." *Journal of Research in Crime and Delinquency* 37:3–30.

Brief, Arthur P., Michael J. Burke, Jennifer M. George, and Brian S. Robinson. 1988. "Should negative affectivity remain an unmeasured variable in the study of job stress?" *Journal of Applied Psychology* 73:193–198.

Britt, Chester L. 1997. "Reconsidering the unemployment and crime relationship: Variation by age group and historical period." *Journal of Quantitative Criminology* 13:405–428.

Burkett, Steven R., and Bruce O. Warren. 1987. "Religiosity, peer associations, and adolescent marijuana use: A panel study of underlying causal structures." *Criminology* 25:109–131.

Burton, Velmer S., Jr., Francis T. Cullen, T. David Evans, Leanne F. Alarid, and R. Gregory Dunaway. 1998. "Gender, self-control, and crime." *Journal of Research in Crime and Delinquency* 35:123–147.

Bushway, Shawn, Robert Brame, and Raymond Paternoster. 1999. "Assessing stability and change in criminal offending: A comparison of random effects, semiparametric, and fixed effects modeling strategies." *Journal of Quantitative Criminology* 15:23–61.

Cairns, Robert B., and Beverley D. Cairns. 1994. *Lifelines and Risks*. Cambridge: Cambridge University Press.

Campbell, Susan B. 1995. "Behavior problems in preschool children: A review of recent research." *Journal of Child Psychology and Psychiatry* 36:113–149.

Canada, Geoffrey. 1995. *Fist Stick Knife Gun*. Boston: Beacon Press.

Caspi, Avshalom. 1998. "Personality development across the life course." Pp. 311–388 in *Handbook of Child Psychology*, ed. Nancy Eisenberg. New York: John Wiley & Sons.

Caspi, Avshalom, Daryl J. Bem, and Glen H. Elder, Jr. 1989. "Continuities and consequences of interactional styles across the life course." *Journal of Personality* 57:375–406.

Caspi, Avshalom, Donald Lynam, Terrie E. Moffitt, and Phil A. Silva. 1993. "Unraveling girls' delinquency: Biological, dispositional, and contextual contributions to adolescent misbehavior." *Developmental Psychology* 29:19–30.

Caspi, Avshalom, and Terrie E. Moffitt. 1995. "The continuity of maladaptive behavior: From description to understanding in the study of antisocial behavior." Pp. 472–511 in *Developmental Psychopathology, Volume 2*, eds. Dante Cicchetti and Donald J. Cohen. New York: John Wiley.

Caspi, Avshalom, Terrie E. Moffit, Phil A. Silva, Magda Stouthamer-Loeber, Robert F. Krueger, and Pamela S. Schmutte. 1994. "Are some people more crime prone? Replications of the personality-crime relationship across countries, genders, races, and methods." *Criminology* 32:163–196.

Catalano, Richard F., Michael W. Arthur, J. David Hawkins, Lisa Berglund, and Jeffrey J. Olson. 1998. "Comprehensive community- and school-based interventions to prevent antisocial behavior." Pp. 248–283 in *Serious and Violent Juvenile Offenders*, eds. Rolf Loeber and David P. Farrington. Thousands Oaks, CA: Sage.

Catalano, Richard F., and J. David Hawkins. 1996. "The social development model." Pp. 149–197 in *Delinquency and Crime*, ed. J. David Hawkins. Cambridge, England: Cambridge University Press.

Cernkovich, Stephen A., and Peggy C. Giordano. 2001. "Stability and change in antisocial behavior: The transition from adolescence to early adulthood." *Criminology* 39:371–410.

Chartrand, Tanya A., and John A. Bargh. 2002. "Nonconscious motivations: Their activation, operation, and consequences." Pp. 13–41 in *Self and Motivation: Emerging Psychological Perspectives*, eds. Abraham Tesser, Diederik A. Stapel, and Joanne V. Wood. Washington, DC: American Psychological Association.

Chesney-Lind, Meda. 1989. "Girls' crime and woman's place: Toward a feminist model of female delinquency." *Crime and Delinquency* 35:5–29.

Chesney-Lind, Meda, and Randall G. Shelden. 2004. *Girls, Delinquency, and Juvenile Justice*, 3rd ed. Pacific Grove, CA: Brooks/Cole.

Chung, Ick-Joong, Karl G. Hill, J. David Hawkins, Lewayne D. Gilchrist, and Daniel S. Nagin. 2002. "Childhood predictors of offense trajectories." *Journal of Research in Crime and Delinquency* 30:60–90.

Claxton, Guv. 1999. *Hare Brain, Tortoise Mind: Why Intelligence Increases When You Think Less*. Hopewell, NJ: Ecco Press.

Coie, John D., and Kenneth A. Dodge. 1998. "Aggression and antisocial behavior." Pp. 779–862 in *Handbook of Child Psychology*, ed. Nancy Eisenberg. New York: John Wiley & Sons.

Colder, Craig R., and Eric Stice. 1998. "A longitudinal study of the interactive effects of impulsivity and anger on adolescent problem behavior." *Journal of Youth and Adolescence* 27:255–274.

Coltrane, Scott. 1998. *Gender and Families*. Thousand Oaks, CA: Pine Forge Press.

Colvin, Mark. 2000. *Crime & Coercion*. New York: St. Martin's Press.

Compas, Bruce E. 1987. "Stress and life events during childhood and adolescence." *Clinical Psychological Review* 7:275–302.

Conger, Rand D., Xiaojia Ge, Glen H. Elder, Jr., F.O. Lorenz, and Ronald L. Simons. 1994. "Economic stress, coercive family process, and developmental problems of adolescents." *Child Development* 65:541–561.

Conger, Rand D., Gerald R. Patterson, and Xiaojia Ge. 1995. "It takes two to replicate: A mediational model for the impact of parents' stress on adolescent adjustment." *Child Development* 66:80–97.

Conger, Rand D., and Ronald L. Simons. 1997. "Life-course contingencies in the development of adolescent antisocial behavior: A matching law approach." Pp. 55–99 in *Developmental Theories of Crime and Delinquency, Advances in Criminological Theory*, Volume 7, ed. Terence P. Thornberry. New Brunswick, NJ: Transaction.

Cornish, Derek, and Ronald Clarke. 1986. *The Reasoning Criminal: Rational Choice Perspectives on Offending*. New York: Springer-Verlag.

Cromwell, Paul, Lee Parker, and Shawn Mobley. 1999. "The five-finger discount: An analysis of motivations for shoplifting." Pp. 57–70 in *In Their Own Words*, ed. Paul Cromwell. Los Angeles: Roxbury.

Cromwell, Paul F., James N. Olson, and D'Aunn Wester. 1991. *Breaking and Entering: An Ethnographic Analysis of Burglary*. Thousand Oaks, CA: Sage.

Crouter, Ann C. 1994. "Processes linking families and work: Implications for behavior and development in both settings." Pp. 9–28 in *Exploring Family Relationships with Other Social Contexts*, eds. Ross D. Parker and Sheppard G. Kellam. Hillsdale, NJ: Lawrence Erlbaum.

Crutchfield, Robert D., and Susan R. Pitchford. 1997. "Work and crime: The effects of labor stratification." *Social Forces* 76:93–118.

Cullen, Francis T. 1984. *Rethinking Crime and Deviance Theory*. Totowa, NJ: Rowan and Allanheld.

——. 1994. "Social support as an organizing concept for criminology." *Justice Quarterly* 11:527–559.

———. 1995. "Assessing the penal harm movement." *Journal of Research in Crime and Delinquency* 32:338–358.

———. 2002. "Rehabilitation and treatment programs." Pp. 253–289 in *Crime*, eds. James Q. Wilson and Joan Petersilia. Oakland, CA: ICS Press.

Cullen, Francis T., and Robert Agnew, eds. 2003. *Criminological Theory: Past to Present.* Los Angeles: Roxbury.

Cullen, Francis T., and Paul Gendreau. 2000. "Assessing correctional rehabilitation: Policy, practice, and prospects." Pp. 109–175 in *Policies, Processes, and Decisions of the Criminal Justice System, Criminal Justice 2000,* ed. Julie Horney. Washington, DC: National Institute of Justice.

Currie, Elliot. 1998. *Crime and Punishment in America.* New York: Owl Books.

De Li, Spencer. 1999. "Legal sanctions and youths' status achievement: A longitudinal study." *Justice Quarterly* 16:377–401.

Decker, Scott H., and Barrik Van Winkle. 1996. *Life in the Gang: Family, Friends, and Violence.* Cambridge, England: Cambridge University Press.

DeFronzo, James. 1997. "Welfare and homicide." *Journal of Research in Crime and Delinquency* 34:395–406.

Denno, Deborah W. 1990. *Biology and Violence.* Cambridge, England: Cambridge University Press.

D'Unger, Amy V., Kenneth C. Land, and Patricia L. McCall. 2002. "Sex differences in age patterns of delinquent/criminal careers: Results from Poisson latent class analyses of the Philadelphia cohort study." *Journal of Quantitative Criminology* 18:349–375.

D'Unger, Amy V., Kenneth C. Land, Patricia L. McCall, and Daniel S. Nagin. 1998. "How many latent classes of delinquency/criminal careers? Results from mixed Poisson regression analysis." *American Journal of Sociology* 103:1593–1630.

Eitle, David, and R. Jay Turner. 2002. "Exposure to community violence and young adult crime: The effects of witnessing violence, traumatic victimization, and other stressful life events." *Journal of Research in Crime and Delinquency* 39:214–237.

Elder, Glen H., Jr., and Avshalom Caspi. 1988. "Economic stress in lives: Developmental perspectives." *Journal of Social Issues* 44:25–45.

Elder, Glen H., Jr., Tri Van Nguyen, and Avshalom Caspi. 1985. "Linking family hardship to children's lives." *Child Development* 56:361–375.

Elliott, Delbert S. 1994. "Serious violent offenders: Onset, development course, and termination." *Criminology* 32:1–21.

———. 1995. "Lies, damn lies, and arrest statistics." Paper presented at the annual meeting of the American Society of Criminology. Boston.

Elliott, Delbert S., Susan S. Ageton, and Rachel Canter. 1979. "An integrated theoretical perspective on delinquent behavior." *Journal of Research in Crime and Delinquency* 16:3–27.

Elliott, Delbert S., and Susan S. Ageton. 1980. "Reconciling race and class differences in self-reported and official estimates of delinquency." *American Sociological Review* 45:95–110.

Elliott, Delbert S., David Huizinga, and Susan S. Ageton. 1985. *Explaining Delinquency and Drug Use.* Beverly Hills, CA: Sage.

Elliott, Delbert S., and Scott Menard. 1996. "Delinquent friends and delinquent behavior: Temporal and developmental patterns." Pp. 28–67 in *Delinquency and Crime: Current Theories,* ed. J. David Hawkins. Cambridge, England: Cambridge University Press.

Elliott, Delbert S., William Julius Wilson, David Huizinga, Robert J. Sampson, Amanda Elliot, and Bruce Rankin. 1996. "The effects of neighborhood disadvantage on adolescent development." *Journal of Research in Crime and Delinquency* 33:389–426.

Ellis, Lee, and Anthony Walsh. 1997. "Gene-based evolutionary theories in criminology." *Criminology* 35:229–276.

———. 2000. *Criminology.* Boston: Allyn and Bacon.

England, Paula, Jennifer Thompson, and Carolyn Aman. 2001. "The sex gap in pay and comparable worth: An update." Pp. 551–565 in *Sourcebook of Labor Markets,* eds. Ivar Berg and Arne L. Kalleberg. New York: Plenum.

Evans, T. David, Francis T. Cullen, Velmer S. Burton, Jr., and Michael L. Benson. 1997. "The social consequences of self-control: Testing a general theory of crime." *Criminology* 35:475–504.

Exum, M. Lyn. 2002. "The application and robustness of the rational choice perspective in the study of intoxicated and angry intentions to aggress." *Criminology* 40:933–966.

Fagan, Jeffrey, and Richard B. Freeman. 1999. "Crime and work." *Crime and Justice: A Review of Research* 25:225–290.

Farrington, David P. 1993. "Motivations for conduct disorder and delinquency." *Development and Psychopathology* 5:225–241.

———. 1994a. "Human development and criminal careers." Pp. 511–584 in *The Oxford Handbook of Criminology,* eds. Michael Maguire, Rod Morgan, and Robert Reiner. New York: Oxford University Press.

———. 1994b. "Introduction." Pp. xiiv–xxxvi in *Psychological Explanations of Crime,* ed. David P. Farrington. Aldershot, England: Dartmouth.

———. 1994c. "Interactions between individual and contextual factors in the development of offending." In *Adolescence in Context: The Interplay of Family, School, Peers, and Work in Adjustment*, eds. Rainer K. Silbereisen and Eberhard Todt. New York: Springer-Verlag.

———. 1995. "The development of offending and antisocial behavior from childhood: Key findings from the Cambridge Study in Delinquent Development." *Journal of Child Psychology and Psychiatry* 360:929–964.

———. 2002. "Families and crime." Pp. 129–148 in *Crime: Public Policies for Crime Control*, eds. James Q. Wilson and Joan Petersilia. Oakland, CA: ICS Press.

Farrington, David P., and J. David Hawkins. 1991. "Predicting participation, early onset and later persistence in officially recorded offending." *Criminal Behaviour & Mental Health* 1:1–33.

Farrington, David P., and Donald J. West. 1995. "Effects of marriage, separation, and children on offending by adult males." *Current Perspectives on Aging and the Life Cycle* 4:249–281.

Faust, Kimberly A., and Jerome N. McKibben. 1999. "Marital dissolution." Pp. 475–499 in *Handbook of Marriage and the Family*, eds. Marvin D. Sussman and Suzanne K. Steinmetz. New York: Plenum Press.

Federal Bureau of Investigation. 2003. *Crime in the United States, 2002.* Washington, DC: U.S. Government Printing Office.

Felson, Marcus. 1998. *Crime and Everyday Life: Insight and Implications for Society, Second Edition.* Thousand Oaks, CA: Pine Forge Press.

Felson, Richard B. 1996. "Big people hit little people: Sex differences in physical power and interpersonal violence." *Criminology* 34:433–452.

Ferber, Marianne A., and Brigid O'Farrell, eds. 1991. *Work and Family: Policies for a Changing Work Force.* Washington, DC: National Academy Press.

Fergusson, David M, L. John Horwood, and Daniel S. Nagin. 2000. "Offending trajectories in a New Zealand birth cohort." *Criminology* 38:525–552.

Finkel, Steven E. 1995. *Causal Analysis With Panel Data.* Thousand Oaks, CA: Sage.

Fishbein, Diana. 2001. *Biobehavioral Perspectives in Criminology.* Belmont, CA: Wadsworth.

Fleming, Charles B., Richard F. Catalano, Monica L. Oxford, and Tracy W. Harachi. 2002. "A test of the generalizability of the social development model across gender and income groups with longitudinal data from the elementary school developmental period." *Journal of Quantitative Criminology* 18:423–439.

Fleming, Zachary. 1999. "The thrill of it all: Youthful offenders and auto theft." Pp. 71–79 in *In Their Own Words*, ed. Paul Cromwell. Los Angeles: Roxbury.

Fox, Greer Linton, and Michael L. Benson, eds. 2000. *Families, Crime and Criminal Justice*. New York: JAI.

Giordano, Peggy C., Stephen A. Cernkovich, and Jennifer L. Rudolph. 2002. "Gender, crime, and desistance: Toward a theory of cognitive transformation." *American Journal of Sociology* 107:990–1064.

Glueck, Sheldon, and Eleanor Glueck. 1950. *Unraveling Juvenile Delinquency*. New York: The Commonwealth Fund.

Gold, Martin. 1963. *Status Forces in Delinquent Boys*. Ann Arbor, MI: Institute for Social Research.

Gottfredson, Denise C. 2001. *Schools and Delinquency*. Cambridge, England: Cambridge University Press.

Gottfredson, Denise C., Richard J. McNeil III, and Gary D. Gottfredson. 1991. "Social area influences on delinquency: A multilevel analysis." *Journal of Research in Crime and Delinquency* 28:197–226.

Gottfredson, Michael, and Travis Hirschi. 1990. *A General Theory of Crime*. Palo Alto, CA: Stanford University Press.

Gove, Walter R., Michael Hughes, and Omer R. Galle. 1979. "Overcrowding in the home: An empirical investigation of possible pathological consequences." *American Sociological Review* 44:59–80.

Grasmick, Harold G., Charles R. Tittle, Robert J. Bursik, and Bruce J. Arneklev. 1993. "Testing the core empirical implications of Gottfredson and Hirschi's General Theory of Crime." *Journal of Research in Crime and Delinquency* 30:5–29.

Greenberg, David F., and Ronald C. Kessler. 1982. "Equilibrium and identification in linear panel models." *Sociological Methods and Research* 10:435–451.

Greene, Jack R. 2000. "Community policing in America: Changing the nature, structure, and function of the police." Pp. 299–370 in *Policies, Processes, and Decisions of the Criminal Justice System, Criminal Justice 2000*, ed. Julie Horney. Washington, DC: National Institute of Justice.

Haas, Linda. 1999. "Families and work." Pp. 571–612 in *Handbook of Marriage and the Family*, eds. Marvin D. Sussman and Suzanne K. Steinmetz. New York: Plenum Press.

Hagan, John. 1991. "Destiny and drift: Subcultural preferences, status attainments, and risk and rewards of youth." *American Sociological Review* 56:567–581.

———. 1993. "The social embeddedness of crime and unemployment." *Criminology* 31:465–491.

———. 1994. *Crime and Disrepute.* Thousand Oaks, CA: Pine Forge Press.

———. 1997. "Defiance and despair: Subcultural and structural links between delinquency and despair in the life course." *Social Forces* 76:119–143.

Hagan, John, and Bill McCarthy. 1997. *Mean Streets.* Cambridge: Cambridge University Press.

Hagan, John, John H. Simpson, and A.R. Gillis. 1979. "The sexual stratification of social control: A gender-based perspective on crime and delinquency." *British Journal of Criminology* 30:25–38.

Hawdon, James E. 1999. "Daily routines and crime: Using routine activities as measures of Hirschi's involvement." *Youth and Society* 30: 395–415.

Hawkins, J. David, Todd I. Herrenkohl, David P. Farrington, Devon Brewer, Richard F. Catalano, Tracy W. Harachi, and Lynn Cothern. 2000. "Predictors of youth violence." Washington, DC: Office of Juvenile Justice and Delinquency Prevention.

Hawkins, J. David, Brian H. Smith, Karl G. Hill, Rick Kosterman, Richard F. Catalano, and Robert D. Abbott. 2003. "Understanding and preventing crime and violence: Findings from the Seattle social development project." Pp. 255–312 in *Taking Stock of Delinquency,* eds. Terence P. Thornberry and Marvin D. Krohn. New York: Kluwer Academic/Plenum.

Hay, Carter. 2001. "Parenting, self-control, and delinquency: A test of self-control theory." *Criminology* 39:707–736.

Haynie, Dana L. 2001. "Delinquent peers revisited: Does network structure matter?" *American Journal of Sociology* 106:1013–1057.

———. 2002. "Friendship networks and delinquency: The relative nature of peer delinquency." *Journal of Quantitative Criminology* 18:99–134.

Heimer, Karen. 1995. "Gender, race, and the pathways to delinquency." Pp. 140–173 in *Crime and Inequality,* eds. John Hagan and Ruth D. Peterson. Stanford, CA: Stanford University Press.

———. 2000. "Changes in the gender gap in crime and women's economic marginalization." Pp. 427–483 in *The Nature of Crime: Continuity and Change, Criminal Justice 2000,* Volume 1, ed. Gary LaFree. Washington: National Institute of Justice.

Hirschi, Travis. 1969. *Causes of Delinquency.* Berkeley, CA: University of California Press.

——. 1979. "Separate and unequal is better." *Journal of Research in Crime and Delinquency* 16:34–38.

——. 1989. "Exploring alternatives to integrated theory." Pp. 37–49 in *Theoretical Integration in the Study of Deviance and Crime: Problems and Prospects*, eds. Steven F. Messner, Marvin D. Krohn, and Allen E. Liska. Albany, NY: State University of New York Press.

Hops, Hyman, Linda Sherman, and Anthony Biglan. 1990. "Maternal depression, marital discord, and children's behavior: A developmental perspective." Pp. 185–208 in *Depression and Aggression in Family Interaction*, ed. Gerald R. Patterson. Hillsdale, NJ: Lawrence Erlbaum Associates.

Horney, Julie, and Ineke Haen Marshall. 1992. "Risk perceptions among serious offenders: The role of crime and punishment." *Criminology* 30:575–592.

Horney, Julie, D. Wayne Osgood, and Ineke Haen Marshall. 1995. "Criminal careers in the short-term: Intra-individual variability in crime and its relation to local life circumstances." *American Sociological Review* 60:655–673.

Howell, James C. 2003. *Preventing and Reducing Juvenile Delinquency*. Thousand Oaks, CA: Sage.

Hoyt, Dan R., Kimberly D. Ryan, and Ana Mari Cauce. 1999. "Personal victimization in a high-risk environment: Homeless and runaway adolescents." *Journal of Research in Crime and Delinquency* 36:371–392.

Hughes, Michael, and Melvin E. Thomas. 1998. "The continuing significance of race revisited: A study of race, class, and quality of life in America, 1972 to 1996." *American Sociological Review* 63:785–795.

Huizinga, David, Anne Wylie Weiher, Rachele Espiritu, and Finn Esbensen. 2003. "Delinquency and crime: Some higlights from the Denver youth survey." Pp. 47–91 in *Taking Stock of Delinquency*, eds. Terence P. Thornberry and Marvin D. Krohn. New York: Kluwer.

Ireland, Timothy O., Carolyn A. Smith, and Terence P. Thornberry. 2002. "Developmental issuers in the impact of child maltreatment on later delinquency and drug use." *Criminology* 40:359–400.

Jacobs, Jerry A. 2001. "Evolving patterns of sex segregation." Pp. 535–550 in *Sourcebook of Labor Markets*, eds. Ivan Berg and Arne L. Kalleberg. New York: Plenum.

Jang, Sung Joon. 1999. "Age-varying effects of family, school, and peers on delinquency: A multilevel modeling test of interactional theory." *Criminology* 37:379–397.

Jarjoura, G. Roger, Ruth A. Triplett, and Gregory P. Brinker. 2002. "Growing up poor: Examining the link between persistent childhood poverty and delinquency." *Journal of Quantitative Criminology* 18:159–187.

Jessor, R.J., J. Van Den Bos, F.M. Vanderryn, and M.S. Turbin. 1995. "Protective factors in adolescent problem behavior: Moderator effects and developmental change." *Developmental Psychology* 31:923–933.

Johnson, Richard E. 1979. *Juvenile Delinquency and Its Origins*. Cambridge, England: Cambridge University Press.

Kashefi, Max. 1999. "Work." Pp. 1381–1390 in *Encyclopedia of Family Life*, Volume 5, ed. Carl C. Bankston. Pasadena, CA: Salem Press.

Katz, Jack. 1988. *Seductions of Crime*. New York: Basic Books.

Kaufman, Robert L. 2001. "Race and labor market segmentation." Pp. 645–668 in *Sourcebook of Labor Markets*, eds. Ivan Berg and Arne L. Kalleberg. New York: Plenum.

Kim, Jae-On, and John H. Mueller. 1978. *Factor Analysis*. Thousand Oaks, CA: Sage.

Kumpfer, Karol L., and Rose Alvarado. 1998. "Effective Family Strengthening Interventions." Washington, DC: Office of Juvenile Justice and Delinquency Prevention.

LaFree, Gary. 1998. *Losing Legitimacy*. Boulder, CO: Westview.

LaGrange, Teresa, and Robert A. Silverman. 1999. "Low self-control and opportunity: Testing the general theory of crime as an explanation for gender differences in delinquency." *Criminology* 37:41–72.

Lanctot, Nadine, and Marc LeBlanc. 2002. "Explaining deviance by adolescent females." *Crime and Justice: A Review of Research* 29:113–202.

Larson, Jeffry H., Stephan M. Wilson, and Beley Rochelle. 1994. "The impact of job insecurity on marriage and family relationships." *Family Relations* 43:138–143.

Laub, John H., Daniel S. Nagin, and Robert J. Sampson. 1998. "Trajectories of change in criminal offending: Good marriages and the desistance process." *American Sociological Review* 63:225–238.

Laub, John H., and Robert J. Sampson. 2001. "Understanding desistance from crime." *Crime and Justice: A Review of Research* 28:1–70.

Lauritsen, Janet L., Robert J. Sampson, and John H. Laub. 1991. "The link between offending and victimization among adolescents." *Criminology* 29:265–292.

Lempers, Jacques D., Dania Clark-Lempers, and Ronald L. Simons. 1989. "Economic hardship, parenting, and distress in adolescents." *Child Development* 60:25–39.

Lin, Nan. 1999. "Social networks and status attainment." *Annual Review of Sociology* 24:467–487.

Liska, Allen E., Richard B. Felson, Mitchell Chamlin, and W. Baccaglini. 1984. "Estimating attitude-behavior reciprocal effects within a theoretical specification." *Social Psychology Quarterly* 47:15–23.

Liska, Allen E., and Mark D. Reed. 1985. "Ties to conventional institutions and delinquency: Estimating reciprocal effects." *American Sociological Review* 50:547–560.

Lockwood, Daniel. 1997. "Violence among middle school and high school students: Analysis and implications for prevention." Washington, DC: National Institute of Justice.

Loeber, Rolf, David P. Farrington, Magda Stouthamer-Loeber, Terrie E. Moffitt, Avshalom Caspi, Helene Raskin White, Evelyn H. Wei, and Jennifer M. Beyers. 2003. "The development of male offending: Key findings from the first decade of the Pittsburg youth study." Pp. 93–136 in *Taking Stock of Delinquency*, eds. Terence P. Thornberry and Marvin D. Krohn. New York: Kluwer Academic/Plenum.

Loeber, Rolf, and Magda Stouthamer-Loeber. 1986. "Family factors as correlates and predictors of juvenile conduct problems and delinquency." *Crime and Justice: A Review of Research* 7:29–149.

Lubinski, David. 2000. "Scientific and social significance of assessing individual differences: 'Sinking shafts at a few points.' " *Annual Review of Psychology* 51:405–444.

Luckenbill, David. 1977. "Criminal homicide as a situated transaction." *Social Problems* 25:176–186.

Luster, Tom, and Stephen A. Small. 1997. "Sexual abuse history and problems in adolescence: Exploring the effects of moderating variables." *Journal of Marriage and the Family* 59:130–142.

Lynch, Michael J., and Paul B. Stretesky. 2001. "Radical criminology." Pp. 267–286 in *Explaining Criminals and Crime*, eds. Raymond Paternoster and Ronet Bachman. Los Angeles: Roxbury.

MacLeod, Jay. 1995. *Ain't No Makin' It*. Boulder, CO: Westview.

Magnusson, David, and Hakan Stattin. 1998. "Person-context interaction theories." Pp. 685–745 in *Handbook of Child Psychology*, ed. Richard M. Lerner. New York: John Wiley & Sons.

Maguin, Eugene, and Rolf Loeber. 1996. "Academic performance and delinquency." *Crime and Justice: A Review of Research* 20:145–264.

Massey, James L., and Marvin D. Krohn. 1986. "A longitudinal examination of an integrated social process model of deviant behavior." *Social Forces* 65:106–134.

Matsueda, Ross L. 1992. "Reflected appraisals, parental labeling, and delinquency: Specifying a Symbolic Interactionist theory." *American Journal of Sociology* 97:1577–1611.

Matsueda, Ross L., and Kathleen Anderson. 1998. "The dynamics of delinquent peers and delinquent behavior." *Criminology* 36:269–308.

Matza, David. 1964. *Delinquency and Drift.* New York: Wiley.

Mazerolle, Paul, and Jeff Maahs. 2000. "General strain and delinquency: An alternative examination of conditioning influences." *Justice Quarterly* 17:753–778.

Mazerolle, Paul, and Alex Piquero. 1998. "Linking exposure to strain with anger: An investigation of deviant adaptations." *Journal of Criminal Justice* 26:195–211.

McClelland, Gary H., and Charles M. Judd. 1993. "Statistical difficulties of detecting interactions and moderator effects." *Psychological Bulletin* 114:376–390.

Mears, Daniel P., Matthew Ploeger, and Mark Warr. 1998. "Explaining the gender gap in delinquency: Peer influence and moral evaluations of behavior." *Journal of Research in Crime and Delinquency* 35:251–266.

Menard, Scott, and Barbara J. Morse. 1984. "A structuralist critique of the IQ-delinquency hypothesis: Theory and evidence." *American Journal of Sociology* 89:1347–1378.

Messerschmidt, James W. 1993. *Masculinities and Crime.* Lanham, MD: Rowman and Littlefield.

Messner, Steven F., Marvin D. Krohn, and Allen E. Liska. 1989. *Theoretical Integration in the Study of Deviance and Crime: Problems and Prospects.* Albany, NY: State University of New York Press.

Messner, Steven F., and Richard Rosenfeld. 2001. *Crime and the American Dream.* Belmont, CA: Wadsworth.

Miethe, Terance D., and Robert F. Meier. 1994. *Crime and Its Social Context.* Albany, NY: State University of New York Press.

Miller, Jody. 2001. *One of the Guys: Girls, Gangs, and Gender.* New York: Oxford.

Miller, Joshua D., and Donald Lynam. 2001. "Structural models of personality and their relation to anti-social behavior: A meta-analytic review." *Criminology* 39:765–798.

Moffit, Terrie E. 1990. "The neuropsychology of juvenile delinquency: A critical review." Pp . 99–169 in *Crime and Justice*, eds. Michael Tonry, and Norval Morris. Chicago: University of Chicago Press.

——. 1993. "Adolescence-Limited and Life-Course-Persistent antisocial behavioral: A developmental taxonomy." *Psychological Review* 100:674–701.

Moffitt, Terrie E., Avshalom Caspi, Michael Rutter, and Phil A. Silva. 2001. *Sex Differences in Antisocial Behavior.* Cambridge, England: Cambridge University Press.

Moffitt, Terrie E., and Hona Lee Harrington. 1996. "Delinquency: The natural history of antisocial behavior." Pp. 163–185 in *From Child to Adult*, eds. Phil A. Silva and Warren R. Stanton. Oxford: Oxford University Press.

Moore, Joan, and John Hagedorn. 2001. "Female gangs: Focus on research." Washington, DC: Office of Juvenile Justice and Delinquency Prevention, U.S. Department of Justice.

Morash, Merry. 1986. "Gender, peer group experiences, and seriousness of delinquency." *Journal of Research in Crime and Delinquency* 23:43–67.

Mueller, Charles W., and Jean E. Wallace. 1996. "Justice and the paradox of the contented female worker." *Social Psychology Quarterly* 59:338–349.

Nagin, Daniel S. 1998. "Deterrence and incapacitation." Pp. 345–368 in *The Handbook of Crime and Punishment*, ed. Michael Tonry. New York: Oxford University Press.

Nagin, Daniel S., and Kenneth C. Land. 1993. "Age, criminal careers, and population heterogeneity: Specification and estimation of a nonparametric, mixed Poisson model." *Criminology* 31:327–362.

Nagin, Daniel S., and Raymond Paternoster. 1993. "Enduring individual differences and rational choice theories of crime." *Law & Society Review* 27:467–496.

——. 1994. "Personal capital and social control: The deterrence implications of a theory of individual differences in criminal offending." *Criminology* 32:581–606.

——. 2000. "Population heterogeneity and state dependence: State of the evidence and directions for future research." *Journal of Quantitative Criminology* 16:117–144.

Nagin, Daniel S., and Gregg Pogarsky. 2001. "Integrating celeritry, impulsivity, and extralegal sanction threats into a model of general deterrence: Theory and evidence." *Criminology* 39:404–430.

O'Brien, Robert M., Jean Stockard, and Lynn Isaacson. 1999. "The enduring effects of cohort characteristics on age-specific homicide rates, 1960–1995." *American Journal of Sociology* 104:1061–1095.

Osgood, D. Wayne, Janet K. Wilson, Patrick M. O'Malley, Jerald G. Bachman, and Lloyd D. Johnstone. 1996. "Routine activities and individual deviant behavior." *American Sociological Review* 61:635–655.

Paternoster, Raymond. 1994. "General Strain Theory and delinquency: A replication and extension." *Journal of Research in Crime and Delinquency* 31:235–263.

Paternoster, Raymond, and Ronet Bachman. 2001. *Explaining Criminals and Crime*. Los Angeles: Roxbury.

Paternoster, Raymond, Robert Brame, Ronet Bachman, and Lawrence W. Sherman. 1997. "Do fair procedures matter? The effect of procedural justice on spouse assault." *Law & Society Review* 57:163–204.

Paternoster, Raymond, and Paul Mazerolle. 1994. "General strain theory and delinquency: A replication and extension." *Journal of Research in Crime and Delinquency* 31:235–263.

Paternoster, Raymond, and Alex Piquero. 1995. "Reconceptualizing deterrence: An empirical test of personal and vicarious experiences." *Journal of Research in Crime and Delinquency* 32:251–286.

Patterson, Gerald R., Barbara D. Debaryshe, and Elizabeth Ramsey. 1989. "A developmental perspective on antisocial behavior." *American Psychologist* 44:329–335.

Patterson, Gerald R., Marion S. Forgatch, Karen L. Yoerger, and Mike Stoolmiller. 1998. "Variables that initiate and maintain an early-onset trajectory for juvenile offending." *Development & Psychopathology* 10:531–547.

Patterson, Gerald R., John B. Reid, and Thomas J. Dishion. 1992. *Antisocial Boys*. Eugene, OR: Castalia.

Pearson, Frank S., and Neil Alan Weiner. 1985. "Toward an integration of criminological theories." *Journal of Criminal Law and Criminology* 76:116–150.

Peterson, Gary W., and Della Hann. 1999. "Socializing children and parents in families." Pp. 327–370 in *Handbook of Marriage and the Family,* eds. Marvin B. Sussman and Suzanne K. Steinmetz. New York: Plenum.

Piquero, Alex R., Robert Brame, Paul Mazerolle, and Rudy Haapanen. 2002. "Crime in emerging adulthood." *Criminology* 40:137–170.

Piquero, Alex R., Randall MacIntosh, and Matthew Hickman. 2000. "Does self-control affect survey response? Applying exploratory, confirmatory, and item response theory to Grasmick et al.'s self-control scale." *Criminology* 38:897–930.

Piquero, Alex R., and Paul Mazerolle, eds. 2001. *Life-Course Criminology*. Belmont, CA: Wadsworth.

Piquero, Alex R., and Greg Pogarsky. 2002. "Beyond Stafford and Warr's reconceptualization of deterrence: Personal and vicarious experiences, impulsivity, and offending behavior." *Journal of Research in Crime and Delinquency* 39:153–186.

Piquero, Alex R., and Stephen G. Tibbetts. 1996. "Specifying the direct and indirect effects of low self-control and situational factors on offenders' decision making: Toward a more complete model of rational offending." *Justice Quarterly* 13:481–510.

Piquero, Alex R., and Stephen G. Tibbetts, eds. 2002. *Rational Choice and Criminal Behavior*. New York: Routledge.

Pogarsky, Greg. 2002. "Identifying 'deterrable' offenders: Implications for research on deterrence." *Justice Quarterly* 19:431–452.

Pogarsky, Greg, and Alex R. Piquero. 2003. "Can punishment encourage offending? Investigating the 'resetting' effect." *Journal of Research in Crime and Delinquency* 40:95–120.

Pratt, Travis C., and Francis T. Cullen. 2000. "The empirical status of Gottfredson and Hirschi's general theory of crime: A meta-analysis." *Criminology* 38:931–964.

Raine, Adrain. 1993. *The Psychopathology of Crime*. San Diego, CA: Academic Press.

———. 2002a. "The biological bases of crime." Pp. 43–74 in *Crime*, eds. James Q. Wilson and Joan Petersilia. Oakland, CA: ICS Press.

———. 2002b. "Biosocial studies of antisocial and violent behavior in children and adults: A review." *Journal of Abnormal Child Psychology* 30:311–326.

Raine, Adrian, Patricia A. Brennan, David P. Farrington, and Sarnoff A. Mednick, eds. 1997. *Biosocial Bases of Violence*. New York: Plenum.

Rankin, Joseph H., and L. Edward Wells. 1990. "The effect of parental attachments and direct controls on delinquency." *Journal of Research in Crime and Delinquency* 27:140–165.

Reckless, Walter C. 1961. "A new theory of crime and delinquency." *Federal Probation* 25:42–46.

Reskin, Barbara F., and Irene Padavic. 1999. "Sex, race, and ethnic inequality in United States workplaces." Pp. 343–374 in *Handbook of the Sociology of Gender*, ed. Janet Saltzman. New York: Plenum.

Riordan, Cornelius. 1997. *Equality and Achievement: An Introduction*. New York: Longman.

Rosenberg, Morris, Carmi Schooler, and Carrie Schoenbach. 1989. "Self-esteem and adolescent problems: Modeling reciprocal effects." *American Sociological Review* 54:1004–1018.

Rowe, David C. 2002. *Biology and Crime*. Los Angeles: Roxbury.

Rowe, David C., Alexander T. Vazsonyi, and Daniel J. Flannery. 1994. "No more than skin deep: Ethnic and racial similarity in developmental process." *Psychological Review* 101:396–413.

———. 1995. "Sex differences in crime: Do means and within-sex variation have similar causes?" *Journal of Research in Crime and Delinquency* 32:84–100.

Rutter, Michael, Henri Giller, and Ann Hagel. 1998. *Antisocial Behavior by Young People*. Cambridge, England: Cambridge University Press.

Sampson, Robert J. 1987. "Urban black violence: The effect of male jobless-ness and family disruption." *American Journal of Sociology* 93:348–382.

——. 1997. "The embeddedness of child and adolescent development: A community-level perspective on urban violence." Pp. 31–77 in *Violence and Childhood in the Inner City*, ed. Joan McCord. Cambridge, England: Cambridge University Press.

Sampson, Robert J., and W. Byron Groves. 1989. "Community structure and crime: Testing Social Disorganization Theory." *American Journal of Sociology* 94:774–802.

Sampson, Robert J., and John H. Laub. 1993. *Crime in the Making: Pathways and Turning Points Through Life*. Cambridge, MA: Harvard University Press.

——. 1997. "A life-course theory of cumulative disadvantage and the sta-bility of delinquency." Pp. 133–161 in *Developmental Theories of Crime and Delinquency, Advances in Criminological Theory*, Volume 7, ed. Terence P. Thornberry. New Brunswick, NJ: Transaction.

Sampson, Robert J., and Janet L. Lauritsen. 1997. "Racial and ethnic dispar-ities in crime and criminal justice in the United States." *Crime and Jus-tice* 21:311–374.

Sampson, Robert J., and William Julius Wilson. 1995. "Toward a theory of race, crime, and urban inequality." Pp. 37–54 in *Crime and Inequality*, eds. John Hagan and Ruth Peterson. Stanford, CA: Stanford Univer-sity Press.

Savolainen, Jukka. 2000. "Inequality, welfare state, and homicide: Further support for an institutional anomie theory." *Criminology* 38:1021–1042.

Sheley, Joseph F. 1983. "Critical elements of criminal behavior explana-tions." *Sociological Quarterly* 24:509–525.

Sherman, Lawrence W. 1993. "Defiance, deterrence, and irrelevance: A theory of the criminal sanction." *Journal of Research in Crime and Delin-quency* 30:445–473.

——. 2000. "The Defiant imagination: Consilience and the science of sanc-tions." Albert M. Greenfield Memorial Lecture, University of Pennsyl-vania, February, 2000.

——. 2002. "Fair and effective policing." Pp. 383–412 in *Crime*, eds. James Q. Wilson and Joan Petersilia. Oakland, CA: ICS Press.

Sherman, Lawrence W. and John E. Eck. 2002. "Policing for crime preven-tion." Pp. 295–329 in *Evidence-Based Crime Prevention*, eds. Lawrence W. Sherman, David P. Farrington, Brandon C. Welsh, and Doris Layton MacKenzie. New York: Routledge.

Sherman, Lawrence W., David P. Farrington, Brandon C. Welsh, and Doris Layton MacKenzie. 2002. *Evidence-Based Crime Prevention*. New York: Routledge.

Sherman, Lawrence W., Douglas A. Smith, Janell D. Schmidt, and Dennis P. Rogan. 1992. "Crime, punishment, and stake in conformity: Legal and informal control of domestic violence." *American Sociological Review* 57:680–690.

Sherman, Lawrence W., Heather Strang, and Daniel Woods. 2000. "Recidivism patterns in the Canberra reintegrative shaming experiments (RISE)" (unpublished manuscript). Law Program, Research School of Social Sciences, Australian National University.

Short, James F., Jr., and Fred L. Strodtbeck. 1965. *Group Process and Gang Delinquency.* Chicago: University of Chicago Press.

Shover, Neal. 1996. *Great Pretenders: Pursuits and Careers of Persistent Thieves.* Boulder, CO: Westview.

Shover, Neal, and Carol Y. Thompson. 1992. "Age, differential expectations, and crime desistance." *Criminology* 30:89–104.

Shover, Neal, and John Paul Wright. 2001. *Crimes of Privilege.* New York: Oxford University Press.

Siegel, Jane A. and Linda M. Williams. 2003. "The relationship between child sexual abuse and female delinquency and crime: A prospective study." *Journal of Research in Crime and Delinquency* 40:71–94.

Sim, Hee-og, and Sam Vuchinich. 1996. "The declining effects of family stressors on antisocial behavior from childhood to adolescence and early adulthood." *Journal of Family Issues* 17:408–427.

Simons, Ronald L., Eric Stewart, Leslie C. Gordon, Rand D. Conger, and Glen H. Elder, Jr. 2002. "A test of life-course explanations for stability and change in antisocial behavior from adolescence to young adulthood." *Criminology* 40:401–434.

Simons, Ronald L., Chyi-In Wu, Rand D. Conger, and Frederick O. Lorenz. 1994. "Two routes to delinquency: Differences between early and late starters in the impact of parenting and deviant peers." *Criminology* 32:247–276.

Smith, Carolyn A., Alan J. Lizotte, Terence P. Thornberry, and Marvin D. Krohn. 1995. "Resilient youth: Identifying factors that prevent high-risk youth from engaging in delinquency and drug use." Pp. 217–247 in *Delinquency and Disrepute in the Life Course*, ed. John Hagan. Greenwich, CT: JAI Press.

Smith, Douglas A., and Patrick R. Gartin. 1989. "Specifying specific deterrence: The influence of arrest on future criminal activity." *American Sociological Review* 54:94–106.

Smith, Douglas A., and Raymond Paternoster. 1987. "The gender gap in theories of deviance: Issues and evidence." *Journal of Research in Crime and Delinquency* 24:140–172.

Snyder, Howard N., and Melissa Sickmund. 1999. "Juvenile offenders and victims: 1999 national report." Pittsburgh, PA: National Center for Juvenile Justice.

Stafford, Mark C., and Mark Warr. 1993. "A reconceptualization of general and specific deterrence." *Journal of Research in Crime and Delinquency* 30:123–135.

Steffensmeier, Darrell, and Emilie Allan. 1996. "Gender and crime: Toward a gendered theory of female offending." *Annual Review of Sociology* 22:459–487.

——. 2000. "Looking for patterns: Gender, age, and crime." Pp. 85–127 in *Criminology: A Contemporary Handbook*, ed. Joseph F. Sheley. Belmont, CA: Wadsworth.

Stern, Susan B., and Carolyn A. Smith. 1995. "Family processes and delinquency in an ecological context." *Social Service Review* 69:703–731.

Stewart, Eric A., Ronald L. Simons, and Rand D. Conger. 2000. "The effects of delinquency and legal sanctions on parenting behavior." Pp. 257–279 in *Families, Crime, and Criminal Justice*, eds. Greer Litton Fox and Michael L. Benson. New York: JAI Press.

——. 2002a. "Assessing neighborhood and social psychological influences on childhood violence in an African American sample." *Criminology* 40:801–830.

Stewart, Eric A., Ronald L. Simons, Rand D. Conger, and Laura V. Scaramella. 2002b. "Beyond the interactional relationship between delinquency and parenting practices: The contribution of legal sanctions." *Journal of Research in Crime and Delinquency* 39:36–59.

Sullivan, Mercer L. 1989. *"Getting Paid": Youth Crime and Work in the Inner City*. Ithaca, NY: Cornell University Press.

Sutherland, Edwin H., Donald R. Cressey, and David F. Luckenbill. 1992. *Principles of Criminology*. Dix Hills, NY: General Hall.

Sykes, Gresham M., and David Matza. 1957. "Techniques of neutralization: A theory of delinquency." *American Journal of Sociology* 22:664–670.

Tanner, Julian, Scott Davies, and Bill O'Grady. 1999. "Whatever happened to yesterday's rebels? Longitudinal effects of youth delinquency on education and unemployment." *Social Problems* 46:250–274.

Teevan, James J., and Heather B. Dryburgh. 2000. "First person accounts and sociological explanations of delinquency." *Canadian Review of Sociology and Anthropology* 37:77–93.

Thornberry, Terence P. 1987. "Toward an interactional theory of delinquency." *Criminology* 25:863–891.

——. 1996. "Empirical support for interactional theory: A review of the literature." Pp. 198–235 in *Delinquency and Crime*, ed. J. David Hawkins. Cambridge, England: Cambridge University Press.

Thornberry, Terence P., and R. L. Christenson. 1984. "Unemployment and criminal involvement: An investigation of reciprocal causal structures." *American Sociological Review* 49:398–411.

Thornberry, Terence P., and Margaret Farnworth. 1982. "Social correlates of criminal involvement: Further evidence on the relationship between social status and criminal behavior." *American Sociological Review* 47:505–517.

Thornberry, Terence P., and Marvin D. Krohn. 2001. "The development of delinquency: An interactional perspective." Pp. 289–305 in *Handbook of Youth and Justice*, ed. Susan O. White. New York: Kluwer Academic/Plenum.

Thornberry, Terence P., Marvin D. Krohn, Alan J. Lizotte, Carolyn A. Smith, and Kimberly Tobin. 2003a. *Gangs and Delinquency in Developmental Perspective*. Cambridge: Cambridge University Press.

Thornberry, Terence P., Alan J. Lizotte, Marvin D. Krohn, Margaret Farnworth, and Sung Joon Jang. 1991. "Testing interactional theory: An examination of reciprocal causal relationships among family, school, and delinquency." *Journal of Criminal Law and Criminology* 82:3–35.

——. 1994. "Delinquent peers, beliefs, and delinquent behavior: A longitudinal test of Interactional Theory." *Criminology* 32:47–84.

Thornberry, Terence P., Alan J. Lizotte, Marvin D. Krohn, Carolyn A. Smith, and Pamela K. Porter. 2003b. "Causes and consequences: Findings from the Rochester youth development survey." Pp. 11–46 in *Taking Stock of Delinquency*, eds. Terence P. Thornberry and Marvin D. Krohn. New York: Kluwer Academic/Plenum.

Thornberry, Terence P., Evelyn H. Wei, Magda Stouthamer-Loeber, and Joyce Van Dyke. 2000. *Teenage Fatherhood and Delinquent Behavior*. Washington, DC: Office of Juvenile Justice and Delinquency Prevention.

Thornton, Timothy N., Carole A. Craft, Linda L. Dahlberg, Barbara S. Lynch, and Katie Baer, eds. 2002. *Best Practices of Youth Violence Prevention*. Atlanta: National Center for Injury Prevention and Control, Centers for Disease Control and Prevention.

Tibbetts, Stephen G., and Alex Piquero. 1999. "The influence of gender, low birth weight, and disadvantaged environment in predicting early onset of offending: A test of Moffit's interactional hypothesis." *Criminology* 37:843–878.

Tibbetts, Stephen G., and Chris L. Gibson. 2002. "Individual propensities and rational decision-making: Recent findings and promising approaches." Pp. 3–24 in *Rational Choice and Criminal Behavior,* eds. Alex R. Piquero and Stephen G. Tibbetts. New York: Routledge.

Tittle, Charles R. 1995. *Control Balance: Towards a General Theory of Deviance.* Boulder, CO: Westview Press.

Tittle, Charles R., and David A. Ward. 1993. "The interaction of age with the correlates and causes of crime." *Journal of Quantitative Criminology* 9:3–53.

Tolan, Patrick. 2002. "Crime prevention: Focus on youth." Pp. 109–127 in *Crime,* eds. James Q. Wilson and Joan Petersilia. Oakland, CA: ICS Press.

Treas, Judith, and Leora Lawton. 1999. "Family relations in adulthood." Pp. 425–438 in *Handbook of Marriage and the Family,* eds. Marvin B. Sussman and Suzanne K. Steinmetz. New York: Plenum Press.

Turner, Michael G., and Alex R. Piquero. 2002. "The stability of self-control." *Journal of Criminal Justice* 30:457–471.

Uggen, Christopher. 2000. "Work as a turning point in the life course of criminals: A duration model of age, employment, and recidivism." *American Sociological Review* 67:529–546.

U.S. Department of Health and Human Services. 2001. *Youth Violence: A Report of the Surgeon General.* Rockville, MD: U.S. Department of Health and Human Services.

Visher, Christy A. 2000. "Career offenders and crime control." Pp. 601–619 in *Criminology: A Contemporary Handbook,* ed. Joseph F. Sheley. Belmont, CA: Wadsworth.

Wadsworth, Tim. 2000. "Labor markets, delinquency, and social control theory: An empirical assessment of the mediating process." *Social Forces* 78:1041–1066.

Walsh, Anthony. 2000. "Behavior genetics and anomie/strain theory." *Criminology* 38:1075–1108.

Walters, Glenn D. 1999. "Crime and chaos: Applying nonlinear dynamic principles to problems in criminology." *International Journal of Offender Therapy and Comparative Criminology* 43:134–153.

Warr, Mark. 2002. *Companions in Crime.* Cambridge, England: Cambridge.

Wasserman, Gail A., and Laurie S. Miller. 1998. "The prevention of serious and violent juvenile offending." Pp. 197–247 in *Serious & Violent Juvenile Offenders,* eds. Rolf Loeber and David P. Farrington. Thousand Oaks, CA: Sage.

Watson, David, Lee Anna Clark, and Allan R. Harkness. 1994. "Structures of personality and their relevance to psychopathology." *Journal of Abnormal Psychology* 103:18–31.

Welsh, Wayne N., Robert Stokes, and Jack R. Greene. 2000. "A macro-level model of school disorder." *Journal of Research in Crime and Delinquency* 37:243–283.

Wesley, Stephen, and Edward M. Waring. 1996. "A critical review of marital therapy outcome research." *Canadian Review of Psychiatry* 41:421–428.

White, Helene Raskin, and D.M. Gorman. 2000. "Dynamics of the drug-crime relationship." Pp. 151–218 in *The Nature of Crime: Continuity and Change, Criminal Justice 2000*, Volume 1, ed. Gary LaFree. Washington, DC: National Institute of Justice.

Wiatrowski, Michael D., David B. Griswold, and Mary K. Roberts. 1981. "Social control theory and delinquency." *American Sociological Review* 46:525–541.

Wikstrom, Per-Olof H., and Rolf Loeber. 2000. "Do disadvantaged neighborhoods cause well-adjusted children to become adolescent delinquents? A study of male juvenile serious offending, individual risk and protective factors, and neighborhood context." *Criminology* 38:1109–1142.

Wilkinson, Deanna L. 2002. "Decision making in violent events among adolescent males: An examination of sparks and other motivational factors." Pp. 163–196 in *Rational Choice and Criminal Behavior*, eds. Alex R. Piquero and Stephen G. Tibbetts. New York: Routledge.

Wilson, William Julius. 1987. *The Truly Disadvantaged: The Inner City, the Underclass, and Urban Poverty*. Chicago: University of Chicago Press.

———. 1996. *When Work Disappears: The World of the New Urban Poor*. New York: Knopf.

Wood, Peter B., Walter R. Gove, James A. Wilson, and John K. Cochran. 1997. "Nonsocial reinforcement and habitual criminal conduct: An extension of learning theory." *Criminology* 35:355–366.

Wright, Bradley R. E., Avshalom Caspi, Terrie E. Moffit, and Phil A. Silva. 1999. "Low self-control, social bonds, and crime: Social causation, social selection, or both?" *Criminology* 37:479–514.

Wright, Bradley R. Entner, Avshalom Caspi, Terrie E. Moffitt, and Phil A. Silva. 2001. "The effects of social ties on crime vary by criminal propensity: A life course model of interdependence." *Criminology* 39:321–352.

Wright, John Paul, and Francis T. Cullen. 2000. "Juvenile involvement in occupational delinquency." *Criminology* 38:863–896.

——. 2001. "Parental efficacy and delinquent behavior: Do control and support matter?" *Criminology* 39:677–706.

Wright, John Paul, Francis T. Cullen, and Nicolas Williams. 1997. "Working while in school and delinquent involvement: Implications for social policy." *Crime and Delinquency* 43:203–221.

Wright, Kevin N., and Karen E. Wright. 1995. "Family Life, Delinquency, and Crime: A Policymaker's Guide." Washington, DC: Office of Juvenile Justice and Delinquency Prevention.

Wright, Richard T., and Scott H. Decker. 1997. *Armed Robbers in Action.* Boston: Northeastern University Press.

Yu, Jiang, and Allen E. Liska. 1993. "The certainty of punishment: A reference group effect and its functional form." *Criminology* 31:447–463.

Zhang, Quauwu, Rolf Loeber, and Magda Stouthamer-Loeber. 1997. "Developmental trends of delinquent attitudes and behaviors: Replications and synthesis across domains, time, and samples." *Journal of Quantitative Criminology* 13:181–215.

Zimring, Franklin E., and Gordon Hawkins. 1995. *Incapacitation: Penal Confinement and the Restraint of Crime.* New York: Oxford University Press. ✦

Author Index

Subject Index

Made in the USA
Lexington, KY
18 January 2014